THE ART OF
SELF-IMPROVEMENT

THE ART OF
SELF-IMPROVEMENT

Ten Timeless Truths

ANNA KATHARINA SCHAFFNER

Yale

UNIVERSITY PRESS

New Haven and London

Published with assistance from the foundation established in memory of James Wesley Cooper of the Class of 1865, Yale College.

Yale University Press books may be purchased in quantity for educational, business, or promotional use. For information, please e-mail sales.press@yale.edu (U.S. office) or sales@yaleup.co.uk (U.K. office).

Set in Janson type by IDS Infotech Ltd.
Printed in the United States of America.

Library of Congress Control Number: 2021931301
ISBN 978-0-300-24771-8 (hardcover : alk. paper)

A catalogue record for this book is available from the British Library.

This paper meets the requirements of ANSI/NISO Z39.48-1992 (Permanence of Paper).

10 9 8 7 6 5 4 3 2 1

It seems to me that we are unfinished business. There is always scope to grow, not just intellectually but morally, epistemically and spiritually.

—JONATHAN ROWSON, *The Moves That Matter: A Chess Grandmaster on the Game of Life*

Contents

Preface

IN ONE OF MY most enduring nightmares, I stare into the mirror only to find that, overnight, my hair has turned white. My eyes are foggy and won't stay open. My skin is old and wrinkled, the consistency of parchment. I touch my face with skeleton fingers and understand that I am dying of old age. My response is one of dread. But it is not death as such that I fear. Rather, it is the realization of a terrible failure on my part. No, this cannot be, I am not done yet, I think in a panic—I have made no progress. I am overwhelmed by the terrifying realization that I have wasted my life agonizing over my various insecurities. The image I see in that dream-mirror is of an old woman with the psychological hang-ups of a teenager. Self-centered, but ineffectively so. It is the stuff of which true horror is made. For my dream-self has sinned against one of my most cherished beliefs: that it is possible to improve ourselves, and that self-improvement is our most important existential task.

We tend to write about the things that matter most to us, the things we wish to learn more about. I have always wanted to improve, to understand more deeply what self-improvement entails. A highly self-conscious introvert, I have battled with a range of frustrating limitations all my life. Constitutionally incapable of small talk, I often feel awkward in social situations, or come across as aloof. I find it challenging to connect with others. I can be preoccupied with my own debilitating inner voice; relentlessly self-critical, it drowns out many of the good things in my life. Because my energy is expended internally, I do not have nearly as much to give to others as I would like. My resources are consumed in the endless battle between that critical inner voice and the wiser parts of my personality. I frequently feel as though I am functioning at a level far below my natural potential.

For decades, I have been searching for a way to direct my energy outward, once and for all, so that I can live a more other- and more purpose-oriented life. As I see it, that is the point of all worthwhile self-improvement: to free up our energies so that we can direct them toward other people and toward creative projects. Fundamentally, self-improvement is a desire to learn how we can best develop our personal faculties and our moral qualities.

I have tried out my fair share of self-help regimes and read hundreds of books on the subject. My reading has always been driven by hope—the hope that the next book really will hold the key, the long-lost formula for a sustainable better life. Self-improvement promises nothing less than salvation, of a secular kind. Crucially, self-improvement is intimately linked to the transcendence of the self. While that may sound paradoxical, I strongly believe that the truly improved self shows itself in its interactions with others. It is less egoistical, humbler, more generous. It is not constantly preoccupied with its own anxieties, perceived shortcomings, and disappointments.

Unfortunately, I have not found any single means of self-improvement, a strategy guaranteed to work for everyone. Indeed, I have come to the conclusion that it does not exist. I have, however, discovered multiple strategies for self-improvement that have survived the test of time. In this book, I have brought together what I consider to be the ten most valuable and enduring ideas about self-improvement. These ideas come from different periods and cultures, and they have undergone variation across the ages. I encountered them while I was working through the vast literature of self-improvement, the origins of which lie thousands of years in the past. One of the things those ideas teach us is that there can be no simple revolution of the self. We cannot improve ourselves once and for all. Rather, self-improvement is an ongoing process, and one that has to be pursued throughout our lives.

While self-improvement is a deeply personal topic for me, it is also a topic with wide-ranging philosophical, psychological, and social significance. For it is based on the belief that we can learn and change for the better, that we are free to shape ourselves (albeit within certain limits) and are not simply destined to turn into our parents. It is a way of kicking against determinism, reassuring us that we all have the potential to mold our lives and that the work we do on ourselves is worth the effort. Self-improvement also entails a humble admission that there is always still so much that we can learn, both through honest self-observation and from others. We are, after all, "unfinished business," our selves constantly evolving.[1]

There is also a significant social dimension to self-improvement. Imagine a society that did not believe in the possibility that we can better ourselves. What place would there be for teaching and learning, for mentoring, for development of any kind? Would not such a society simply abandon or punish those experiencing difficulties and those who have fallen on hard times, rather than helping them to help themselves? Would it not ultimately be the least humane of societies? Arguably the most persuasive argument against the death penalty is precisely that it rules out the very possibility of self-improvement. To sentence someone to death is to assume that they cannot transcend the self that committed the crime for which they are being punished. I, for one, would not wish to live in a world that rejected the idea that change for the better is possible, and I do not believe that anyone else would either, if they really thought about it.

On the surface, Anglo-American cultures enthusiastically embrace the notion of the improvable self—a fact to which our current multibillion-dollar personal development industry attests. And yet there are cracks and contradictions in this construct, and many questions to which we do not have answers: Where exactly does our agency to shape ourselves begin and end? Which parts of us are innate, determined by our genes, and which are learned behavior, the result, in part, of upbringing and specific socioeconomic circumstances? What can we realistically hope to change about ourselves, and what is destined to remain fixed, no matter how hard we rattle the cage?

Crucially, our beliefs about our fundamental improvability (or lack thereof) translate into our politics. Are all self-improvers in principle created equal, or is self-improvement much harder for some than it is for others? Do we hold those of us who fail to improve ourselves personally responsible, or do we take into consideration our individually unique circumstances? Do we assign personal blame to those who struggle with their weight, with social anxiety, with impulse control, with substance abuse, with relationship problems, or who find themselves in financial hardship? For, to be sure, with the theoretical possibility of self-improvement comes practical responsibility.

Some theorists of self-improvement believe in limitless agency, with which comes a high degree of personal accountability, while at the other end of the spectrum the determinists focus on dependency and helplessness. Where we position ourselves on that spectrum reflects our fundamental ideas about what it means to be human. Our views on self-improvement ultimately tell us not only who we are, but how we think about others. Nothing, to my mind, could be more important than that.

THE ART OF
SELF-IMPROVEMENT

Introduction

IT WAS UNTHINKABLE IN THE Middle Ages that a celestial being could descend from heaven to earth other than in a spiral movement. The notion that angels might approach the terrestrial sphere in a straight line was quite simply unimaginable. Today, to suggest that the self cannot be improved is, for most of us, similarly unthinkable. Perhaps we believe in the possibility of complete, even magical transformation, as in the fairy tales of old. Or we might trust in more humble forms of improvement—that, like a good wine or cheese, we will simply get better with age. In part, this widespread belief in self-improvement grows out of our belief in the idea of progress. Just as most of us assume that humanity has made huge leaps forward over the centuries, so most of us assume that we are—or at least should be—developing as individuals.

Our appetite for self-improvement has never been greater: in 2020, the personal development market was valued at $39.99 billion worldwide, and is forecast to grow rapidly over the next few decades.[1] We consume self-help books voraciously, ever hungry for new offerings. Self-help apps, podcasts, online workshops, and personal growth webinars are booming. We spend large sums on life coaches, tasked with enhancing our mental and emotional fitness, while our employers invest heavily in developing our resilience and soft skills. Where does this idea of helping the self come from? Is it new, or has the desire to improve ourselves always been part of the human experience? And why does it define us so strongly?

The idea of the improvable self may appear to be a recent phenomenon. Firmly married to our belief in progress and personal agency, it also seems to have become entwined with a wider cultural drive for efficiency enhancement that includes the human. Self-improvement is, however, far from a modern concept. In fact, it has a long and rich history that stretches back to antiquity. Wishing to improve ourselves is a ubiquitous human desire. That said, it finds distinctive expressions in various historical periods and cultures.

It is important to distinguish between the literature of self-improvement and that of self-help. The self-help genre as we know it today first emerged in the mid-nineteenth century with the publication of Samuel Smiles's bestselling book *Self-Help* (1859). It has gone on to constitute a highly visible and commercially extremely successful subgenre within the much older corpus of the literature of self-improvement—a literature rooted in texts addressed to lay readers containing concrete advice on how we can develop ourselves positively. This literature aims to provide us with the tools and skills consciously to self-improve without the further involvement of any third parties, such as theologians, teachers, or psychologists.

While researching the long history of the idea of self-improvement I read widely, starting with works from ancient China and concluding with recent publications by bestselling writers such as Anthony Robbins, Eckhart Tolle, and Marie Kondo. I focused not only on modern self-help but also on philosophical works, religious texts, medical treatises, wisdom literature, ancient myths, and popular psychology. I read books on magic and astrology, as well as almanacs for medieval princes, Renaissance courtiers, and Victorian housewives. The more I read, the clearer it became that we today are far from being the only generation to have dreamed of improving ourselves.

The more I read, too, the more clearly I saw certain themes reoccurring. Beneath the many historical and cultural differences, ten core strategies run through the literature on self-improvement, both ancient and modern. We tend to know them today mainly in their packaged and marketed form, which often dilutes or distorts the wisdom of the original versions. We therefore have much to gain by tracing these strategies for self-improvement back to their origins. By exploring their evolution through the ages, and across cultures, we can discover much about our own shifting cultural values and anxieties.

Each chapter of this book focuses on one of these ten core themes from the long history of self-improvement. I examine the different guises they assume in changing cultural contexts, as well as how and why they resonate with our present-day concerns. It is from these enduring ideas about how we can improve ourselves that we have most to learn. For new is not always better. Sometimes, we forget what we already know. History holds many answers to our most pressing contemporary challenges.

The ancient wisdom has endured for a reason. The very best works on self-improvement are philosophies of life. As the Roman Stoic Seneca defined it, such a philosophy shapes our personality, provides structure and moral guidelines for our behavior, and generally "sits at the helm and keeps one on the correct course as one is tossed about in perilous seas."[2] This is a perfect description of any self-help literature worth its salt, with "improvement" meaning simply that we hone our ability to deal with being so tossed, to exist in these perilous seas. Indeed, the greatest works in the literature of self-improvement have always managed to function as an "axe for the frozen sea within us," as the writer Franz Kafka put it. They not only appeal to our reason but also manage to activate our emotions and our imagination.

The idea of self-improvement is bound up with a number of profound philosophical, psychological, and sociological questions. These include our very notion of selfhood, as well as concepts of agency, willpower, and personal responsibility. Moreover, self-improvement literature provides a powerful barometer of the aspirations and fears that preoccupy us at a particular historical moment. All successful works of self-improvement speak to our most acute concerns. The most common personal development aims in our current self-help landscape are self-realization and self-optimization. Our self-help literature promises to help us unleash our true potential (whatever that may be), raise our self-esteem, and enhance our personal effectiveness. In the self-improvement literature of the past, however, other values were more important. These included virtues such as altruism, humility, fortitude, and courage.

We also have much to learn from examining shifting trends in our own self-help literature. What, for example, are we to make of the current craze for minimalist living and decluttering, for mindfulness and digital detoxing, for Stoic ideas, and for invitations to learn from other species? All of these trends provide insights into the spirit of our age. They reveal a desire for cleansing (literally and metaphorically), living more sustainably, consuming more consciously, and privileging experiences over objects. They reveal our unease about the ways in which our smartphones and social media bleed into our experience of the present moment, and point to our growing concerns around what the attention economy is doing to our sense of self.[3] The neo-Stoic models reveal an intensifying sense of hopelessness in the face of the political and environmental challenges we face. Last but not least, the growing number of works that invite us to learn the art of living well from animals and plants indicates a profound disenchantment with our own kind.

The literature of self-improvement not only tells us about the aspirational values of different historical moments, but also reveals changing conceptions of selfhood. Is the self seen as atomistic or relational? As fundamentally good or bad? As primarily rational or emotional? Did our ancestors think of themselves as powerful agents able to exercise free will or as shaped by internal or external forces? The literature of self-improvement is always embedded in wider cultural paradigms. It offers views on what constitutes a good life—what we should strive for and what we need in order to live fulfilling and meaningful lives.

The literature of self-improvement also reveals how we think about the relation between the mind, the body, and the social communities to which we belong. It is for that reason that there is always an ethical, even a political, dimension to all self-improvement regimes. The various suggested paths to improving ourselves rest on assumptions about what we can and what we cannot change about ourselves. They outline the scope of our agency and, by implication, our personal responsibility for overcoming the forces that shape us. These include our genes, our upbringing, our experiences, our broader sociocultural environments, and our economic circumstances.

For over two and a half thousand years, the art of self-improvement was the domain of philosophers, sages, and theologians. Today, however, many of our philosophers have abandoned the project of reflecting on the good life and dispensing advice on how we may achieve it. Our religious thinkers have lost their influence. As a result, the task of instructing us in how to improve ourselves is now largely in the hands of the self-help industry. This state of affairs is problematic. The desire to improve ourselves, to learn and develop, is an ancient impulse, manifest in our enduring quest for self-knowledge and for guidance on how to live well. Like all of our aspirations, this desire can be exploited. Today's self-help industry is profit-driven and, alongside serious and inspirational work, also markets many unsound regimes that promise instant transformation with no effort.

This matters. For self-help literature not only reflects but also shapes our values, our aspirations, and our behaviors. It shapes how we attempt to manage our emotions and cognitions. Even if we have never picked up a self-help book, our life will have been influenced by the many tropes that have infiltrated our everyday language. They shape the news we consume, the films we watch, and the narratives through which we understand our lives. At work, our line managers will have tried to enhance our productivity, hone our team spirit, improve our capacity to empathize, and sharpen our communication skills. Friends will have told us to feel the fear and do it anyway, to silence our inner critic, to be co-dependent no more, to listen to our inner child, to make our superego our amigo, to embrace the power of now, or to seek out the roads less traveled.

The language of self-help, its metaphors and imagery, also reveals much about the conceptions of selfhood that are at work in our society. Consider, for example, "self-management." This term understands the self as an HR problem, requiring managerial interventions, like a dysfunctional team. According to this model, there are parts of us that need to be disciplined or performance-managed, perhaps even retrained or retired. "Self-optimization" and "self-enhancement," by contrast, suggest that the self is like a machine in need of fine-tuning.

Many self-help regimes compare our minds to computers. They recommend that we change our hardwired beliefs and reprogram our operating systems, and that we eliminate behavioral glitches and malfunctions. They suggest memory wipes and new software. But as complex and constantly evolving organisms that interact dynamically with our environments, we actually share very little with machines. We are embodied, embedded, and encultured. Thinking of ourselves as akin to computers is harmful. So are the equally ubiquitous financial and business metaphors—references to our social capital, emotional bank accounts, portfolios, and assets, with self-improvement being a form of long-term investment that will eventually pay off, yielding higher profits.[4] Their aim is to show us how to sell ourselves more professionally and effectively on the social marketplace. Even the term "self-worth" has a monetary ring to it.

Other much-used metaphors in modern self-help include the idea of life as a journey, a work of art, a battle, a jungle, a game, and a competition. Many writers rely on images of social ascent, such as rising to the top, climbing a ladder or a mountain, or getting over the wall. Depending on which of these metaphors we adopt, as the American sociologist Micki McGee observes, we may imagine ourselves as "combatants, contestants, or players; travelers or explorers; and entrepreneurs, salespersons, or managers. For the combatants, contestants, and players, winning is the goal, while power and wealth are typically the prizes. For the traveler or explorer, rewards tend to be experiential, nonmaterial, and spiritual."[5] The entrepreneurial cluster, finally, is motivated by material gains.

Our current notion of self-optimization contrasts starkly with the much older idea of self-cultivation. Prominent in the ancient literature, both Asian and Western, self-cultivation evokes a slower, less dramatic mode of developing our good qualities, an approach that is incremental and sustainable. It encourages us to nurture our virtues patiently and calmly, as we would nurture seedlings in a garden. The ancient self is often represented in botanical terms, as something that needs to be carefully nourished so that it may grow and blossom. We might be urged to prune and gently guide it. We must find the right climate and soil for our selves to flourish, and eradicate problems at their roots. We might have to plant new seeds and pull out weeds. Modern esoteric texts that borrow from these traditions, in contrast, tend to write of the self in a more nebulous language of flows and energies. They favor metaphors of liquidity, light and dark, and natural power. They also tend to rely upon the imagery of networks, webs, and rhizomes, suggesting the connectedness of all life forms.

Metaphors matter.[6] In the literature of self-improvement, the choice of metaphors reveals how we see ourselves and our purpose. We may, for example, think of ourselves as part of a wider social community with shared aims and obligations, or as lone fighters in a hostile environment, out there to secure a personal advantage. The Stoic philosopher Seneca writes: "Our relations with one another are like a stone arch, which would collapse if the stones did not mutually support each other, and which is upheld in this very way."[7] His concept of our relational nature and communal purpose could not differ more from Jordan B. Peterson's. In his bestselling *12 Rules for Life: An Antidote to Chaos* (2018), Peterson recommends that we copy the ways of the "top-lobster." For it is "winner-take-all in the lobster world, just as it is in human societies, where the top 1 percent have as much loot as the bottom 50 percent."[8] The posturing of the strutting shellfish intimidates less confident members of the species, thus enhancing its chances of securing prey, territory, and sexual partners. Peterson, then, simply advocates we emulate natural dominance hierarchies, whereas Seneca's vision is ethically and socially more ambitious.

As the long literature of self-improvement reveals, our drive to better ourselves is related to our basic human needs. Perhaps the best-known attempt to identify these core needs is that by the humanist psychologist Abraham Maslow in 1943.[9] Primitive physiological needs form the basis of his model, followed by safety, belongingness, and esteem, and at the very top, self-actualization.[10] Other theories of our most fundamental needs prioritize attachment, terror management, and self-determination.[11] The psychologist Robert Kegan, for example, argues that there are only two "great human yearnings"—our striving for autonomy and independence and our need for inclusion and communion—and they are in conflict with one another.[12] We could also add a need for beauty in its various forms.

There is truth to all of these models. However, the specific self-improvement aims I encountered in my research for this book tend to revolve predominantly around social relations, status, learning, variety, and altruism.[13] Most, if not all, of our historically and culturally changing self-improvement aims can, I believe, be traced back to these five basic needs.

Social relations encompass our desire to feel connected, accepted, and part of a community. They also include our longing for understanding, friendship, and love. This need captures classic modern self-help aims such as increasing both the quantity and quality of our friendships, and finding our soulmate. It also relates to our desire to feel rooted in a particular place and community. Many twentieth- and twenty-first-century self-help books focus on pain points that are directly tied to these desires, such as loneliness, isolation, alienation, and feeling unloved or undesirable. They aim to teach us how to connect with others in a deeper way, or at least more effectively.

Status includes our need for respect and attention, but also for power, influence, and control. Concerns about status may be manifest in a preoccupation with what others think about us and a desire to impress them—be that via looks, wit, ideas, clothes, cars, or other objects of conspicuous consumption. It may also be manifest in our need for professional recognition in the form of promotion, for social media "likes" and followers, or simply in feeling that our voices and opinions are heard and that we are taken seriously. At a deeper level, status relates to the hope that our existence matters and that it is positively acknowledged by others.

Learning is connected to our thirst for knowledge and understanding, as well, of course, to our desire to improve ourselves. Throughout our lives, most of us seek to continue to expand our understanding of the world. This includes the spiritual and the metaphysical, and questions pertaining to the meaning of our existence. It also includes skills and aptitude—we may wish to learn Arabic or Mandarin, to scuba dive, or to meditate. Perhaps we want to learn how to grow bonsai trees or how to draw animals. We may seek enlightenment, or simply new recipes for vegan brownies.

Most importantly, learning includes learning about ourselves—to understand ourselves more deeply, and to gain insight into our own patterns, preferences, and deeper motivations. It also includes our appetite for learning how to improve our character, interpersonal skills, and the management of our thoughts and emotions. We could even flip this argument on its head: rather than seeing self-improvement as an aspect of learning, we could consider all forms of learning as modes of self-improvement. Whichever way we look at it, learning and self-improvement are the closest of allies.

This alliance is perhaps best captured by the German concept of *Bildung*. Denoting a complex psychosocial process of character formation, this notion was dear to many eighteenth-century German philosophers. Wilhelm von Humboldt (1767–1835), for example, understood *Bildung* not just as the acquisition of knowledge and specific skills and aptitudes, but as a much broader and also deeper process of development and socialization.[14] Our formation, moreover, is based on a constant critical dialogue with cultural norms and other people. Most importantly, it includes learning about our inner life and our place in society, resulting in a more reflective and nuanced understanding of our selves, others, and the world.

Our desire for *variety* is what motivates us to travel to faraway places, to get to know new people, and to build new relationships. A form of epistemic and experiential curiosity, it leads us to try new foods and new sexual partners, or to climb mountains. Our thirst for novelty sometimes makes us restless, driving us to search for new jobs and new challenges. If we do not seek variation, we end up dead in life, shutting out those new experiences that keep our minds and hearts active. Our horizons will shrink, our learning will stagnate, and we will become nothing but creatures of habit.

Our fifth and final basic desire, *altruism*, includes our wish to be good and to care for others. It centers on helping those around us to grow and to achieve happiness. It can find expression in social and community engagements, such as working in a charity shop or a food bank, volunteering, or agitating for political change; it includes caring for a child or an elderly parent, supporting friends through difficult times, or taking in a rescue cat. Closely related to our ability to empathize, it is a desire to translate kindness into concrete actions. At a deeper level, altruism relates to the need to know that our actions are meaningful and that they contribute, in some way, small or big, to making the world a better place. Our yearning for self-transcendence, too, is therefore a core facet of altruism.

Most of our aspirations—whether they be material, emotional, cognitive, or spiritual—can be located within these five categories. However, each period and culture tends to value some needs more than others. Maintaining a good balance between the five basic needs is an important task not only for individuals, but for societies. If, say, a culture privileges status well above the other needs, it will inevitably be out of kilter. This state of imbalance will be clearly visible in the values that shape its literature of self-improvement.

As the following chapters show, the ancients held altruism, social relations, and learning in higher esteem than we seem to today. It is fair to say that status-related desires have become much more important in the self-improvement literature of our era. That said, the number of other-oriented, pro-social self-help texts seems to be on the rise again. COVID-19, the climate emergency, growing inequality, psychological alienation, and a resurgence of populism have prompted an increasing proportion of us to reflect anew on our atomistic conception of the self, and its adverse impact on social structures and the environment.

The desire to improve ourselves is above all related to our need to learn and to develop our faculties and moral qualities. Many consider this to be quite simply our primary existential task. The belief in the possibility of self-improvement gives us purpose and hope for a better future. It rests on the conviction that our qualities can be cultivated and that we have the capacity for lifelong learning. The American psychologist Carol S. Dweck refers to this attitude as the "growth mindset." As opposed to people with a fixed mindset, who believe that our skills, abilities, and intelligence are immutable, people with a growth mindset believe that they can develop.[15] Dweck has shown that these two mindsets have wide-ranging consequences. They dramatically impact the degree to which we seek new challenges, attempt proactively to develop our skills and abilities, and learn from our failures. While we may all have different temperaments and talents, our belief in our ability to learn is a significant determinant of our success in life.

Crucially, this belief is also of wider social importance. As the German *Bildung* philosophers knew well, inner and outer transformation are interrelated. What would happen if we all simply let our potential go to waste? If nobody sought to stretch themselves, there would be no progress—neither social, emotional, nor technological. We would collectively stagnate, perhaps even regress. There would be no innovation and no creativity. None of the global challenges that we face today would be addressed. We would not seek to develop new social imaginaries and would stop searching for solutions to the many urgent crises we need to tackle. Moreover, as a society we would not seek to hone potential, but would instead fixate only on talent that is already in evidence. Individually and collectively, then, we must take our desire for self-improvement seriously. For we all have a lot to learn—including from history and from other cultures.

At the most fundamental level, our desire to improve ourselves, and the belief that this is possible, is an act of rebellion against the idea of determinism. Engaging in the act of self-improvement is our—however flawed—effort to exert control over our lives. It is an attempt to defy whatever forces we may blame for our perceived insufficiencies: nature or nurture, genes or the environment, God, karma, fate, or the constellation of the planets. Our belief in the improvability of the self can therefore be seen as a powerful proclamation of defiance, an assertion of agency in a world where it is all too easy to feel powerless and adrift.

CHAPTER ONE

Know Thyself

GENUINE SELF-KNOWLEDGE HAS to be the starting point for any attempt to improve ourselves. Without a proper understanding of our strengths and weaknesses, we cannot determine what needs to be improved and how that might be possible. The Delphic maxim "Know Thyself" is therefore an ever-present mantra in the literature of self-improvement. But knowing ourselves—truly understanding who we are—is by no means easy. The ancient Greeks not only appreciated the vital importance of self-knowledge, but also knew how difficult it is to achieve. To remind themselves of this most essential of tasks, they carved the motto above the portal to the Temple of Apollo.

The Greek philosopher Socrates (470–399 BCE) went even further, declaring that the unexamined life is not worth living. He proclaimed self-knowledge as an absolute good, indeed as our highest virtue. While he put it rather starkly, it is true that if we remain in the dark about our natural preferences, our values, and our hopes for the future, it will be very difficult to change anything at all about ourselves. If we do not understand our basic motivations and fears, we will be tossed around by our emotions like small vessels adrift on a choppy sea. We will be controlled by forces that remain incomprehensible to us, and we will not be able to navigate toward the shore.

When he was put on trial for corrupting the youth of Athens in 399 BCE, Socrates's defense was that he did not know much about anything at all. But his strategy backfired, for, as Socrates knew well, admitting the limits of our knowledge is in fact a sign of wisdom. In Plato's *Five Dialogues*, Socrates reflects: "So I withdrew and thought to myself: 'I am wiser than this man; it is likely that neither of us knows anything worthwhile, but he thinks he knows something when he does not, whereas when I do not know, neither do I think I know; so I am likely to be wiser than he to this small extent, that I do not think I know what I do not know.' "[1] The jury, unconvinced by his defense, found him guilty, and Socrates was sentenced to death.

Socratic self-knowledge, then, is anchored in knowing what we do not know, in a lucid awareness of our own shortcomings and prejudices. Importantly, however, Socratic self-knowledge is not the fruit of solitary introspection alone. The philosopher's favored method was naturally the Socratic one, which involves asking probing questions and pointing out inconsistencies in other people's arguments and beliefs. That way, Socrates hoped to guide us toward a fuller grasp of the truth.

Conversations with wise teachers, analysts, and friends can be powerful catalysts for acquiring self-knowledge. But how can we deepen our self-knowledge on our own? One tool, though ultimately limited, is personality theories, which give us an idea of our basic preferences. The idea that we can be classified according to our personality type can be traced all the way back to the ancient physicians Hippocrates and Galen. Their model of the four basic temperaments continues to shape current personality type theories and a range of widely used psychometric tests.[2]

According to the depth psychologist C. G. Jung, we can also acquire self-knowledge by studying myths, fairy tales, dreams, and folklore.[3] The tales of old can be windows into the collective unconscious, revealing the hidden archetypal patterns that structure our lives. Stories that follow the hero's journey blueprint, for example, can teach us about the important threshold moments that we all have to master.

The most nuanced understanding of ourselves, however, is gained by paying careful attention to our cognitive processes, by observing our emotional reactions, and by reflecting on our past experiences. The founding father of psychoanalysis, Sigmund Freud, has shown in troubling detail just how much we are shaped by our pasts. That said, there continues to be a lively debate about the extent to which we can emancipate ourselves from our established patterns of thought and behavior.

Before we analyze more thoroughly the different ways of gaining a deeper knowledge of ourselves, we need to clarify our conception of that self. For there is no universal agreement on what a "self" really is. There are, for example, crucial differences between East Asian and Western notions of selfhood.[4] The philosopher Julian Baggini argues that there are three main ways of conceptualizing the self: the "no-self" (as found in Buddhist traditions), the relational self (as found in Confucianism and certain Japanese traditions), and the atomized self (as found in most, but by no means all, Western accounts of selfhood).[5]

The Buddhist notion of the self is the trickiest one for Westerners to understand, for it is rooted in a conception of the world that is not dualistic. Buddhists believe that our selves have no lasting, unchanging essence. Instead, we consist of five impermanent aggregates: our physical body, sensations and feelings, perceptions, mental activity, and consciousness. These aggregates bundle together in constantly changing constellations. What we think of as the self is therefore merely an assemblage of fleeting processes.[6] And neither is the self a separate and discrete entity—for we are connected with all things living and dead. Paradoxically, then, true Buddhist self-knowledge is to understand that there is no permanent self to begin with. Understanding the self in a Buddhist manner means fathoming our true nature, and letting go of our preoccupation with the self as a fixed and isolated unit.

The question of whether we are relational at heart—social animals, born to cooperate and support one another—or whether we are selfish, designed to secure advantages for ourselves and to maximize our pleasure, is both crucial and highly divisive. How we view the human—our basic nature and our core mission—depends to a large extent on our politics and values. What is more, conceptions of selfhood have not only changed dramatically throughout history and across cultures, but they are also discipline-dependent. Biologists, psychologists, sociologists, and anthropologists will all come up with radically different answers as to how to define the self.

Historians can identify the beliefs about selfhood that were dominant at a particular time relatively easily because they were widely shared. Our own age, however, is marked by eclecticism. Our self-help landscape testifies to the often wildly conflicting scientific, spiritual, and political views of the self that coexist. Today, we may imagine ourselves as isolated or as relational, as rational or as predominantly governed by our emotions. We may understand ourselves in purely material terms or as embodied. We may still think of the self as a spiritual entity amenable to salvation. Or we may experience ourselves as autonomous agents, able to control our own destinies—or else as helpless, irrevocably shaped by our upbringing and environment. These different conceptions have wide-ranging consequences. Are we preprogrammed to behave and feel in a certain way, as many evolutionists, psychoanalysts, and behaviorists would have it? Or is our bio-social makeup characterized by plasticity, as most neuroscientists and self-help writers argue? Is the self a work-in-progress, or does it have fixed attributes? And, perhaps most importantly, which of our qualities are changeable and which are not?

Theorists of temperament and personality type tend to assume that we are defined by a fairly fixed set of behavioral preferences, which can be used to classify and categorize us. This idea can be traced all the way back to ancient Greece and the physician Hippocrates (ca. 460–370 BCE). His typology of the four basic temperaments is rooted in humor theory. Established in the fifth century BCE, this theory was developed further by the Greek physician Galen of Pergamum (129–ca. 216 CE). Humor theory was so influential that it remained the dominant medical paradigm until the advent of modern medicine in the nineteenth century.[7] The idea of four basic human temperaments, too, persisted for millennia. We can still feel the repercussions of the Hippocratic temperament typology today.

Humor theory suggests that we are made up of four bodily fluids, or humors: blood, yellow bile, black bile, and phlegm. These four humors need to be in balance; otherwise, serious disturbances to our physical and mental health will ensue. Each humor is also associated with specific qualities and with one of the four elements: blood is aligned with warmth and moisture, and the element air; yellow bile with warmth, dryness, and fire; black bile with coldness, dryness, and earth; and phlegm with coldness, moisture, and water. Furthermore, each of the humors is also related to a particular temperament. Blood is associated with the sanguine temperament, yellow bile with the choleric temperament, black bile with the melancholic temperament, and phlegm with the phlegmatic temperament. The characteristics of the soul, Galen writes in *On the Temperaments*, follow the mixtures of the body. Humor theory, then, explained not only acute and chronic physical disturbances, but also our long-term psychological dispositions.

The sanguine type is thought to be relaxed, optimistic, and outgoing, while the phlegmatic character is stable, calm, and self-contained, bordering on the lethargic. Those with a choleric temperament are dominant, prone to wrath and outbursts of aggression, while the melancholic is brooding, depressive, and inward-looking. The many typologies of temperament that have emerged since Galen are essentially variations of this model. We can clearly see here the origins of Jungian and other more recent theories of personality types. We might now describe the sanguine, for instance, as extroverted feelers with a high social intelligence, and the choleric as extroverted thinkers, happy to lead and, on occasion, to bully. The phlegmatic map onto the category of introverted feelers, who are in touch with their intuition. The melancholic are introverted thinkers, prone to brooding. Knowing our temperament, then, and accepting the core traits that are associated with it, constitutes one of the oldest and most basic forms of self-knowledge.

The temperament that attracted most attention in the past was the melancholic. Melancholia was associated with "causeless sorrow and fear"—which we might now describe as symptoms of depression and anxiety. It was also aligned with a bitter, withdrawn, and occasionally misanthropic disposition. Melancholics often caused concern and sometimes evoked dislike. There were those who even thought of them as a danger to social cohesion. At the same time, however, melancholia was also associated with genius, art, scholarship, and creativity. In some circles, it was valorized, even celebrated—most notably by the Romantics.[8]

Three Books on Life (1489) is the first self-improvement handbook specifically addressed to melancholics and "learned people." Written by the Italian humanist Marsilio Ficino (1433–1499), it instructs gloomy knowledge-seekers on how to stay healthy and to live long and productive lives. In his wild mélange of astrology, astronomy, alchemy, and white magic, Ficino shows us how we can benefit from planetary constellations and draw on their specific energies. It is only by living in harmony with cosmic patterns that we can truly thrive, he believes. His thinking was very much in line with the then-current assumption that there were essential analogies between the micro- and the macrocosmic patterns of the universe.

But it is Ficino's advice on the recognition of our "natural bent" that is most important for our exploration of self-knowledge. "To live well and prosper," he writes, "first know your natural bent, your star, your genius, and the place suitable to these; here live. Follow your natural profession." First and foremost, we must find out and embrace our true calling, the one activity we enjoy most in life: "Assuredly for this above all else you were made by nature— the activity which from tender years you do, speak, play-act, choose, dream, imitate; that activity which you try more frequently, which you perform more easily, in which you make the most progress, which you enjoy above all else, which you leave off unwillingly." Only if we find and follow our natural bent will our undertakings be supported by the heavens.

If we fail to discover our natural bent, and our natural work, and even our natural habitat, we cannot prosper. If, for example, we choose a profession contrary to our genius, we "will find fortune adverse and will sense that the heavens are [our] enemy." There are two kinds of people, Ficino warns, who are unfortunate beyond the rest: the do-nothings and the misfits. The former "vegetate lazily when all the time the ever-moving heavens are continually inciting them to activity."[9] The misfits, however, labor in vain, because they are working not just against the grain of their own nature, but against the patterns of the cosmos. Living in harmony with our celestial patron enables us to tap fully into our potential, while battling against the order of the universe will result in complete exhaustion. The heavens will drain our resources and thwart our ambitions, and all our efforts will be for naught.

Ficino's self-improvement philosophy, then, amounts to a "know thyself" creed with both an astrological and a very practical spin. Beneath the astro-magical aspects of his model hides a time-less lesson: the importance of recognizing our natural talents and preferences. First of all, we need to establish what they are. In a crucial second step, they must inform our professional choices. By asking us to choose the external conditions that are most suitable to our internal dispositions, Ficino goes further than his predecessors. Socrates was interested in showing us the limits of our knowledge. Galen encouraged us to understand our basic temperament. Ficino's emphasis, by contrast, is on deliberately engineering fit. He urges us consciously to choose the environment that harmonizes most with our needs.

Applying Ficino's insight, we can draw some fairly obvious conclusions. Nervous introverts, for example, would be well advised not to work in a bar. People-loving adrenalin-cravers might not be suited to life as a librarian. Kind-hearted carers might make wonderful social workers and nurses, but in all likelihood be abysmal insurance salespeople. In this, we are not dissimilar to plants, for fig and olive trees will flourish in the sun, but not in the shade. Richard N. Bolles knew this well. His book *What Color Is Your Parachute?* (1970) has been described as "the world's most popular job-hunting guide."[10] It is structured precisely around Ficino's idea of engineering as good a match as possible between our "natural bent" and our profession. According to Bolles, it is necessary to take an inventory of the self, which enables us first to establish and then to plan our careers around our key passions and preferences.

Our current concept of self-knowledge includes not only an understanding of our temperament and natural preferences, but also an acknowledgment of how our past may have shaped us. By introducing the notion of the unconscious, the Austrian founder of psychoanalysis, Sigmund Freud (1856–1939), ushered in a dramatic paradigm shift. Our mind, Freud argues, is like an iceberg: only a small part of it is observable, while the rest drifts in the murky depths of our unconscious. Only when we pull our darkest desires into the light of the conscious, where we can examine them calmly and analytically, will they begin to lose their monstrosity, and much of their influence. Although Freud demonstrated in great detail the disconcerting power of the unconscious over our emotions and behaviors, he also remained a firm believer in reason as a panacea for our problems. He suggests that all of our seemingly irrational actions in the present can be explained rationally, by understanding our repressed desires and our past patterns.

"Psychoanalysis is often about turning our ghosts into ancestors," the neurologist Norman Doidge writes. "We are often haunted by important relationships from the past that influence us unconsciously in the present. As we work them through, they go from haunting us to becoming simply part of our history."[11] The things that tend to haunt us most are those we most rigorously try to repress. But, like the monster in any horror movie, the repressed has a tendency to return and to wreak havoc. It is very hard, if not impossible, to kill it off once and for all. The repressed is, of course, also what we do not know consciously—it is the true "other" to genuine self-knowledge.

Strictly speaking, psychoanalysis is not a form of self-help, since it requires the involvement of a third party—an analyst who acts both as an interpreter and as a projection screen. Via transference, the analyst allows us to reenact and eventually reframe key beliefs in the safe space of the consulting room. But Freud's ideas have substantially shaped modern conceptions of selfhood, and many of his basic assumptions are at work in the self-help literature of the twentieth and twenty-first centuries. First and foremost, these are manifest in the notion that we have basic psychological patterns that are determined by childhood events. These experiences may be responsible for our conflicts in the present. No less important is Freud's conception of critical superegos in overdrive. He has clearly shown that there is a part within ourselves that may be hostile, and that may even turn into our tormentor by constantly castigating and judging us. Last but not least, there is also Freud's famous three-part model of the human psyche, divided into the id, the ego, and the superego. It enjoys a vivid afterlife in various "mind model"–based self-help regimes.

In what is perhaps his darkest text, *Civilization and Its Discontents* (1930), Freud argues that culture constantly urges us to repress our aggressive impulses, which we therefore tend to internalize. Mostly in the form of guilt and self-hatred, we learn to turn them against ourselves rather than outward. Our superego can become a persecutory and even a sadistic agency, viciously lacerating the ego, constantly berating it for its failures. It is so powerful that it can even drive us to abandon the will to live altogether.

The melancholic is a classic example of someone tormented by a cruel superego. In his essay "Mourning and Melancholia" (1917), Freud outlines the core features of the melancholic, which traditionally include causeless sorrow and fear. Yet he throws a new symptom into the mix: self-hatred. As he puts it: "The distinguishing mental features of melancholia are a profoundly painful dejection, cessation of interest in the outside world, loss of the capacity to love, inhibition of all activity, and a lowering of the self-regarding feelings to a degree that finds utterance in self-reproaches and self-revilings, and culminates in a delusional expectation of punishment."[12]

Melancholia is associated with loss. In a complex psychological procedure, the melancholic transforms emotions originally triggered by the loss of a love object into the loss of a stable sense of self. Above all, Freud writes, the melancholic suffers from a persistent "delusion of (mainly moral) inferiority." As he explains: "In mourning it is the world which has become poor and empty; in melancholia it is the ego itself. The patient represents his ego to us as worthless, incapable of any achievement and morally despicable; he reproaches himself, vilifies himself and expects to be cast out and punished."[13] The melancholic's energies are spent on sadistic attacks inflicted on the vulnerable ego by a judgmental superego. In other words, melancholics are quite literally consumed by self-hatred. They use up all of their energy in psychological battles with themselves. Consequently, they have very little energy left to direct outward—that is, toward other people or external projects. In the more recent literature of self-help, the ongoing impact of this idea is evident in concepts such as "negative thoughts," "negative self-talk," and "limiting beliefs."

As psychoanalysts well know, in order to become genuine self-knowledge, any kind of rational insight into our nature needs to be accompanied by emotional change. Otherwise it will remain sterile and ineffective. We may be given a sharp and accurate diagnosis of what is wrong with us, and we may even accept it intellectually, but it is unlikely that this will change our behavior in a sustainable way. For transformation can only happen when an insight permeates deeper, to a place where it affects the very structure of our feelings. It needs to change the way we experience and interpret the world. In psychoanalysis, it is the analyst who tries to build these bridges. Their main tool for bringing about such deeper transformations in the patient is transference. The analyst helps us to change our stories about ourselves, assisting us in reframing our experiences and creating kinder, more productive narratives. Analysts are existential detectives, trying to trace the origins of our discontent back to its source. Then they put this information to work to disempower our less helpful self-beliefs.

The crucial act of reframing, of "self-story" or "script" changing, is much harder to achieve by reading self-help books than it is in a therapy or coaching setting. While we may be intellectually convinced or even deeply moved by what we read, information obtained from books is bound to be less effective in challenging our more deep-seated beliefs. Self-help writers attempt this task with stories. They tend to include numerous inspirational narratives or case studies of others who may have struggled with difficulties that are similar to our own. These stories reach us on an emotional, not just intellectual, level. They are designed to pull on our heartstrings, to appeal to our empathy, and to activate our imagination. They provide us with positive visions of what could be. It is via artfully told and inspiring case studies, combined with insightful analysis, that psychoanalytic self-help works, too. Irvin D. Yalom's *Love's Executioner and Other Tales of Psychotherapy* (1989) and, more recently, Stephen Grosz's *The Examined Life: How We Lose and Find Ourselves* (2013) are beautiful examples. Both are based on the assumption that by understanding more about the inner lives of others, we will be able to gain a kind of transferable self-knowledge that we can adapt to fit our own situations.

The greatest contribution of psychoanalysis to the deeper understanding of ourselves is, paradoxically, that it reconfirms our fundamental rationality. Psychoanalysis comes up with hyperrational explanations for our seemingly most irrational behaviors. It assumes that there are patterns in our lives and that we can trace the origins of these patterns back to our childhood experiences. If we feel undesirable or deficient in some way, it is because we have had this feeling at some point in our past. If we think nobody can ever love us, or are prone to erupt in anger at seemingly trivial incidents, there will be a pattern to discover there, too. If we trace it back carefully to its beginnings, it will reveal an old wound to our ego that has continued to fester in the shadows. We are, then, much more reasonable creatures than we may think. In fact, our behaviors only seem irrational if we lack the deeper self-knowledge to provide a rational explanation.

Many modern psychologists and self-help writers are highly critical of Freud. They dislike his fairly deterministic view of human nature, the importance he places on sexuality, and the interminable and indeterminable nature of analysis. They also take issue with his emphasis on past traumas and working through our bad experiences. And they are not alone. There can be no doubt that the grand narrative of psychoanalysis has dramatically lost purchase in the twenty-first century. We tend now to prefer cheaper, quicker, science-based, and more future-oriented ways of enhancing our psyches. But in spite of their renunciation of Freud, many self-help writers continue to adhere to a number of fundamental Freudian ideas.

It is now commonly accepted that basic psychological detective work is essential for genuine self-knowledge. If we want to improve ourselves, we need to understand our past patterns. This insight features centrally in M. Scott Peck's *The Road Less Traveled: A New Psychology of Love, Traditional Values, and Spiritual Growth* (1978), for example. It is present in all books that operate on the idea of "healing the inner child." In *You Can Heal Your Life* (1984), Louise L. Hay neatly sums up the Freudian notion of childhood patterns and how they may affect us later in life: "When we grow up, we have a tendency to re-create the emotional environment of our early home life," she writes. "This is not good or bad, right or wrong; it is just what we know inside as 'home.' We also tend to recreate in our personal relationships the relationships we had with our mothers or with our fathers, or what they had between them."[14] In fact, because they are so common and so widely accepted, statements of this kind now sound like truisms. But they simply show how firmly Freud's basic ideas have been woven into our wider cultural fabric.

Equally important in modern self-help is the Freudian idea of the castigating saboteur inside us that can make our lives hell. Books such as Anthony Robbins's *Awaken the Giant Within: How to Take Control of Your Mental, Emotional, Physical, and Financial Destiny* (1991) urge us to work on our inner critic. They advise us to eradicate negative self-talk and negative self-beliefs, and replace them with more positive mantras. Their key priority is the strengthening of our self-esteem. But the less conscious motive of works of this kind, and also of our wider cultural obsession with self-esteem, may well be different. It relates to the desire to guard ourselves precisely against the internal horror scenario that Freud describes so vividly—that is, the danger not just of constantly sabotaging ourselves but of becoming our own torturer.

The third prominent way in which Freudian ideas persist in modern self-help is manifest in models that attempt to manage our irrational side. Freud famously divided our psychological apparatus into id, ego, and superego. Others have created their own "mind models." Thomas A. Harris, in his bestselling *I'm OK—You're OK* (1973), for example, argues that our psyche is divided into a parent, an adult, and a child. In our interactions with others, we tend to adopt one of these positions. Ideally, we should not just be aware of the particular relational dynamics in which we find ourselves, but relate to others on an adult-to-adult basis. If we know ourselves and also understand where the other is coming from, Harris believes, we can avoid most interpersonal misunderstandings and conflicts.

Perhaps the most famous work of "mind model"–based self-help is Steve Peters's *The Chimp Paradox* (2012). Peters refers to our three "psychological brains": the "chimp" (roughly corresponding to the id, and resident in our limbic brain), the "human" (more or less the ego, located in our frontal lobes), and the "computer" (the superego, situated in our parietal brain).[15] Depending on the situation we are in, our blood supply flows from one part of the brain to another, activating specific behaviors and emotional responses. Like Freud's, Peters's is also a model based on conflicting agendas, in which different parts of our psyche do battle with one another in an endless psychomachia. Peters's self-improvement regime, too, is based on the idea that understanding more fully how our mind works will allow us to master it more effectively. However, he uses neurological language and offers evolutionary rather than psychoanalytic explanations. He promotes cognitive behavioral therapy techniques for correcting glitches in our "computer" brain and learning to manage our "chimp" brain.

Most of Peters's book focuses on chimp management techniques. For the chimp cannot be controlled, only coaxed. Crucially, we need the chimp on our side. Without it, we lack energy, instinct, and passion in our lives. In that sense, too, there are parallels to Freud's model. Freud famously compares the relationship between the ego and the id to that between a rider and his horse. The horse, he writes, provides the locomotor energy, whereas the rider has to determine the direction in which this energy is led. Without the rider's directive powers, the horse will run wild, taking the rider places he does not want to go. Without the horse, however, the rider has no powers of movement and cannot get where he wants to go either.

The American psychologist Daniel Goleman, too, knows that simply repressing our nonrational parts is not the solution. If we want to live fulfilling and balanced lives, we need to cultivate and master our emotions. Our emotions do not just provide impulses to act but can also serve as wise guides. Our aim should not be simply to let reason reign supreme—that would lead to a dull, cold, and lifeless existence. We would, in Freud's terms, lack the vital energy and drive of the id-horse. We would lack passion and the ability to connect emotionally with others. Instead, we should seek to establish a solid balance between our two forms of intelligence.

Goleman popularized the notion of "emotional intelligence." "Emotional aptitude," he writes, "is a *meta-ability*, determining how well we can use whatever other skills we have, including raw intellect."[16] Emotional intelligence involves self-control and the ability to empathize with others and to read their emotions. Crucially, emotional intelligence rests on an understanding of our own core emotional processes.[17] The keystone of emotional intelligence is *"knowing one's emotions."* It is a form of self-awareness that is manifest in "recognizing a feeling as it happens." For, Goleman writes, the "inability to notice our true feelings leaves us at their mercy."[18]

Those of us who know our feelings are generally better pilots of our lives. Indeed, for Goleman, knowing our emotions *is* knowing ourselves.

There is a crucial difference between simply being caught up in a feeling and developing an awareness that we are being taken over by that feeling. We might, for example, feel angry about not being served quickly enough in a restaurant. Our raw anger might lead us to shout at the waiter, get testy with our partner, storm out, and write a scathing online review. If we are better trained, however, it is likely that we will not do any of these things. We might recognize the physical and emotional symptoms of anger in the moment they occur. We might explore where our anger really comes from. We might be able to detach our emotions from the situational trigger and realize how they relate to deeper anxieties. Perhaps there was a time when we felt we were not taken seriously or were not treated with respect. In other words, by noticing, naming, and analyzing our feelings, we take the wind out of their sails.

Detached self-observation is essential for knowing our emotional selves. Such self-observation entails stepping back from our experience. It is about cultivating an awareness of our conscious thought that hovers above it rather than becoming entangled in it. Both Freud and Goleman believe that knowing ourselves is essential. Yet Goleman's emphasis is firmly on the present rather than on the past. And while Freud ultimately wishes for reason to reign supreme in our inland empires (it is, after all, the rider in his image), Goleman advocates a more harmonious power-sharing between reason and the emotions. For our head- and heart-based intelligences would both be impoverished without the input of the other.

While Freud was interested in the unconscious of the individual, his rival C. G. Jung (1875–1961) turned his attention to what he called the "collective unconscious." Jung, too, believed that we all have an individual unconscious, but he argued that there is another layer beneath it that is transpersonal. We share this second layer, which holds latent memories from our ancestral and evolutionary past, with all other members of the human species. Jung was keenly interested in myth and in symbolism in art, literature, and in our dreams. He considered all of them rich repositories of the imagery and archetypes that derive from the collective unconscious.

Jung's construct of the archetype is a timeless one, primordial and archaic in character. It expresses material from the collective unconscious in a condensed and concise form. Jung understands the archetype as a memory deposit that has arisen "through the condensation of countless processes of a similar kind." It gives a distinctive shape to "certain ever-recurring psychic experiences."[19] Jung's four most important archetypes are the persona, the anima/animus, the shadow, and the self. A classic set of twelve characters is particularly popular in the coaching and self-help world. This dozen comprises the ruler, the creator, the sage, the trickster, the explorer, the rebel, the hero, the magician, the everyman, the innocent, the caregiver, and the lover. Jungian archetypes, too, can be tools for self-knowledge. They can help us to identify the ancient blueprints for the roles we play, the behaviors in which we engage, and our natural predilections.

Jungian archetypes are also highly relevant for self-knowledge in relation to myth. According to Joseph Campbell (1904–1987), the teaching of self-knowledge is one of the primary functions of myth. A comparative mythologist by training, Campbell established the theory of the "monomyth"—the idea that all myths are essentially variations of some basic archetypal narratives. One of the most important myths is the hero's journey, which Campbell explores in depth in *The Hero with a Thousand Faces* (1949). Hero's journey myths follow a cyclical departure/return structure. Their key stages include the call to adventure, with the hero venturing forth into the unknown. The unknown may take the form of a dark wood, an underground kingdom, caves, the sea, the belly of a beast, or lands in which fabulous creatures roam. The hero then encounters an obstacle and needs to engage in battle—with a creature, an enemy, or a temptation—finally winning a decisive victory. He returns from his adventure transformed, often with a boon, an elixir, or a message in tow. There may also be magical helpers, protectors, and mentors, and, of course, dangerous temptations—frequently in the form of seductive women.

The hero's adventure often begins with a lack or a loss, and ends in a recovery of what has been lost or was lacking. Like many other successful Disney productions, the plot of *Frozen II* (2019) follows the hero's journey pattern. At the beginning, something is not right in Queen Elsa's kingdom. She hears voices, and nature is acting up. Elsa is, quite literally, called upon to venture into the unknown. She embarks on a journey into an enchanted forest, and later seeks the mythical river Ahtohallan, which, as legend has it, contains the answers to all secrets. Entering into the glacial heart of the frozen river, she penetrates deeper and deeper in search of the answers she seeks, putting her life in peril. Eventually she discovers the disconcerting truth about herself and her family's past. Armed with new self-knowledge, and aided by the brave actions of her sister Ana, Elsa finally emerges from the cold depth of her unconscious onto a higher spiritual plane. Her outfit is now all white. She returns to save the people of her kingdom, and henceforth lives happily in the woods, in harmony with nature and the elements.

The basic motif of the universal hero's journey, Campbell writes in *The Power of Myth* (1988), is "leaving one condition and finding the source of life to bring you forth into a richer or mature condition."[20] The hero's journey is about self-discovery and learning to control our darker passions. Monsters and other creatures of evil symbolize the irrational savage within us. Via trials, tribulations, and illuminating revelations, the hero's journey chronicles the transformation of consciousness from a state of unawareness to a state of deep self-understanding.

Myths, then, furnish us with a collective kind of self-knowledge—at the species level—helping to guide us safely through the different stages of life. In the West, we have grown ever worse at collectively celebrating the rites of passage that mark our most important moments of transition. These initiation and threshold moments include birth, death, marriage, mother- and fatherhood, and the passage from childhood into adulthood. Myths can also provide solace, by showing us that we are far from alone with our troubling experiences. They impart knowledge not in the form of explicit advice, but in the language of symbols, metaphors, and imagery. This language speaks to our imagination and our unconscious, and resonates with our more deeply imprinted latent memories. "Myths inspire the realization of the possibility of your perfection, the fullness of your strength, and the bringing of solar light into the world," Campbell writes. "Slaying monsters is slaying the dark things."[21]

There is also a frequently neglected but essential social dimension to the hero's quest. The hero's true function is "neither release nor ecstasy for oneself, but the wisdom and the power to serve others."[22] "A hero," Campbell observes, "is someone who has given his or her life to something bigger than oneself."[23] The true objective of the hero is to save others. It is thus of vital importance for the hero to return from the magical kingdom in which she has achieved victory. She must share her life-transforming trophy with her people. The true hero does not selfishly hold on to the holy grail or elixir of life, or nail the Golden Fleece on his living-room wall where he alone can see it. Nor does he stay on the Island of the Sun, or in a state of self-contained bliss. The Buddha, for example, returns to the earthly realm to communicate his message to others in spite of having achieved Nirvana. Odysseus stays with neither Calypso nor Circe, and he rejects Nausicaa's offer of marriage. Although briefly tempted, the ancient Mesopotamian hero Gilgamesh does not eat the plant of life himself, but instead shares it with his people back home. Queen Elsa, too, only retires to the woods after having saved her people from a potentially devastating flood and having installed her sister as her worldly successor. Compassion and altruism, then, are the true aims of successful heroic transformation.

By activating archetypal patterns, myths communicate a collective form of self-knowledge. They nourish our spirit and provide guidance. Pointing to our deeper spiritual potential, they have a therapeutic function: they show us how to interpret and confront our suffering. Similarly, many modern self-help texts operate with archetypes. Carol S. Pearson's bestselling *The Hero Within: Six Archetypes We Live By* (1986) is a case in point. The Jungian psychoanalyst Clarissa Pinkola Estés, in her classic *Women Who Run with the Wolves: Contacting the Power of the Wild Woman* (1992), explores the archetype of the wild woman and uses folk tales to activate the powers of this archetype in the unconscious of her readers. The male counterpart to Estés's book is Robert Bly's equally Jungian-in-spirit *Iron John: Men and Masculinity* (1990).

As the publication dates of Campbell's and these other books show, the idea of the Jungian collective unconscious captured the public imagination in the late 1980s and early 1990s. This may have been at least in part a reaction to the celebration of competitive individualism in the era of Thatcher and Reagan. To counter the growing emphasis on material success and essentially selfish pursuits, these self-help books emphasize what we share instead—above all in the form of deep and collective imagery. It is also noticeable that the more corporate we became, the more we appeared to long for wildness, as the particular appeal of the wild woman and the wild man archetypes indicate. But just like Freudian psychoanalysis, this aspect of Jungian thought has fallen from favor in our current millennium.

There is no doubt that Jung's theory of the collective unconscious has lost its relevance in the self-help literature of the twenty-first century. Many tend now to associate talk of the collective unconscious with an esoteric, new-agey kind of mysticism. Jung's personality type model, by contrast, is still proving influential. As we have seen, the idea that we can be classified according to our basic temperaments is not new, but reaches back all the way to Greek antiquity. Modern psychologists have continued to search for universal types and models that capture our fundamental differences. But by far the most influential attempt to establish such a characterology is Jung's.

In *Psychological Types* (1921), Jung argues that there are two main categories of people: introverts and extroverts. The key difference between these two types is the direction of their interest. Extroverts direct it outward, toward people and external objects, whereas introverts are primarily preoccupied with their inner self. This difference is crucial, because it determines how we interpret and perceive the world. For introverts, the subjective factor rules supreme. This can result in a "devaluation of the object. The object is not given the importance that belongs to it by right. Just as it plays too great a role in the extraverted attitude, it has too little meaning for the introvert."[24]

Jung presents an evolutionary reason for our fundamental differences. Always intent on expending and propagating themselves, extroverts are characterized by a high rate of fertility and low powers of defense. Introverts, by contrast, invest the lion's share of their energy in self-preservation, with a resulting lower fertility rate.[25] By producing both introverts and extroverts, nature tries it on both ways. Sometimes the proactive and sometimes the defensive and cautious approach is bound to be more suitable for ensuring the survival of the species.

While introversion and extroversion are the basic "attitudes of consciousness," Jung also specifies four "functions of consciousness": feeling, thinking, sensation, and intuition. According to our predilections, there can thus be extroverted thinking types, introverted sensing types, extroverted feeling types, and so on. If we have a preference for sensing, for example, we will privilege seeing and hearing over our intuition. We may be realists, empiricists, and lovers of "tangible reality" with a highly developed sense for objective facts.[26] As an extroverted intuitive type, by contrast, we may not be bound by accepted reality-values, but may have a keen nose for novelty and possibilities. We may feel suffocated by stable conditions and constantly ferret out new possibilities, choosing entrepreneurial or speculative professions, such as investment banking.

It is fair to say that Jung is generally not particularly positive about introverts. Partly this is because he was an introvert himself, so we can interpret this negativity as a form of self-criticism. But we can also see his stance as the result of a broader cultural bias against introversion. His negative take contrasts starkly with that of Susan Cain, whose beautiful hymn to introversion, *Quiet: The Power of Introverts in a World That Can't Stop Talking* (2012), perceptively analyzes the wider cultural prejudice against introverts. Whereas Cain bolsters introverted egos by outlining their many gifts and special talents, Jung writes that introverts' strong disregard for external objects, including other people, can make others feel unimportant or unwanted. If we fall into the introverted category, we may be shy, taciturn, and aloof, and appear arrogant, cold, and inflexible. If we are thinking introverts, moreover, we may overcomplicate things and constantly become entangled in our own scruples and misgivings. If we are really tragic cases, we may even "develop into a misanthropic bachelor with a childlike heart."[27]

While Jung sometimes found it difficult to hide his distaste for introverts, the intention behind his characterology was neither to judge nor to rank the different types, but simply to understand them. The core lesson to learn from his reflections on type is that we all have natural preferences, resulting in different ways of looking at the world. We all perceive through specific lenses, filtering out information or focusing on completely different things. As Jung puts it, "Although it is true that everyone orients himself in accordance with the data supplied by the outside world, we see every day that the data in themselves are only relatively decisive."[28] The better we understand what our preferences and lenses are, then, the better we understand ourselves.

During the Second World War, Katharine C. Briggs and her daughter Isabel Briggs Myers, both ardent fans of Jung's work, decided to develop his ideas further. The result was the Myers-Briggs Type Indicator (MBTI). The MBTI accepts extroversion and introversion as basic type indicators, along with the four functions of consciousness, thinking, feeling, sensing, and intuition. However, Briggs and Briggs Myers also added a preference for judging or perceiving as a further function pair. Today, the Myers-Briggs typology is still a widely employed personality assessment tool. It is used for personal and leadership development, recruitment purposes, team enhancement, and even on dating sites.

Another widely used Jungian psychometric tool that has much traction in today's business world is Insights Discovery Profiles. Users of the Insights product answer twenty-five questions; the responses are converted into a detailed personality report listing our natural preferences, strengths, and weaknesses. Insights uses color coding, dividing people into cool blue types (thinking introverts), fiery red types (extroverted thinkers), sunshine yellow types (extroverted feelers), and earth green types (introverted feelers). These types and the colors are clearly related to Hippocrates's four temperaments, with blue mapping onto the melancholic, red onto the choleric, yellow onto the sanguine, and green onto the phlegmatic temperament.

On its website, Insights describes its services in the following terms: "We bring self-awareness to people, teams, leaders and organisations. That's where business breakthroughs happen. We provide insights for your people—increasing their self-awareness, helping them form better relationships, and becoming more effective at their jobs. ... Self-understanding is transformative for your people; self-aware people are transformative for your business."²⁹ In this marketing snippet, we can clearly see the instrumentalization of self-knowledge. It is presented as a tool for productivity enhancement and gaining competitive advantages. Here, self-knowledge is presented not so much as a value but as a skill, even a product that we may purchase. It is worth having because it turns us into better communicators, more productive team players, more effective relationship builders, and generally more efficient workers.

These may indeed all be consequences or welcome side effects of self-knowledge. There is nothing wrong with these aims per se; indeed, most of us aspire to possessing these qualities. It is also perfectly reasonable that our employers would wish for us to have them—for nobody enjoys working with catastrophic communicators, bad team players, and colleagues with poor impulse control who constantly clash with their clients and coworkers. And it is very likely that such people are also bad for business. However, self-knowledge has been recast here as a means to achieve an end. Stripped of its ancient connection to wisdom, it is no longer considered a value in its own right. Instead, self-knowledge has been turned into yet another tool for realizing the diktat of relentless efficiency enhancement.

While still very popular in the self-help and business world, typological approaches such as Jung's have fallen from favor among psychologists. Instead, they have searched for more scientific ways to capture our fundamental differences. The most famous attempt, the so-called "Big Five" trait theory, rose to prominence in the early 1990s. It is based on a lexical analysis of descriptors of common language. The five factors used to describe the human psyche in this model are openness, conscientiousness, extroversion, agreeableness, and neuroticism (they form the acronym OCEAN). How we score on these traits is measured by rating statements such as "I am the life of the party," "I don't mind being the center of attention," and "I have a soft heart." Openness refers to the degree to which we seek and appreciate new experiences and intellectual stimulation. It also relates to our ability to tolerate ambiguity. Conscientiousness measures how organized, disciplined, industrious, and goal-orientated we are. Extroversion relates to our need for stimulation from others and from the outside world. Agreeableness measures our potential for aggression, politeness, compassion, and the extent to which we care about what others think about us. Neuroticism, finally, encompasses our general emotional stability, our ability to cope with stressful situations, and our tendency to withdraw.[30]

According to psychologist and self-help author Richard Wiseman, not only do these character traits "tend to remain unchanged" throughout our life, but they also influence almost every aspect of our behavior, including "relationships, performance in the workplace, leisure activities, consumer choice, religious and political beliefs, creativity, sense of humor and health."[31] Wiseman puts forth an even more disconcerting claim: "Most psychologists now believe that the apparent complexity of human personality is an illusion. In reality, people vary on just five fundamental dimensions."[32] Judging by the prevalence of Big Five and other personality tests in modern self-help texts, many self-help writers appear to agree with this rather reductive view of the human psyche.

There is no doubt that these and other kinds of personality tests can capture some of our basic traits and cognitive preferences. Often, they can be surprisingly, almost spookily, accurate, as in the case of Insights Discovery Profiles. However, they remain limited tools. The Big Five model, for example, has been shown to be methodologically flawed. It is not nearly as effective in explaining or predicting behavior as is often claimed. And in no way does it include all of the "normal" traits of human personality, let alone those deemed "abnormal."[33] The Big Five have also been described in terms of a "psychology of the stranger." The test refers to the obvious parts of our personality, while revealing very little about our more private selves.[34]

Personality tests based either on Jung's typology or on the Big Five model can give us important pointers to our preferences, ones we may not have been consciously aware of, and in that respect, these tests are useful. However, they are also reductive, each with its specific flaws and blind spots.[35] While they may provide appealing labels that resonate with us, by putting us into boxes they can also halt growth rather than stimulating it. Labels can be experienced as positive and helpful, but they can also lead to selective attention and create fixed mindsets. If we grow too attached to them, we may become blind to the many instances when we do not live up (or down) to our type. Our behavior, moreover, tends to be highly context-dependent, and our type affiliations may vary accordingly. We might be quite extroverted and chatty when in a family setting, for example, but very reluctant to speak during meetings at work.

What is more, while they may present a fairly accurate picture of the status quo, personality tests tend not to show us how we might improve ourselves.[36] Guidance about what we should do with this kind of information is usually provided by third parties—coaches, mentors, and therapists. Personality tests, then, may furnish us with more or less accurate information about ourselves, but not with genuine self-knowledge. Proper self-knowledge has to be experienced and put to the test—often through trials and tribulations, as in the hero's journey. It has to be acquired in action, not simply given to us. Personality tests alone do not have the capacity to generate wisdom. They do not take into account our past and how it may be affecting us in the present, and they tend to ignore the many more intricate aspects of our personalities.

According to Hippocrates, I am a full-blown melancholic. In Jungian terms, I am a thinking introvert with a strong preference for sensing, and my MBTI type is ISTJ (introverted, sensing, thinking, and judging). I am also very blue on my Insights Discovery profile, a focused coordinating observer. My main archetypes are engineer and architect, as well as custodian, scribe, seeker, and challenger. The Big Five test tells me I am a fairly neurotic, extremely introverted, but highly conscientious person, anxious not to offend others but very open to new experiences. While there is an undeniable theme running through my results (blue in color), they really do not tell you very much at all about me in all my messiness and complexity.

My test results will not, for example, tell you what my favorite smells are (tea shops, dunes, and gorse bushes), nor that I have a phobia of birds because of their reptilian eyes and prehistoric claws, and because I was once bitten by a swan that I tried, unwisely, to feed popcorn. I do not like unmade beds, very small teeth, crumbs, and the sound of chewing, and I often find the company of the jolly and the overconfident taxing. I prefer the sea to shallow water, and I find mountains and small children dressed like adults uncanny. For almost two years now, I have played almost nothing but Pachelbel's Canon in D Major on the piano. In others I most envy big hair and the skill of small talk—both of which I lack. When I was little, I was mortally afraid of angels. My favorite animal is the wolf. I like symmetry in gardens, as well as in architecture and faces, but I like it even more when it is disturbed by a gnarly tree or a mole. Along with solar panels, I would like to put some gargoyles on our roof. I tend to drink too much red wine, although I really try not to, and I am a great lover of salty things, beautiful but succinct writing, and clear thinking. I have two Siberian cats and a daughter who is my complete opposite in almost every respect: she talks nonstop, loves to dance in the limelight, and is the most relentlessly social creature I know. But she, too, is impatient and loves to watch films with positive transformations at their core. We both loathe the sound of bagpipes and shrill brass instruments.

A final important question remains to be answered. Why should we aspire to self-knowledge in the first place? Why is it a good thing to possess? Self-knowledge directly relates to one of our five basic needs, the desire to learn. It includes learning about our own patterns, preferences, and processes. The opposite of self-knowledge is ignorance—about who we really are, our true motives, and how others may perceive us. Freud would argue that self-knowledge emancipates us from being a slave to our unconscious and its many seemingly irrational whims. Only when we know our patterns, and whence they came, can we manage and perhaps even change them. Self-knowledge, then, yields mastery and realism, as well as congruence and alignment. It is the necessary first step in initiating change. Only by taking stock of what is—in as objective a way as possible—can we truly plan what we want to change. Self-knowledge, moreover, quite simply improves our chances of making wiser life choices on a regular basis.[37]

But self-knowledge can only be a catalyst for change when it comes from the inside. It cannot just be passed on to us in the form of a snappy diagnosis or a test result. In order for information about ourselves to impact on our behavior and the way we feel about and perceive the world, this information needs to be transformed into something we hold to be true at a deeper level. In this process, our imagination and our emotions need to be involved. We also need repeatedly to experience this information as true in action. This means that genuine self-knowledge can never be gained purely by theoretical introspection or reading about different models of the mind, but only through trials and tribulations, and in dialogue with others. It needs to be acquired on our own journeys—heroic or otherwise.

CHAPTER TWO

Control Your Mind

T HE BELIEF THAT WE can control our feelings by controlling our thoughts is both the most simple and also the most radical premise on which most modern self-help rests. The promise of sovereignty over our minds is highly attractive. If we were truly able to control our thoughts, nothing could ever rattle us, no matter how bad the cards we are dealt in life. The prospect of control over our cognitive processes is even more appealing in times of uncertainty and change. The more unstable our external circumstances are, the more we long to establish stability within ourselves. But the dream of being master in our own house is much older than we may think.

The idea first emerged in ancient Greece around 300 BCE among the philosophers of the Stoa. The school of Hellenistic philosophy known as Stoicism flourished in the Greek and Roman worlds until the third century CE, its name deriving from the place where the early Stoics taught their doctrine, the *stoa poikile*, or "painted porch," which looked out to the ancient agora of Athens. The significance of the porch is that it was an open public space rather than an enclosed private one, like Speaker's Corner in London's Hyde Park. One of the many achievements of the Stoics was that they democratized the venture of philosophy: anyone could drop by and listen to their teachings.

We now tend to associate the Stoics with the repression of the emotions and imagine them to have been cold and heartless, lacking empathy and a sense of humor. A bit like Data in *Star Trek*, we are inclined to think of them as people who have trouble computing human emotions. But this is a misconception. Rather than arguing that we should put a lid on our emotions, the Stoics believed we should evaluate them rationally and reason ourselves out of upsetting emotional states. Their method was a "working-through" maneuver, but one that was purely analytical in spirit. Reason, not repression, was their solution to all of our emotional challenges.

In that respect, Stoic thought is strikingly modern. Stoics such as Seneca (ca. 2 BCE–65 CE), Epictetus (ca. 55–135 CE), and Marcus Aurelius (121–180 CE) believed that all suffering is in our minds. It is caused not by external events but by our reactions to those events—that is, by faulty judgments and unrealistic expectations. The Stoics also held fantastically pragmatic views about how we should spend our mental energies. Given that most external events are beyond our control, they believed that it is pointless to worry about them. Our evaluations of these events, by contrast, are completely within our control, for we are ultimately rational animals. Therefore, they recommend that we should not attach significance to any external phenomena or circumstance. Instead, all our mental energies should be directed inward, with a view to controlling our minds.

Stoic thought has a rich and thriving afterlife. A modern Christian version of Stoic principles can be found in Reinhold Niebuhr's serenity prayer. The prayer has become a core mantra in twelve-step programs such as AA: "God grant me the serenity to accept the things I cannot change; courage to change the things I can; and wisdom to know the difference." Cognitive behavioral therapy (CBT), with its emphasis on disempowering our negative thoughts and limiting beliefs by confronting them with more rational and objective assessments, is also based on Stoic principles. The notion of resilience, too—the idea that if we cannot change our circumstances, we should concentrate on building up our inner resources instead so that we can cope more effectively with adversity—belongs in this tradition. Resilience is essentially about "bouncing back better."

The Stoic approach is highly reasonable—perhaps to a fault. There are other advocates of mind control who are situated on the opposite end of the spectrum, with theories more akin to magical than to rational thinking. The Stoics were absolutely clear about what we can control (our inner world) and what we cannot control (external events). Yet a highly influential group of self-help writers alleges that by controlling our inner world we *can* influence the outer world as well. Writers such as Napoleon Hill, who wrote the bestselling *Think and Grow Rich* (1937), and more recently Rhonda Byrne, author of *The Secret* (2006), argue that our thoughts are "magnetic." If we think positive thoughts, we will automatically attract positive outcomes—and vice versa: if we are gloomy pessimists, bad things will happen to us. The illusion of omnipotence that Byrne and other mystic-esoteric self-help writers promote is dangerous in many ways. According to their logic, everything bad that happens to us is entirely our fault, and that includes illnesses, assault, poverty, and other misfortunes.

Positive psychology, which rose to prominence in the 1990s, sits somewhere between the two extremes of the Stoic and the magical thinking traditions. It argues that how we think about ourselves can have an impact on our performance and achievements. However, it sidesteps the overestimation of the powers of our rational faculties, and also avoids unsubstantiated claims about the ability of our thoughts to influence external events. Positive psychology is particularly concerned with self-belief and positive self-talk. It, too, advocates that we control our minds, by urging us to focus on the importance of positive and optimistic thinking. Positive psychology also mobilizes the powers of our imagination in this task. The Stoics, by contrast, trusted only reason with managing our emotions. It is to their ideas that we shall turn first.

The greatest Stoic thinkers, Seneca, Epictetus, and Marcus Aurelius, all believed that philosophy's key function is to help us reform our character and to provide practical advice on how we may achieve this aim.[1] They propose philosophical action plans for living a good and virtuous life, in harmony with divine providence and society. Epictetus's famous essay *Of Human Freedom* includes chapter titles that could easily feature in a modern self-help book, such as "Concerning what is in our power and what is not," "How a person can preserve their proper character in any situation," "On satisfaction," "How we should struggle with circumstance," and "Every circumstance represents an opportunity."

It is no coincidence that Stoicism flourished in times of great political instability. Changeable and often cruel emperors held absolute power over the life and death of their subjects. It was not uncommon for men in influential political positions suddenly to fall from grace and to be banished from Rome. Some were be-headed or instructed to commit suicide simply because they had aroused the emperor's jealousy. Epictetus knew a thing or two about such dramatic changes of fortune. Consequently, he sought to establish robust psychological defenses against them. Before he became a philosopher, he was a crippled Greek slave. He was even-tually freed by his Roman master, who recognized his considerable intellectual gifts. But even as a free man he was not safe. Banished from the capital by governors envious of his popularity, Epictetus had to set up his school in the provinces and start all over again.

Seneca's life provides another captivating case study in instabil-ity. Early in his career, the statesman, philosopher, and author of tragedies was sentenced to death by Caligula. He was accused of having committed adultery with the emperor's sister. Although Ca-ligula's successor, Claudius, commuted the death sentence to banish-ment, Seneca had to spend eight long and lonely years in exile in Corsica. Eventually, he was recalled to Rome to teach Claudius's son, who would become the infamous emperor Nero. But Nero clearly ignored the teachings of his mentor. Violent and vindictive, he became renowned for his cruelty. In 59 CE, Nero ordered the killing of his own mother. Justifiably worried, Seneca withdrew from public life and, as a precaution, donated his entire fortune to his for-mer charge. But the gesture failed to appease. In the aftermath of a botched plot to kill Nero, in which Seneca may or may not have been involved, the philosopher was ordered to commit suicide.

Given Seneca's and Epictetus's biographies, and those of many other Greeks and Romans besides, we can see why the Stoics were so concerned with how best to negotiate the fickleness of fortune. The mood swings of their rulers could, quite literally, be deadly. Power, public office, money, and reputation could be granted and withdrawn on a whim. They saw empires rise and fall, great cities burn to cinders, and men of noble families killed or enslaved.

It is also unsurprising that interest in Stoicism has surged in our own troubled times. Our challenges are many. Political and economic uncertainty, the threat brought by pandemic and irreversible climate change, and the rapid digitization of our professional and private lives have no doubt contributed to the present-day renaissance of Stoic thought. Yet while these challenges may have sharpened our desire to shore up our psychological defenses, the appeal of gaining control over our inner lives never really weakened in the first place. Many of the Stoics' promises possess a timeless allure. Our specific woes may well change throughout the centuries. But illness, death, loss of loved ones, and changes of fortune remain perennial human sorrows with which all of us have to contend.

Stoics accept that there are many things we cannot control. All outer circumstances, they believe, are predetermined by fate and nature and are thus by definition beyond our sphere of influence. But rather than despairing about what they could not master, the Stoics decided to direct all of their mental energy to what they could: our *responses* to external events. Most would agree with their reasoning so far. But the Stoics went further. Because we cannot control external phenomena, they argued that we should not attach significance to *any* external phenomena at all—that is, to anything that can be taken away from us. This list includes possessions, reputations, food and drink, and all pleasures of the flesh, but also our health, friends, partners, children—and even our very lives. It is at this point that their doctrine becomes much harder to accept.

"There is nothing either good or bad but thinking makes it so," writes Seneca (as Hamlet knew well).[2] And he adds: "We are attracted by wealth, pleasures, good looks, political advancement and various other welcoming and enticing prospects: we are repelled by exertion, death, pain, disgrace and limited means. It follows that we need to train ourselves not to crave for the former and not to be afraid of the latter."[3] To cope with the frailty of human existence, we must refuse to allow anything that goes badly for us to affect us emotionally. Only if we carry our valuables inside us—in the form of our beliefs and cognitive skills—can we become invincible, no matter what fortune hurls at us.

A key strategy for achieving this aim of absolute equanimity in the face of hardship is to regulate our desires. According to the Stoics, we should completely align our desires with nature and divine providence. We can do this by never wanting anything we cannot have or that we may lose. All we should ever desire is to exercise the right kind of judgment when we respond to the external world. If we do not struggle against circumstance, we gain something much more precious: we become free. "Freedom," Epictetus writes, "is having events go in accordance with our will, never contrary to it."[4] In other words, if we always want exactly that which happens to us, we can never be disappointed.

One of the most common human desires, both now and then, is for money and luxury goods. These, in turn, are driven by our need for status. While it is perhaps the ultimate cliché to state that money cannot buy us happiness, there is also no other truism that we fail more spectacularly to take to heart. For millennia, sages have preached that accumulating possessions cannot ever bring us lasting joy. The most extreme spiritual seekers—ascetics and hermits—even try to live entirely without them. Epictetus, too, argues that all of the external things we crave, and that we work so hard to acquire, turn to ashes once we attain them. We will always find that our longing is unchanged, and our anxiety unappeased.

Modern psychologists are familiar with this phenomenon, too. They call it "hedonic adaptation." If we buy a new coat, for example, it will boost our happiness level for a few weeks at most. But soon our new coat will have become the new normal. It will cease to make our heart skip a beat when we touch its fabric, put it on, and admire it in the mirror. Instead, we will quickly start to crave a newer model. The same is true of bigger houses, handbags, cars, watches, and so on. Our happiness level will never change sustainably as a result of any purchase. If we are lucky, it may spike for a few days or weeks, only to return to where it was before. What is worse, our possessions also make us more vulnerable to the pain of loss. For while we will feel no increase in our contentment in the long run whenever we purchase stuff or gain in status, we are very able to feel acute pain when we lose these things. The more we value things beyond our control, then, the less control we have. Freedom, Epictetus concludes, is "not achieved by satisfying desire but by eliminating it."[5]

But how realistic is it to aspire to such a high-minded nonmaterialistic mindset? Even the Stoics were ready to admit that some of the external phenomena beyond our control are preferable to others. It is obviously nicer to be wealthy, healthy, loved, and sated with a roof over our head than the opposite. Seneca writes that he is not against us possessing these things as such. But he wants to ensure that we possess them "without tremors." We can only achieve that by convincing ourselves that we can live happily without them, and "by always regarding them as being on the point of vanishing."[6]

By contrast, Epictetus—generally more hard-nosed than Seneca —seems positively to welcome blows of fortune. They provide us with essential training and ultimately turn us into better, stronger people. Life is suffering; bad things will happen. And when they do, we can use our bad luck to test our resolve: "So when trouble comes, think of yourself as a wrestler whom God, like a trainer, has paired with a tough young buck. For what purpose? To turn you into Olympic-class material."[7] Adversity, then, is to be seen as a sparring partner. All our challenges are opportunities to strengthen our inner resolve. Everything that fortune throws at him, Epictetus writes, "I will transform into a blessing, a boon—something dignified, even enviable."[8]

Predictably, the Stoics do not abide self-pity. They are particularly unsympathetic to people complaining about their parents. There is no room in their philosophy for the idea of victimhood or psychological damage. On parents and childhood wounds—a topic on which much ink is expended in modern self-help—Epictetus has the following to say: "'It's my bad luck to have awful parents.' Well, you couldn't very well choose them beforehand, saying 'Let this man have intercourse with this woman, at this particular moment, so that I can be conceived.' Your parents had to come first, then you had to be born the way you are, of parents the way *they* are. Does that mean you have to be miserable?"[9] Both Epictetus and Seneca cavalierly eliminate all the drama and sense of injustice from our formation years. Their hyper-rational view runs completely counter to our psychoanalytically inflected understandings of our mental troubles. The Stoics make no allowance at all for the impact of traumatic experiences. There is also no attempt to understand why some of us are more resilient than others. This is clearly a blind spot in their philosophy. Almost everything that is of interest to present-day psychologists the Stoics would dismiss as weakness and a failure of our logical faculty to control our passions.

The question of responsibility in Stoic thought, finally, is also provoking. On the one hand, we are completely released from any blame for external events. In some cases, this lack of accountability may be experienced as a relief. The Stoics believe that we can do very little indeed to impact our surroundings. Epictetus writes: "The gods have released you from accountability for your parents, your siblings, your body, your possessions—for death and for life itself. They made you responsible only for what is in your power— the proper use of impressions. So why take on the burden of matters which you cannot answer for? You are only making un- necessary problems for yourself."[10] Many of us might feel uncom- fortable with this deterministic worldview—we like to think of ourselves as possessing much more agency than the Stoics suggest we have. However, the Stoics compensate by arguing that we are 100 percent responsible for our inner life—our judgments, beliefs, values, and desires. According to that logic, experiencing grief, sad- ness, anxiety, depression, or anger is our own fault, too. Epictetus and Seneca would judge that these emotions are the result of false interpretations and wrong expectations. They would remind us that it is not just within our power but indeed our primary duty to man- age these. In reality, this is far from easy, and not always possible.

The Roman emperor-by-adoption Marcus Aurelius (121–180 CE) was not a professional philosopher, but his famous *Meditations* read like the (albeit highly sophisticated) journal of a Stoic trainee. Pri- vate reflections, they include self-examinations, mental exercises, and numerous maxims that beautifully capture Stoic thought, re- vealing the efforts of someone who tried to put Stoic doctrine into practice in his everyday life. They also demonstrate just how much cognitive discipline being a Stoic requires. Aurelius's text is teeming with imperatives such as "remember," "keep in mind," and "do not forget." The *Meditations* not only record the journey of a man in search of self-mastery, but function as a spiritual-philosophical guidebook for its author.

The *Meditations* focus solely on the inner life. There is no men- tion of any of the external events with which Aurelius had to contend during his reign—in spite of the fact that they included fairly major ones such as the flooding of the Tiber, famine, and the plague, which broke out in 166–167 CE, as well as various attempts to usurp him. The *Meditations* are not about mastery of the external world but, in true Stoic fashion, purely about cognitive self-mastery. They chronicle Aurelius's attempt to reassert his rule not over his subjects and his enemies but over himself. For him, philosophy was above all a form of self-therapy.

Aurelius practiced various mental exercises. One entails the act of disassembling something into its constituent parts, thereby rendering it strange and alien. The purpose of this technique is to create emotional distance. We should seek to show things "naked, see their shoddiness, strip away their own boastful account of themselves."[11] This "denuding of human experience" is an excellent Stoic strategy for putting things into perspective.[12] On food and sex, for example, Aurelius writes: "How good it is, when you have roast meat or suchlike foods before you, to impress on your mind that this is the dead body of a fish, this the dead body of a bird or pig. . . . And in sexual intercourse that it is no more than the friction of a membrane and a spurt of mucus ejected."[13] Another technique Aurelius favors for honing our ability to respond more rationally to external events is to remember the vanity of all our desires. He constantly reminds himself of the transience of phenomena, the flux and cyclical nature of change, and, of course, the great equalizer that is death. Like Epictetus and Seneca, Aurelius is cavalier about the end. Death, so what, he shrugs: "You embarked, you set sail, you made port. Go ashore now. . . . You should always look on human life as short and cheap. Yesterday sperm: tomorrow a mummy or ashes."[14]

For Aurelius, too, the crux is the control of both our desires and our judgments. We should only desire that which happens to us. In other words, we should completely align our wishes with the workings of divine providence. Assuming any kind of agency over external events and wanting what we do not have is not just illogical but sets us up for failure. One of his most beautiful lines, which captures in a nutshell the importance of adjusting our expectations, is "Only a madman looks for figs in winter."[15] There is much wisdom in that image. If we want a friend who is caring and supportive, for example, we need to befriend someone who has the ability to act in this way. We should not choose someone who is completely preoccupied with their own dramas and has little or no capacity to give. If we know that our mothers, fathers, or partners are constitutionally incapable of expressing approval, we need to seek that approval elsewhere. There is no point in trying to impress the unimpressible. In the same spirit, if we want our portrait painted, we need to go to someone who can actually paint. We often have expectations of people that they simply cannot fulfill. The Stoics argue that it is always our unwise expectations that do us harm, not the actions of others. Aurelius advises: "Harm to you cannot subsist in another's directing mind, nor indeed in any turn or change of circumstance. Where, then? In that part of you which judges harm. So no such judgment, and all is well."[16] In other words, it is we alone who can make ourselves hurt. We are the sole creators of our inner pain. This is an insight that is both frightening and liberating.

Finally, Aurelius, like the other Stoics, puts great emphasis on man not just as a rational but also as a quintessentially social animal. His conception of the self is fundamentally relational—we are all part of a larger social collective. We should treat each other with kindness and respect, and always think about the social consequences of our actions: "What does not benefit the hive does not benefit the bee either."[17] "We were born for cooperation," he writes, "like feet, like hands, like eyelids, like the rows of upper and lower teeth. So to work in opposition to one another is against nature: and anger or rejection is opposition."[18] We can also recall here Seneca's equally beautiful image of our communal nature, comparing our relations with one another to "a stone arch, which would collapse if the stones did not mutually support each other, and which is upheld in this very way."[19]

It is precisely this understanding of ourselves as social, relational, and interdependent, as deeply embedded parts of a larger community, that falls by the wayside in many twentieth- and twenty-first-century models of self-help. Rather, they tend to paint us as isolated monads navigating through a largely hostile environment. Our only purpose is to secure the best deal we can get for ourselves, regardless of the wider social costs. But there is growing discontent with this competitive vision of the self, which reduces all our activity to economic advantage-seeking. Is it not better to think of ourselves as bees belonging to one hive or small but essential parts of a beautiful stone arch that would crumble without us, rather than as lone warriors, out there to eat or be eaten?

Stoic conceptions of the self and how to master it differ from our contemporary notions of selfhood in other areas as well. The Stoics, for example, tend to overestimate the power of reason and willpower. Although they assume we are in possession of a completely autonomous and free human will, they would reject the now widely accepted idea that our "will" (itself a contested concept) may be so adversely affected by childhood experiences or genetic predisposition that some of us may simply find it much harder, if not impossible, to "will" ourselves out of our own cognitive swamps. What if our cognitions and our reasoning itself have become so distorted that we no longer realize them as being distorted? Would using our twisted reason then not be like trying to wash dishes in dirty dishwater? The Stoics also ignore another important source for managing our thoughts and emotions—our creative imagination. It is not just reason that can break through the walls of our negative thoughts, but also art, stories, music, stunning landscapes, and smell, taste, and touch.

The Stoics have no time for feelings of bitterness about the cards we may have been dealt by fate, rejecting the very notion of victimhood. Our culture of *ressentiment* would be completely alien to them. Everyone suffers bad fortune: that is simply the way things are. The sooner we accept that fact, the better. The Stoics expect life to involve suffering. Our own horizon of expectation, by contrast, has shifted quite dramatically in the modern period. We expect not just happiness and well-being but also a largely trouble-free existence. Many of us feel a strong sense of injustice when that life is not granted.

Finally, the Stoics understood that self-improvement requires hard, sustained, and indeed lifelong effort. As Aurelius knew well, becoming a Stoic requires absolute commitment to the cause. This is also an optimistic thought, for the Stoics believed in lifelong learning and continuous improvement: we can all train our minds, and our minds can continue to learn and change. But unlike many of us, the Stoics did not embark on this quest in order to avoid

pain and displeasure. An increase in their general happiness levels
was also not what they aimed for. Instead, they simply sought to
cultivate a mental attitude that met whatever fate threw in their
way with poise and composure. Their aims and methods could not
contrast more starkly with many of the self-help titles that populate our bestseller lists today, which promise quick-fix transformation without effort.

Rhonda Byrne's spectacularly successful *The Secret* (2006) exempli-
fies a highly influential strand of self-help literature. It, too, is
based on the "control your mind" dictum. However, it blends in
mystic and esoteric ingredients. This tradition of self-help could
not be more different from the sane and sober Stoic approach,
with its claim that we have no control over external phenomena at
all. "Mind over matter" writers such as Byrne, by contrast, argue
that our thoughts are omnipotent and have the power to shape the
external world. This self-help tradition dates back to the final decades of the nineteenth century. Its beginnings lie in the American
"New Thought" or "mind cure" movement. Proponents of this
movement argued that all sickness originates in the mind; consequently, right thinking has a healing effect. The American clock-
maker Phineas Parkhurst Quimby (1802–1866) was among the first
to articulate this idea. In Quimby's view, disease "is the offspring of
the mind," a false belief that manifests in the body in the form of
physical symptoms.[20] If we accept that our disease is in our minds
alone, we can heal ourselves. Quimby claimed that those who embraced his ideas could henceforth walk without crutches and see
without glasses. His insight made their wounds, inflammations, and
even their tumors disappear.

The most prominent mind-cure sect is the Church of Christ
(Scientist), founded by Mary Baker Eddy (1821–1910). Drawing
heavily on Quimby's ideas, Eddy completed the first edition of the
sect's alternative bible, *Science and Health with Key to the Scriptures*,
in 1875. Her book has now sold over nine million copies. Christian
Scientists categorically reject all medicine and surgical interventions. They believe that sickness is an illusion that can be cured by
prayer alone. Eddy's theology is based on the mystical notion that
reality is purely spiritual and that the material world is an illu-

sion.[21] It therefore follows that disease is nothing but a mental error—the consequence of our faith in matter and in our senses. Prayer should be used to correct these false beliefs.[22] Like Quimby, Eddy holds that illness is not a physical disorder but a mental one. We can only heal ourselves if we realize that there is actually nothing to heal—apart from an incorrect mental assumption, that is.[23] Unsurprisingly, the Christian Scientists' dangerous approach to healthcare has led to the deaths of numerous sect members and their children. A number of Christian Scientists have been successfully prosecuted for manslaughter and gross neglect.

The philosopher and psychologist William James (1842–1910) was deeply interested in the mind-cure movement and the idea of the psychological origins of disease.[24] In *The Varieties of Religious Experience* (1902), he describes the mind-cure movement as an "optimistic scheme of life": "The leaders in this faith have had an intuitive belief in the all-saving power of healthy-minded attitudes as such, in the conquering efficacy of courage, hope, and trust, and a correlative contempt for doubt, fear, worry, and all nervously precautionary states of mind."[25] We can clearly see here that the basic tenets of the mind-cure movement contain the seeds of both positive psychology and positive thinking. Positive thinking was first popularized by the American pastor Norman Vincent Peale in *The Power of Positive Thinking* (1952). It is as influential as it is controversial.

Another important "mind cure" thinker, Prentice Mulford (1834–1892), set out the principles of the "law of attraction." In *Thoughts Are Things* (1889), he explains that positive thoughts attract positive outcomes and that negative thoughts attract negative ones.[26] The first self-help author to combine the spiritual idea of the law of attraction with materialist aspirations was Napoleon Hill. His proved to be a highly lucrative recipe. Hill published his mega-bestseller *Think and Grow Rich!* in 1937, during the American depression. It became the blueprint for a new type of self-help book that centers solely on the pursuit of money. *Think and Grow Rich!*, we are told, is based on twenty years of research and interviews with five hundred famous wealthy men, allegedly including Andrew Carnegie, Henry Ford, and Franklin D. Roosevelt.

Hill's message is simple: we can all become rich if only we want to badly enough. If we focus strongly on thoughts about money and abundance, the universe will magically resonate with our sub-conscious and send infinite riches our way. Success comes to those who become "SUCCESS CONSCIOUS," Hill claims. "TRULY, THOUGHTS ARE THINGS—and powerful things at that when they are mixed with definiteness of purpose, persistence, and a BURNING DESIRE for their translation into riches or other material objects."[27] All we need in order to become rich is to develop a definite desire. Then our thoughts, "like magnets, attract to us the forces, the people, the circumstances of life which harmonize with the nature of our *dominating* thoughts." If we "magnetize our minds" and become "money conscious," we will be millionaires in no time.[28] It is unsurprising that such a message would have been very soothing to readers who were struggling with the economic fallout of the Great Depression. But this message has remained attractive ever since. Hill's book is one of the few perennial classics of the genre that can still be found on the personal development shelves in many bookshops today.

Byrne's *The Secret* rehashes the same idea. Her "secret" is the law of attraction, and she reiterates its principles again and again. She also mobilizes a number of "moneymaking experts" with job titles such as "metaphysician," "visionary," and "personal transformation specialist." All of them, too, talk about nothing but the wonders of the law of attraction. *The Secret* is teeming with stories about unexpected checks in the mail and magical transformations of personal circumstances. It promises its readers that they can easily attract ten million dollars using "the Secret." "The Secret can give you whatever you want," Byrne reassures us, for "you are the most powerful magnet in the Universe! . . . Your thoughts become things!"[29] Our thoughts, apparently, have a frequency. We emit this frequency into the universe and thus magnetically attract all things that are on the same frequency as our thoughts. We are therefore not just the equivalent of a "*human* transmission tower," but one that is "more powerful than any television tower created on earth."[30] Science proves this: "Quantum physicists tell us that the entire Universe emerged from thought!"[31]

Many of us may find these overblown promises of effortless transformation suspicious. But, what is worse, Byrne's doctrine is victim-blaming. She and her band of metaphysicians hold those who experience misfortunes personally responsible for their sufferings. This includes cancer, rape, car accidents, and acts of violence. For Byrne seriously suggests that *all* of life's calamities are caused by our failure to think positive thoughts and to transmit our cheerful requests for luxury items loudly enough into space. She makes it perfectly clear that the rule of the law of attraction also applies to the six million Jews who perished in the Holocaust. Apparently, it was the Jews' "thoughts of fear, separation, and powerlessness" that attracted them "to being in the wrong place at the wrong time."[32] The masters of *The Secret* sternly assert: "Nothing can come into your experience unless you summon it through persistent thoughts."[33]

Why do books such as *Think and Grow Rich!* and *The Secret* appeal to so many of us? It is, of course, nice to be told that we can all become rich without lifting a finger, and that checks for ten million dollars will start arriving in our mailbox if only we think about money hard enough. Books that suggest that all lasting change requires effort, grit, and time champion a less attractive—if perhaps more grown-up—message. Byrne also argues that "all good things are your birthright!"[34] It is, she suggests, our prerogative to be happy and rich—a notion that clashes dramatically with the Stoic and Buddhist conception that life is suffering.

But it is not just our strong sense of entitlement, our aversion to effort, and our desire for quick-fix solutions that render these kinds of books so popular. Another central reason is our age-old desire for empowerment. The magical thinking advocated by thinkers of the mind-cure tradition feeds our yearning for omnipotence and invincibility. It hooks into our ancient desire to guard ourselves against the twin threats of vulnerability and loss of control. The problem, however, remains that while reading these kinds of books may make us feel temporarily hopeful, perhaps even giddily expectant, reality will inevitably catch up with us at some point. We will end up feeling worse, not better, when our promised riches fail to arrive. Not a single one of our problems will have been resolved. We will have learned nothing new about ourselves, and gained no useful insights that may help us genuinely to improve.

Psychotherapists frequently nominate *The Secret* as one of the potentially most damaging self-help books on the market. The most widely recommended self-help manual, by contrast, is David D. Burns's *Feeling Good: The New Mood Therapy*. It is one of very few self-help books that is proven to have measurable and lasting positive effects on its readers.[35] Published in 1980, its scientific underpinnings may no longer be particularly cutting-edge now. Given that its 688 pages include some at times very dense technical prose, it is also by no means an easy read. But its core message is a powerfully soothing one, and it is full of pertinent practical insights. In many ways, it presents a more down-to-earth and applicable version of Stoicism. Based on the premises of cognitive behavioral therapy (CBT), it contains numerous worksheets and self-assessment questionnaires. It is also peppered with many moving anecdotes drawing on Burns's practice as a psychiatrist. It is precisely these examples that breathe life into the book, ensuring that its message reaches us not just at an intellectual level but also engages our emotions and our creative imagination.

Feeling Good is based on the idea that our feelings are created by our thoughts. If we learn to control our thoughts, we can control how we feel. Burns's book builds on depression research by Abraham Low, Albert Ellis, and Aaron Beck, who realized the devastating effects on their patients of damaging self-talk and negative views of the self.[36] They concluded that the depressed suffer from a disturbance in their thinking. Their low mood is caused by thoughts that constantly revolve around their own inadequacy. The depressed think that they are fundamentally flawed—not intelligent, attractive, or talented enough, unlikable, unlovable, or even evil at their core. Their self-reproaching thoughts encompass every aspect of their lives. These thoughts dramatically affect their mood, motivation, view of the world, and relationships with others. Ellis and Beck concluded that these thoughts are not merely a symptom of depression, but rather constitute the very essence of the condition. The symptom, in other words, is the disease.

Depression attacks our self-esteem, and is often accompanied by strong feelings of shame, worthlessness, and despondency. For that reason, it is one of the most insidious forms of suffering. Eroding our healthy and stable sense of self, it can "seem worse than terminal cancer, because most cancer patients feel loved and they have hope and self-esteem."[37] Although *Feeling Good* takes its core lessons from the workings of depression, its insights are relevant for all of us. Burns's thought-management techniques can help us to work on challenges ranging from low self-esteem, anger, guilt, shame, and hopelessness to procrastination.

In essence, CBT is a thought (and, by implication, mood) modification program. Its first and most essential principle—beautifully in line with Stoic thought—is that what makes us feel bad is not external events, but our cognitive evaluations of these events. It follows that only we can make ourselves feel sad, angry, hopeless, or ashamed. Nobody else has the power to do so. Our moods and feelings are created by our cognitions—that is, our thoughts, perceptions, and core beliefs.

CBT practitioners believe that there are ten core cognitive distortions that muddy our thinking. First, we must learn to recognize these distortions. In a second step, we must seek to replace our thoughts with less biased assessments of the situations that tend to cause us grief. In that way, we can learn to reason ourselves out of our unproductive emotional states. The most common cognitive distortions include all-or-nothing thinking (assuming that everything is either black or white with no gray zone in between); overgeneralization; mental filtering; jumping to conclusions; blowing bad things out of proportion and shrinking the significance of good things; and labeling. Cognitive distortions can also be present in stifling "should" statements and in personalization—that is, assuming responsibility for everything, including things that are completely beyond our control.

Consider this case of all-or-nothing thinking (with labeling, catastrophizing, and overgeneralization thrown into the mix): We have made a small mistake at work. Immediately, we jump to the conclusion that we are no good, a total failure and complete loser. We disregard the fact that we rarely ever make mistakes and are highly respected by our colleagues. Instead, we blow the event dramatically out of proportion. We do this so well that we genuinely expect to be publicly shamed and fired with immediate effect. We cannot sleep for days and rehearse our mistake and its potential consequences over and over again in our mind.

Now contemplate an example of filtering. We may just have had a beautiful evening at a friend's house, filled with laughter, music, many compliments, and invigorating conversations. We were in great spirits about 98 percent of the time. But when we get home, we remember only one fleeting bad moment, when a distant acquaintance seemed to cut us off and failed to respond to our greeting. We use this as an opportunity to unravel the entire experience. Did this person shun us because we were we too loud and over the top? Did we offend with the stories we told? Will we never ever get invited to anybody's party again? Did the non-greeter recognize that, deep down, we are simply no good? All of the cognitive distortions are brilliant methods for turning feasts into famines, achievement into failure, and joy into misery.

Unlike psychoanalysis, CBT does not expect us to be like Orpheus, descending into our own netherworlds to sort out the chaos at its source. Instead, it asks us to stay in our heads and in the present. CBT aims for "a rapid and decisive transformation" in the way we *"think, feel,* and *behave."*[38] Our emotions are not simply to be vented, nor are they to be taken at face value. Rather, we are encouraged to turn them into the objects of a critical examination. As Burns puts it, "One of the cardinal features of cognitive therapy is that it stubbornly refuses to buy into your sense of worthlessness."[39]

The most important CBT technique that we can practice at home includes learning to talk back rationally to the inner critic in our head. To do so, we can use a simple three-part worksheet. In the left-hand column of the paper we write our "Automatic Negative Thoughts" about a situation. In the middle column, we should identify the cognitive distortions at work in these automatic thoughts that made us feel bad. In the right-hand column, finally, we are invited to present a "rational response" to our negative thoughts. This response should be written in the manner in which we would advise a good friend if they had shared thoughts of that kind with us.

This way, we can gradually challenge our automatic negative thoughts and replace them with kinder and more objective ones. Eventually, we do not need to do this on paper anymore. Whenever negative thoughts occur, we can simply follow the three steps in our heads. In a similar vein, Burns invites us to investigate our core negative beliefs about ourselves. What are they? Where might they have come from? Which distortions are at work here? What might be a more rational and objective way of looking at ourselves?

What renders the CBT method so appealing is precisely this insight: our very worst thoughts about ourselves tend not to be based on facts. More often than not, they are simply not true. If we work hard, we can manage to retrain our minds to think more clearly and less emotionally about ourselves and our core qualities. For there is nothing more crippling than this clandestine sense of intangible inadequacy. Franz Kafka knew this well—more than one of his skittish characters was haunted by this fuzzy, faulty feeling, ready to accept whatever negative judgment the world deemed fit to cast, and to jump off the next bridge if commanded to do so.

Positive psychologists, too, take the power of our self-talk and self-belief extremely seriously. But unlike CBT practitioners, they shift the focus away from our dysfunctions and instead explore how we can best flourish in our lives. Positive psychology was established in the 1990s by the American psychologist Martin Seligman (b. 1942). Seligman and his colleague Mihaly Csikszentmihalyi, who popularized the notion of "flow," define positive psychology as "the scientific study of positive human functioning and flourishing."[40] Positive psychology, too, advocates a form of mind control, urging us to identify negative thoughts and counterproductive beliefs about ourselves. But the emphasis is more strongly on the positive and more productive beliefs with which we should replace them. In his book *Flourish: A New Understanding of Happiness and Well-Being—and How to Achieve Them* (2011), Seligman argues that there are five basic elements that enable human flourishing: positive emotion, engagement, relationships, meaning, and accomplishment—the initials of which form the acronym PERMA.

The Stoic and the CBT approach are purely rational in spirit. The opposite is true for mind cure– and magical thinking–inspired self-help approaches. Positive psychology presents a combination of the best of the two traditions. It takes seriously the power of our thoughts to shape our feelings, but it also shows how positive self-talk and self-belief, combined with a focus on values and meaning, can impact our performance and success in the world. In addition, it asks us to get our imagination on board, by urging us to visualize positive outcomes rather than negative ones.

In *Learned Optimism* (1991), Seligman proposes that there are two ways of thinking about life: optimistically and pessimistically. Pessimistic thinking is based on the belief that our actions and efforts do not have any consequences. This results in "learned helplessness," which shapes the way we explain to ourselves the causality of events in our lives. Pessimists tend to explain bad events as permanent, pervasive, and personal. If we belong to that camp, we believe that our bad luck will last forever, will affect everything in our lives, and is our own fault. Good events, by contrast, are understood in exactly the opposite manner: pessimists perceive them as something fleeting that will not last, as isolated chance incidents, and as undeserved good luck.

The belief that our own actions are futile is not just the core of pessimistic thinking and learned helplessness; it is also the primary cause of depression. Moreover, Seligman holds that this kind of thinking is responsible for various health problems, shorter life spans, more catastrophes in our lives (in that expecting them to happen can become self-fulfilling), lethargy, passivity, and poor achievement.[41] But the good news is that even if we happen to be pessimists, we can change the way we think.

Seligman, too, views depression and pessimistic thinking as disorders of conscious thought. Because our conscious thought has gone awry, the cure is a direct positivity-enhancing assault on the way we think. He proposes a CBT-based regime with a positive-thinking spin. But his version of positive thinking remains much more firmly married to reason and reality than the positive thinking espoused by the magical magnetists. Seligman does not recommend the chanting of empty positive mantras, and also quite sensibly promotes "flexible optimism" rather than "blind optimism." Importantly, his is an evidence-based intervention. It is based on research that suggests that a more optimistic vision of our selves, our skills, and our potential is more likely to make us happier, more successful, and healthier.[42] Scoring much higher in areas such as self-belief, self-efficacy, and motivation, optimists are more likely to achieve their aims than pessimists. There is, then, a solid case to be made for seeking to control our pessimistic thoughts and to replace them with more hopeful ones.

Although they fly in the face of all logic and evidence, the appeal of magical-thinking self-help regimes continues to be strong. Like fake news, they are hard to eradicate. Their allure is rooted in their no-effort, instant quick-fix, and optimistic feel-good messages. Moreover, by promising fabulous riches that are in direct conflict with our economic realities, they weaponize our materialistic cravings. Ultimately, self-help of this kind hooks into ancient fantasies of being able to control the environment with our thoughts and desires alone. In other words, they present dreams of magical powers, manifest in mind-driven dominance over matter.

We could easily dismiss the popularity of this kind of self-help as a symptom of a hubristic overvaluation of our own agency. We could even see it as an outgrowth of an ever more unconstrained, indeed unhinged, entitlement mentality. But there is a kinder reading of this trend. The promises of *The Secret* and Co. are so clearly the stuff of fantasy that we can also see these texts as escapist. They offer us feel-good daydreams. In that way, they provide respite from our socioeconomic circumstances, and perhaps also offer some solace. For in reality, our chances of social mobility are nothing like the stuff of fairy tales.

There is no doubt that Stoic-style mind-control models continue to be influential in our current self-help literature. But these models are not without their critics, who argue that such hyperrational control strategies do not work. Indeed, they might even make matters worse, resulting in us feeling doubly bad: for thinking negative thoughts in the first place, and for not succeeding with controlling our unproductive thoughts in the long run.[43] There is also very little room for the imagination in these theories—the imagination being a potent transformative force the powers of which we should not underestimate. And neither do Stoics and cognitivists take into account the very noticeable differences in our abilities to pull ourselves out of our own misery by the bootstraps of our reason. For some, such approaches may work well, but for others perhaps less so. Critics of CBT also argue that it is the most prescribed therapeutic intervention in the West simply because it is the cheapest. It is significantly faster, and therefore much more cost-effective, than depth-psychology-based approaches.

Stoic-style methods, moreover, turn our minds into a combat zone in which we need to exercise constant vigilance, dividing intruding thoughts into "friends" and "enemies." This costs considerable energy, and we have to become our own thought police. Our task is not so much to chase the spawns of unreason back to where they came from, but to argue them out of existence, until they admit they have no rational legitimacy and voluntarily dissolve. And yet we are not pure creatures of reason. The philosopher Jonathan Rowson reminds us that our default behavior is "much more automatic, more profoundly social and more embodied" than we like to think. "Rationality is a mode of enquiry, not a feature of being; rational is one of many things we can do, not something we are."[44]

Nor should we aspire to be exclusively rational agents. After all, the notion of the purely rational, self-interested *homo economicus* has caused tremendous damage to our social imaginaries and economic models. This figure continues to haunt us in zombie-esque form, a dead man stalking, still talking. We are, after all, also emotional and imaginative by nature, and this, too, is what makes us human. Many of us are already too head-dominated as it stands, having learned not to listen to our feelings and intuitions. There is a danger that this imbalance could be exacerbated by following the Stoic way too rigidly.

Perhaps the most fundamental problem with Stoicism, however, is that it rigorously draws the lines between what can and cannot be changed between the outside and the inside. Whereas the magical thinkers clearly overestimate their agency in the external world, the Stoics may, perhaps even quite dramatically so, underestimate it. Under absolutist rulers, opportunities for positively influencing external circumstances were no doubt more limited than they are now. Our own times are very different. As a consequence, we have to make much more nuanced assessments about the potential scope of our agency in the external world. This is by no means easy. What we can and what we cannot control remain a crucial question. Again, positive psychology may offer a more pragmatic way of looking at this dilemma. If we succeed in adopting a more hopeful outlook on life, less hampered by negative self-talk and core beliefs, it is simply more likely that we will also be more successful in achieving our external aims.

CHAPTER THREE

Let It Go

A<small>T THE HEART OF</small> the Disney film *Frozen* (2013) there is
a moment of dramatic liberation, when Queen Elsa,
having left her old life behind and fled into the mountains, bursts into song. The song she sings, "Let It
Go," merges ancient archetypes and current self-help clichés into
a highly seductive message celebrating magical transformation
via radical liberation. It suggests that if we cease trying to please
others by repressing our true nature, we can unleash unstoppable
powers. Only if we embrace our authentic selves and become
who we truly are can we realize our full potential. Like many self-
transforming heroes and heroines before her, Elsa theatrically
sheds her cultural skins. Her cape and gloves are thrown to the
winds; she hurls her crown into the night, shakes free her hair, and
emerges in a glittering new ice-blue outfit that announces her dramatic inner transformation. Together with the symbols of external
conformity, Elsa lets go of the social expectations that have caused
her suffering. Rather than trying to hide the gift that rendered her
suspiciously different from everybody else, she now openly embraces it, and henceforth has elemental powers at her command.
The only fly in the ointment is that she is alone, in an ice palace on
the top of a mountain. Her liberating moment of self-realization is
also one of radical isolation.

Most twenty-first-century Western interpretations of the ancient injunction to let go follow a similar pattern. Many self-help books encourage us to let go of social expectations where these collide with our personal needs. They advocate breaking convention and instead celebrating our uniqueness. It is not just OK to be different; it is in fact a special power. There is now an entire subgenre of self-help (much of which features a variant of "F**k It" in the title) that expresses contempt for social norms where they interfere with the realization of our individual desires.

These kinds of books are extreme upshots of Jean-Jacques Rousseau's (1712–1778) belief that we are born good and that it is society and its twisted values that make us bad. This Romantic idea of culture as a negative, even toxic, force rose to prominence once more in the 1960s. Psychologists associated with the Human Potential movement and the Esalen Institute in California declared that authenticity and self-realization are our highest goods. They urged us to become who we truly are by unrepressing our desires and by freeing ourselves from damaging cultural norms. It was in that same decade that the antipsychiatry movement valorized madness, or complete social alienation, as a more authentic manner of being in the world.

The original Eastern art of letting go, by contrast, could not be more different in spirit. Letting go of our desires is a central tenet of Buddhism. In Buddhist thought, letting go necessitates above all the quenching of the flames of our cravings. If we learn to let go of our sensual and worldly wants, we will also learn how to let go of our attachment to our ego, the root cause of all our suffering. Gradually, we will be able to see ourselves as part of a larger whole, rather than as a distinct and separate entity.

The most prominent advocate of letting go as a self-improvement strategy was Lao-tzu. In the *Tao te ching* (ca. fourth century BCE), Lao-tzu advocates a mindset based on acceptance and yielding, and on an absence of striving and conscious effort. In Daoism, letting go centers on the idea of offering no resistance to the natural order of things. It promotes a sophisticated form of submitting our will to cosmic forces, by accepting what is and loosening our attachments to specific outcomes. Daoism exhorts us to adopt a mindset of radical reconciliation with whatever life throws at us—not least because everything is in flux. What we judge to be bad one moment, fate might soon turn into its opposite.

This nonjudgmental acceptance of present circumstances is beautifully captured in the famous Daoist parable about the farmer.

Once upon a time in ancient China there was a farmer who owned a horse. "You are so lucky!" his neighbors told him. "You have a horse that can pull the cart for you." "Who knows," the farmer replied.

One day he forgot to close his gate and the horse ran off. "Poor you! This is terrible news!" his neighbors cried. "Such bad luck!" "Who knows," the farmer replied.

A couple of days later the horse returned, bringing with it six wild horses. "How wonderful! You are the luckiest person ever," his neighbors told him. "Now you are rich!" "Who knows," the farmer replied.

The following week the farmer's son tried to break in one of the wild horses. It kicked out and broke his leg. "Oh no!" the neighbors cried, "such misfortune, all over again!" "Who knows," the farmer replied.

The next day the Emperor's soldiers came to the village and took away all the young men to fight in the war. The farmer's son was left behind. "You are so lucky!" his neighbors proclaimed. "Who knows," the farmer replied.[1]

The farmer wisely yields to whatever fate presents him with, neither rejoicing nor despairing. He offers no resistance to what happens to him because he knows that our circumstances keep changing. In each case, our conceptions of what might seem desirable or undesirable outcomes are dramatically altered. We simply cannot know what will turn out to have been good or bad events in our lives.

While Western-style letting go serves to empower our ego and to enable us to pursue the fulfillment of our desires more effectively, the ancient Eastern ways of letting go strengthen us in a very different way. If we free ourselves from as many of our desires, assumptions, and attachments to specific outcomes as possible, we gain a precious kind of freedom—a kind of equanimity and inner peace that allows us to accept calmly whatever happens in the here and now. The two different strands of letting go are brought together in intriguing ways in self-help based on acceptance and commitment therapy, which seeks to combine radical acceptance with commitment and action.

The evolution of the idea of letting go as a self-improvement technique illustrates particularly clearly some of the core differences between Eastern and Western values. It first emerged in the form of yielding to and accepting what is, as well as stilling our desires. It then took the shape of theories promoting the idea that we should free ourselves from social conventions, which in turn were countered by suggestions that we need to let go of our narcissistic preoccupation with ourselves and seek meaning that is located outside our own psyches. It culminated in models that advocate selfishness and that turn letting go into a recipe for entrepreneurial flexibility and adaptability. When it comes to the idea of letting go, then, the ambiguities are multiple.

Surpassed in popularity only by the Bible, Lao-tzu's *Tao te ching* is the second most widely translated text in the world. Poetic in style and richly ambiguous, it teems with insights that transcend time and place.[2] Its central theme is spiritual self-cultivation by practicing the art of letting go. In stark contrast to Confucianism's emphasis on conformity and respect for tradition and ritual, the *Tao* suggests that we can improve ourselves by returning to a simpler, more authentic, and intuitive way of life.[3]

Both the text and its author are steeped in mystery.[4] *Te* means "virtue" or "power," *ching* "classic," and *tao* "the way," and thus the title is usually translated as "The Classic of the Way and Virtue." The "way" refers to the right course of action as well as the teachings that outline the path toward them.[5] Lao-tzu may well be a legendary rather than a historical figure. Revered as a divinity in the religious strand of Daoism, he was, some sources suggest, an older contemporary of Confucius (551–479 BCE), possibly even his teacher.[6] One myth relates that Lao-tzu worked as an archivist at the court of Zhou, where he encountered and advised Confucius. Witnessing the state disintegrating around him, Lao-tzu decided to leave China, preferring a secluded life far from the court, turning his back on culture and returning to nature. At the gates of the kingdom, however, a guard blocked his way. Before he would let him cross the border, the guard ordered Lao-tzu to write down his teachings. So Lao-tzu scribbled down the five thousand characters of the *Tao*, handed them to the guard, and then departed, never to be seen again.[7]

At the time of Confucius, the Zhou dynasty (ca. 1100–222 BCE) was in sharp decline. The Spring and Autumn period (722–479 BCE), followed by the Warring States period (479–221 BCE), saw increasingly venomous intrigues and even civil war. It was an age of division in which "one hundred schools of thought" were said to be vying for dominance. Both Confucius and Lao-tzu provided what can be described as "philosophical action plans," wishing to tackle the grave social and political disorder that marked their age. In both of their philosophies, self-cultivation occupied a pivotal place and was seen as a precondition for political transformation. But their proposals could not have been more different. Confucius focused his efforts on the public sphere, offering conformist solutions based on respect for social hierarchies, ritual, ancestral reverence, and a nostalgic glorification of the past. Lao-tzu, by contrast, was more interested in the private sphere, advocating the power of authenticity, creativity, and spontaneity.[8]

Apart from *tao*, the other core concepts in Daoist thought are *ziran* (naturalness) and *wu wei* (nonaction). The right mode of being is to follow our original nature and to embrace our natural goodness. This natural way to live, however, had been lost in the declinist climate of the Zhou dynasty. Lao-tzu felt that culture had become a noxious and perverting force. He therefore advises his followers to reject any cultural assumptions that alienate them from their natural state of being,[9] and recommends that we let go of all conventions that are detrimental to our well-being. However, distinguishing clearly between those traits that are "natural" and those that are "cultural" is, of course, far from straightforward: it is a knotty task with which psychologists, biologists, anthropologists, and sociologists still wrestle today.

Wu wei, or "nonaction," has also been translated as "nonpurposive action," "nonassertive action," and "effortless action." *Wu wei* is perhaps best understood as a state of freedom from the dictates of desire. But desiring to be desire-free is a paradoxical aim, the complex logical repercussions of which many of us are likely to find bewildering: "He who does anything will ruin it," Lao-tzu writes; "he who holds will lose it. Hence the sage, because he does nothing, never ruins anything; and because he does not hold, loses nothing. . . . Hence the sage desires not to desire."[10] *Wu wei* is a concept that is difficult to grasp rationally. It is open not just to various translations but also to radically different interpretations. It can perhaps most comprehensively be described as a spiritual state that is marked by simplicity, quietude, and the absence of self-serving desire.[11]

Throughout his famous text, Lao-tzu privileges the female principle over the male, associating it with passivity and submission: "In the intercourse of the world, the female always gets the better of the male by stillness" (ch. 24), he writes. "The most submissive thing in the world can ride roughshod over the most unyielding in the world—that which is without substance entering that which has no gaps. That is why I know the benefit of taking no action" (ch. 6). *Wu wei*, then, is a subtle but at the same time highly effective mode of soft or passive power. It is a means of returning to our natural, virtuous state, freed from arbitrary moral regimes and twisted desires. An authentic way of thinking, feeling, and experiencing the world, it is a general ethical orientation rather than a willed, rational state of mind.

However, the role of effort and willpower in this process remains highly paradoxical. In stark contrast to most other models, self-improvement is not to be achieved via exertion or determination here, but instead by yielding and acceptance, and by giving up all resistance. It is unsurprising that suppleness is one of the most celebrated qualities in the *Tao:* "A man is supple and weak when alive, but hard and stiff when dead," according to Lao-tzu. "The myriad creatures and grass and trees are pliant and fragile when alive, but dried and shrivelled when dead. Thus it is said, the hard and the strong are the comrades of death; the supple and the weak are the comrades of life" (ch. 41). Variations on this idea are frequently expressed through metaphors that relate to the force of water, the hidden power of valleys and the feminine: "Know the male / But keep to the role of the female," Lao-tzu advises; be a "ravine to the empire," and always seek to "return to being the uncarved block" (ch. 72).

The uncarved block is a particularly potent image for our natural way of being: unadorned yet full of potential, it symbolizes the plain beauty of our precultural selves. Here, and in many other passages besides, Lao-tzu radically reverses conventional values, deliberately elevating traditionally less cherished concepts, such as the lower position, that which is crude and unembellished, and the valley rather than the mountain.

Daoist self-cultivation, then, differs radically from most other models in that it does not privilege reason, willpower, and effort as pathways to growth. It is one of the first major philosophies of life that celebrates intuition, simplicity, spontaneity, creativity, and authenticity. As we will see, similar sets of values were to be embraced by European Romantics in the nineteenth century. The key way of achieving this natural state of being is by letting go—of our cravings, aims, fixed ideas, and even social customs. Daoism has a strong antiauthoritarian and anticonformist streak.[12] By dealing in paradoxes and enigmatic brainteasers, it also shows us the limits of rational modes of apprehending ourselves and the world. By celebrating the innate goodness of nature and humans, and declaring culture a corrosive force, Daoist thought anticipates later countercultural rebellions against the primacy of instrumental reason and social conventions. Urging us to become who we truly are and always have been, it invites us to realign ourselves with the natural order and flow of the cosmos.

The injunction to let go of our desires is even more important in Buddhist thought, where it takes center stage. Before the Buddha achieved enlightenment, so the legend goes, he was a prince called Siddhartha Gautama, who lived in circa the fifth century BCE in northeast India.[13] He enjoyed a life of great luxury, shielded from the sight of suffering and hardship. At the age of twenty-nine, however, he ventured out of the palace enclosure and saw, for the first time, an old man, a sick man, and a corpse. He quickly came to the realization that life is suffering. Having also seen a wandering ascetic monk, he renounced his life of self-indulgent pleasure-seeking and embarked on a spiritual quest. For six years, he experimented with diverse philosophical, yogic, and ascetic practices. But he came to the conclusion that radical self-denial did not constitute the path to enlightenment. Instead, he embraced what was to be called the "Middle Way"—a moderate way of life, avoiding the extremes of excessive indulgence and complete abstinence. One day, sitting in deep meditation beneath what became known as the Bodhi tree, he finally achieved the state of enlightenment he had sought: he realized that he had managed to still all of his cravings and to fathom the true nature of existence. Although forever liberated from *samsāra*, the cycle of birth, death, and suffering, the Buddha decided to continue his earthly existence. He set in motion the Wheel of the Dharma, teaching his insights to a rapidly growing number of disciples.

The ultimate goal of Buddhism is to bring to a halt the cycle of suffering and rebirth that is fueled by our cravings. Our suffering can be ended by practicing nonattachment and understanding the impermanent nature of all phenomena. Letting go of our desires and attachments—which includes attachments to our very sense of self—is therefore the most central imperative in Buddhist thought. Buddhists recognize the Dharma, or law, which states the four Noble Truths: life is suffering; suffering is caused by craving; suffering can have an end; and there is a path that leads to the end of suffering. The main causes of human suffering are ignorance and desire. Like a fire, desire "consumes what it feeds on without being satisfied. It spreads rapidly, becomes attached to new objects, and burns with the pain of unassuaged longing."[14]

Nirvana literally means "quenching" or "blowing out" the flames of desire. Craving produces nothing but sorrow and fear. According to the Buddha, craving reduces us to erratic death-bound monkeys, unable to learn from experience, pointlessly chasing fleeting experiences: "If a man watches not for NIRVANA, his cravings grow like a creeper and he jumps from death to death like a monkey in the forest from one tree without fruit to another. . . . But whoever in this world overcomes his selfish cravings, his sorrows fall away from him, like drops of water from a lotus flower."[15]

Yet Buddhists know well that letting go of our desires is an arduous, lifelong process. It requires a radical, permanent cure in order to be effective: "Just as a tree, though cut down, can grow again and again if its roots are undamaged and strong, in the same way if the roots of craving are not wholly uprooted sorrows will come again and again."[16] The cure involves meditation, ethical living, and genuine insight. Ultimately, Buddhism urges us to let go not only of our cravings and attachments, but also of our very conception of the self as a separate and distinct entity. None of this is easy, of course, which is why there are very few who actually reach Nirvana. But then again, given that Buddhists believe in rebirth, we have much longer than a single lifetime to work toward this aim.

One of the earliest and most captivating first-person accounts of the difficulty of letting go of our desires was penned by the bishop Augustine of Hippo (354–430 CE). Augustine is the author of one of the greatest autobiographies in Western literature, entitled simply *Confessions*. His psychological insights are particularly astute on the mechanics of postponing change. Augustine writes with moving openness on the torturous state of indecision and hesitation, when we find we are torn between genuinely wanting change and at the same time seem unable to let go of our bad habits. For many years of his life, before his conversion to Christianity in 386 CE, Augustine simply could not let go of his sensual appetites. Again and again, he privileged "fugitive delights" over spiritual values. At the same time, he also strongly wished to heed his spiritual calling. It is no coincidence that Augustine is most famous for the phrase "Grant me chastity and continence, but not yet."[17] He is truly troubled by the fact that all of his culture and learning are powerless in the face of his sexual appetites. Why does his reason not simply triumph over passion? "What is the cause of this monstrous situation?" he wonders. "The mind commands the body and is instantly obeyed. The mind commands itself and meets resistance."[18] Augustine describes his state of mental anxiety and inner division as the "grand struggle" in his "inner house."[19] He frequently compares the time before his conversion with being asleep. Like a man who would like to get up but is overcome by sleepiness and sinks back again, he continues to defer his decision to shake off his spiritual slumber.[20]

Augustine's inner conflict tears him apart. His flesh struggles against his spirit, or as Freud would have it, his id revolts against the ego. He considers his state of indecision a result of the primal sin that dwells within all of us. Whatever explanation we prefer, his is a timeless description of why many of us simply cannot let go of unwanted behaviors—however badly we may want to: "Vain trifles and the triviality of the empty-headed, my old loves, held me back. They tugged at the garment of my flesh and whispered: 'Are you getting rid of us?' and 'from this moment this and that are forbidden to you for ever and ever.' ... They were not frankly confronting me face to face on the road, but as it were whispering behind my back, as if they were furtively tugging at me as I was going away, trying to persuade me to look back. Nevertheless they held me back. ... The overwhelming force of habit was saying to me: 'Do you think you can live without them?'"[21] Augustine here puts his finger on the force of bad habit. He reflects on the very considerable anxieties that accompany all change, and he gives an honest account of the benefits we may derive from our sins. He owns up to the reluctance many of us feel about letting go of short-term rewards. Psychologists now have a different name for the tugging and whispering forces that prevented Augustine from letting go of his attachment to his sensual appetites for so many years: they call it secondary gain. All of our bad habits provide some sort of gratification. More often than not, we simply privilege these immediate rewards over our long-term aims.

Many twentieth-century esoteric writers, such as Deepak Chopra in *The Seven Spiritual Laws of Success* (1994), also promote the idea of letting go. But they add an important twist: letting go is presented not as the actual aim but instead as a more effective way of achieving other, more worldly, goals. In order to acquire anything at all in the physical world, Chopra writes, we have to relinquish our attachment to it. This includes our attachment to money—we will only become rich if we first let go of certain ideas that we generally associate with money. He believes that we need to surrender ourselves completely to "the creative mind that orchestrates the dance of the universe."[22] But he specifies further that we should only abandon our attachment to specific results, rather than give up on our deeper intentions. We can still desire to be rich, for example, but should keep an open mind about how we get there. This is an important distinction. Many modern psychologists also argue that we thrive best when we remain flexible about specific outcomes, but are led by a stable value-based approach to life.[23] In other words, we need situational adaptability, a willingness to adjust our behavior, especially if it is not effective; but we should also stick to our long-term hopes.

The Austrian psychiatrist, Holocaust survivor, and founder of "logotherapy" Viktor Frankl (1905–1997) also argues that we should let go of specific goals while firmly holding on to our deeper values. In *Man's Search for Meaning* (1946), Frankl maintains that our primary task in life is to furnish it with meaning—whatever form this may take. We must, he argues, find meaning even in our suffering. In the autobiographical part of his moving book, he relates that those who managed to stay in touch with what made their lives meaningful in the Nazi extermination camps were more likely to survive. This could be a strong desire to return to a beloved person, to complete a creative or intellectual project, or simply the wish to help others. According to Frankl, the will to meaning is our primary and most powerful motivational force. Paraphrasing Nietzsche, he writes that if there is a potent "why" that drives us, we can tolerate almost any "how."

Frankl warns, however, that we need carefully to differentiate meaning from pseudo-values, such as the desire for power, riches, or success. Crucially, he argues that meaning has to be located outside ourselves—discovered in the world rather than in our own psyches. Our desire to self-realize and to self-improve, for example, are not legitimate meaning-generating aims in their own right. Instead, Frankl advocates "self-transcendence" in the sense of letting go of our preoccupation with ourselves: "being human always points, and is directed, to something, or someone, other than oneself—be it a meaning to fulfill or another human being to encounter." Paradoxically, then, the more we forget ourselves, by dedicating ourselves to an external cause or to people we love, the more we actualize ourselves. "Self-actualization," he sums up, "is possible only as a side-effect of self-transcendence."[24]

The idea of self-transcendence radically questions some basic psychoanalytical assumptions. According to Frankl, we cannot simply say that our aim in life is to become the best possible version of ourselves. Neither is it enough merely to wish to realize our potential, deepen our self-understanding, or overcome our limitations.

Instead, we must identify meaning that is located outside our own psyche. Ironically, then, in order to self-actualize, we first need to let go of self-actualization as our aim. We must seek to direct our energies to external causes and other people. In this sense, Frankl's existentialist approach challenges the foundations on which most modern self-help advice rests. Essentially, he asks us completely to let go of our obsession with ourselves, and to focus instead on meanings that are connected with the well-being of others.

Like Frankl, the Australian doctor and therapist Russ Harris believes that we have to let go of many of our most basic ideas about self-improvement. Current Western conceptions of happiness, Harris argues, are counterproductive; in fact, they actively prevent us from ever achieving it. In his international bestseller *The Happiness Trap* (2007), he popularizes the principles of acceptance and commitment therapy (ACT). ACT, created in the early 1980s by Steven C. Hayes, is an evidence-based intervention that seeks to blend cognitive behavioral therapy (CBT) with mindfulness-based approaches. Acceptance and letting go are at the heart of this new therapeutic approach. Unlike CBT, ACT does not encourage us rationally to challenge our negative thoughts and feelings. Instead, it asks us simply to recognize and accept them, and then to let them go.

There are two main reasons, Harris believes, why so many of us fail to be happy. The first is evolutionary in nature. Through natural selection and adaptation, our brains have been shaped in certain ways so that we are now hardwired to suffer psychologically. For millennia, our minds have been trained to predict, detect, and avoid danger. The better we were at that task, the more likely we were to survive. As a result, our minds are constantly on the alert, assessing and judging everything we encounter. Yet what used to be a crucial survival skill in the age of the saber-toothed tiger has turned into a curse in the age of social media. Now, we simply cannot stop comparing and criticizing ourselves, focusing on what we lack, and imagining "all sorts of frightening scenarios, most of which will never happen."[25] Although the tendency of our hyperalert minds to generate psychological suffering is obviously not desirable, it is, Harris argues, entirely normal. He therefore assumes that our baseline is unhappiness—rather than arguing, as others do, that unhappiness is a pathological aberration from our naturally happy state of being. This is a radical turning of the tables. What makes matters worse—and this is Harris's second main point—is that our naturally edgy and slightly anxious state of mind has been pathologized in our feel-good society. Unhappiness about our unhappiness is thus thrown into the mix, aggravating our bad feelings further.

It is certainly the case that most modern self-help writers advise us to control and eliminate our negative thoughts and painful feelings. As we have seen, this tradition has a long history that begins with the Stoics. They suggested that negative emotions are merely the result of false judgments and wrong expectations. Harris, by contrast, argues that we have far less control over our thoughts and feelings than we like to think. The idea that we can cure ourselves by controlling our unwanted thoughts is simply an illusion. This stance is in direct contradiction to that of the Stoics, and also challenges CBT's dictum that we should attempt to reason ourselves out of unwanted states of mind. ACT is much more closely aligned with Lao-tzu's idea that we need to let go of unhelpful social presuppositions and return to a more natural way of being. Because willpower is a limited resource, it is much better to manage our condition than to expend all our energies on trying to avoid or change our bad thoughts.

Our cognitive control strategies, then, often make matters worse. They result in our feeling doubly bad—for being unhappy in the first place, and for not succeeding in controlling our unproductive thoughts in the long run. They can also result in avoidance behaviors, in attempts to numb our thoughts with damaging activities or substances, and in constant self-bullying. Harris suggests that our counterproductive control strategies are in fact our core problem—the assumed cure having become a poison in its own right. Our attempts to curb negative thinking take up huge amounts of time and energy, and rarely prove effective over the long haul.

Instead, we should adjust our expectations regarding happiness, completely stop trying to control our thoughts, refrain from labeling them as good or bad, and aim for a value-led approach to life. We can do so by practicing the six core principles of ACT: *defusing* (learning to let unhelpful thoughts happen and then to let them pass by, like clouds in the sky); *expansion* (deliberately making room for unpleasant feelings and thoughts rather than avoiding them); *connection* (connecting with what is happening in the here and now); *tuning into our observing self* (our pure, nonjudgmental awareness, not our thinking self); *connecting with our values;* and *taking committed action* that is guided by these values.[26]

The concept of defusing is based on the idea that our mind relies heavily on stories, opinions, judgments, and beliefs. Often, we completely fuse with these stories and thoughts—that is, we experience them as real. ACT teaches techniques for separating thought and event, that is, for "de-fusing" with our thoughts. The psychologist Robert Kegan, too, considers the move from "being" our impulses, experiences, thoughts, and emotions to "having" them as the most crucial process in the evolution of the self. This process revolves around turning the subject of our experiences into the object—something from which we are detached, and on which we can therefore reflect. By differentiating ourselves from our emotions and recognizing them as such, we are no longer "embedded" in them. Instead, they can become objects of our critical attention.[27] This act of detaching ourselves from and observing our thoughts and emotions from a disinterested perspective is also essential in Buddhist meditation practices. It is akin to adopting a meta-perspective on our affects and cognitive processes.

ACT theorists suggest that we may, for example, practice thinking "Thank you, mind" whenever it bombards us with unhelpful thoughts, and not take the content of these thoughts too seriously. We may want to remind ourselves that our thoughts are just words, opinions, assumptions—nothing more than the noise of our endlessly chattering minds. Another defusing strategy involves naming our core self-bullying stories, the ones we tell ourselves over and over again. This could be a "nobody likes me" story, an "I'm not lovable" story, an "I'm fat and ugly" story, or an "I'm a loser" story. By naming these unhelpful narratives, we accept them, but simultaneously remind ourselves that they are just tales we tend to tell ourselves. It is in that way that we can disempower them and let them go. In the same vein, we should also nonjudgmentally observe our feelings and emotions, and then simply let them pass.

In conclusion, then, ACT would have us abandon our attempts to control our thoughts and feelings, accepting them as they present themselves, and instead invest our freed-up energies in controlling our actions. It proposes a radical countermodel to currently dominant approaches to self-improvement: by reactivating ancient wisdom practices, it presents us with concrete psychological tools for helping us to let go of both the thoughts and the social preconceptions that cause us distress.

Addressing the wider cultural assumptions that cause our sufferings has a history. As we have seen, Lao-tzu recommended that we let go of all those social conventions that interfere with our authenticity and that hamper our spontaneity and creativity. He believed we are all born good, and should remain "uncarved blocks." The Geneva-born philosopher Jean-Jacques Rousseau's most famous idea, too, is that we are naturally good but are rendered corrupt by society. As he famously puts it in *Of the Social Contract* (1762): "Man was born free, and everywhere he is in chains."[28] When human societies and our ways of collaborating with one another became more complex, Rousseau believes, we all became more competitive. Our increased desire for social success and recognition inevitably led to more conflict. Inequality, private property, and the necessity constantly to hide our true beliefs in order to gain social recognition have resulted in a sharp increase in self-alienation in modern societies. Authentic living has become ever more impossible.[29] In order to thrive, Rousseau argues, we have to throw off the shackles of cultural conventions and return to our naturally good and uncorrupted selves. It goes without saying that his is a deeply idealist notion of the self, and one that has since been criticized by many.

An even stronger anticonformist, anticonventional, and antiauthoritarian ethos surfaced in the context of the countercultural revolution of the 1960s, when humanistic psychology and the Human Potential movement rose to prominence. Based on the theories of Abraham Maslow and others, humanistic psychology emphasizes our uniqueness and individuality, and focuses on self-actualization as our highest good.[30] Like Rousseau and Lao-tzu, humanists hold that we are essentially good and that most of our problems are caused by corrupting social forces. Like Wilhelm Reich and other revolutionary Marxist psychoanalysts in the twentieth century, many humanists view repression as the true enemy of human potential.[31] They advocate becoming who we truly are by letting go of social expectations and ready-made values, urging us instead to rediscover our authentic core. In order to heal ourselves, we must stop repressing our desires.

Humanists go beyond even Freud on the question of civilization and its discontents. The price we have to pay for security and social belonging, they feel, which is the repression of many of our desires, is ultimately too high. According to Freud, civilization feeds on the energy derived from our sublimated drives (mainly sexual in nature).[32] We channel our originally sexual energies into more culturally acceptable ventures—such as working, learning, and creating. We readily agree to this transaction because it promises us safety and community. "Civilized man," Freud states laconically, "has exchanged a portion of his possibilities of happiness for a portion of security."[33] However, many theorists question the wisdom of this choice. They consider culture itself our true enemy. The very institution that was to offer us protection has, in their view, turned into an oppressive force that does us more harm than good.

In *Happy Ever After: Escaping the Myth of the Perfect Life* (2019), the behavioral scientist Paul Dolan confirms some of these intuitive suspicions with hard statistics. He analyzes common choices that tend to make the majority of people happy, and also those that do not. Most importantly, he shows that what makes us truly happy may well run counter to our dominant aspirational social values, or "metanarratives." The most influential of these is the "thou shalt reach higher" narrative, which urges us to strive to maximize our wealth, status, and education at all costs. Yet studies show that once all our basic needs have been satisfied, and beyond a certain income threshold, ever-increasing amounts of money do not yield ever greater returns of happiness—when, for example, the price we pay is long commutes, less time with loved ones, more stress, and dramatically plummeting mental and physical health. Our income satisfaction, moreover, is also relative, in that what matters most to us is that we earn more than, or at least as much as, the people with whom we compare ourselves.

Dolan, too, recommends that we let go of all metanarratives that harm our chances of happiness. We should, for instance, adopt a "just enough" approach to wealth, rather than blindly continuing to strive for more. He also presents statistics that show that getting married, living monogamously, and having children are not royal roads to happiness either. He concludes that unthinkingly following social conventions can be bad for us. And he is, of course, right to emphasize the insidious power of broader cultural values that often influence our principal goals, and many of our smaller life choices besides.

The most recent, if also the most impoverished, version of letting go–based advice can be found in self-help of the "fuck it" variety, which has recently enjoyed considerable popularity. In *F**k It: The Ultimate Spiritual Way* (2007), for example, John C. Parkin writes: "When you say F**k It, you carry out a spiritual act (the ultimate one, actually) because you give up, let go, stop resisting and relax back into the natural flow of life itself (otherwise known as the Tao, God, etc.)."[34] Saying "F**k It," Parkin claims, "is the perfect Western expression of the Eastern spiritual ideas of letting go."[35] But this statement is as deep as it gets. Delivering his teenage message in a matching adolescent register, Parkin advises us to chillax and do whatever we want, without worrying unduly about the consequences. He tells us to "say F**k It to the cleaning and get a cleaner instead," to walk out of jobs we don't like, to eat chocolate whenever we feel like it, and to take plenty of sick days. For this, apparently, is freedom: "Finally doing what you really want. Saying F**k It to the world and what people think of you and going for it."[36]

Parkin's and books of a similar kind—other examples include Sarah Knight's *The Life-Changing Magic of Not Giving a F**k* (2015) and Mark Manson's *The Subtle Art of Not Giving a F*ck* (2016)— present a profound idea in a manner that makes it sound banal and often objectionable. Not only do they strip away the ethical implications of its sources, but they actually turn them on their head. Simply saying "fuck it" to various things because they get in the way of our short-term desires for pleasure is clearly very different from working at letting go of our worldly attachments. In an almost caricatural "Western" manner, Parkin manages to convert a concept based on a relational, cosmologically attuned, and humbly yielding notion of selfhood into a silly tantrum-stance. Moreover, he sells what amounts to nothing but an extremely selfish, if not outright antisocial, way of being as a "spiritual act." Yet it is hard to discern the deeper spiritual dimension in the response "You are asking me to clean the house? Me??? Fuck it, get a cleaner instead."

While we should examine social conventions critically, we must do so with a view to finding a healthy balance between our own desires and respect for those of others. After all, quitting our job, not cleaning our house, and eating nothing but sweets all day is highly unlikely to give us long-lasting satisfaction either. Because we have bills to pay and children to feed, we may not wish to give up our job entirely; but we might consider going part-time and trying to earn money in a more passion-driven way on the side. We may decide to stop dieting for good, but not completely disregard commonsensical ideas about healthy eating. We may try to worry a little less about how our choices and opinions might be perceived by others, but not go so far as to shout "Fuck you!" whenever someone's requests conflict with our hedonic impulses. Finally, we may wish to find a better balance between self-realization and external meaning-orientated living.

Letting go in its highest spiritual forms is very different from the Western versions of letting go. While Daoism and Buddhism promote the idea of letting go of our worldly attachments and desires, Western-style letting go tends to be presented as a strategy for reaching our long-term goals in more flexible and creative ways. Attaining those goals, rather than loosening our attachments to them, however, remains the ultimate aim. The popular business parable *Who Moved My Cheese?* (1998) by Spencer Johnson neatly illustrates this tendency. This bestselling little book, which is apparently "a firm favorite with businessfolk,"[37] tells the tale of the two mice Sniff and Scurry and two "Littlepeople" called Hem and Haw. Together, they pass through a maze in search of sustenance. Eventually, they find a large supply of cheese and then feed comfortably at the same cheese station for a long time. The humans grow complacent and begin to structure their entire lives around the cheese station. The mice, by contrast, are always ready to move on and never take off their running shoes.

One day, the humans find that the cheese is gone. The mice—having less complex brains and better instincts than the humans—were aware of the declining cheese stock, and that it was getting old and stale besides. They scurried out into the maze to sniff out new cheese supplies long before the humans even noticed the problem. The humans, however, hem and haw. They become angry and scream, "Who moved my cheese?" Taking it all very personally, they complain bitterly about their fate and feel very, very sorry for themselves. For a long time, they remain in denial, hoping that their cheese supply will magically return. They are afraid to go out into the maze to look for new supplies. They grow ever weaker and more bitter in the now entirely empty cheese station.

In the meantime, the mice discover a new, even bigger cheese supply and are happily stuffing themselves. Slowly, Haw, the more flexible of the two humans, adapts to the new situation. He realizes that if he wants to survive, he needs to leave the empty cheese station, too. He understands that he has to let go of the idea of the old, stale cheese that is gone. Afraid at first, he continues to visualize the new cheese supplies he might find out there in the unknown. Eventually, he puts on his running shoes and goes sniffing and scurrying in the maze, like the mice, whom he soon finds at the new, much more richly stocked cheese station. Haw is happy there but vows never to become complacent and lazy again. He pledges never to take things for granted, instead keeping a sharp eye on the cheese supply and looking out for alternative sources as well. He never again takes off his running shoes.

Hem, however, is unable to let go of the idea of the old cheese. He overthinks and overanalyzes, regarding the disappearance of the cheese as a personal affront. Angrily, he insists he is smarter than the mice. He strongly feels that he is entitled to the cheese that is now gone. He simply wants his old cheese back, and refuses to follow his friend Haw in search of new cheese. Drowning in self-pity, he grows weaker and weaker. We do not find out whether he eventually manages to put on his running shoes to search for new cheese, or whether he dies waiting for his old cheese to come back.

Just in case we missed it, Johnson spells out the moral of the story for us: "The Quicker You Let Go of Old Cheese, the Sooner You Find New Cheese."[38] Advocating flexibility, adaptability, entrepreneurial go-getting, and an opportunistic mindset, he encourages us to embrace change rather than being afraid of it. "If You Do Not Change, You Can Become Extinct," Haw sternly warns his intransigent friend.[39] There is no denying that this not very subtle parable promotes instinct over intellect. The thinking human being is shown to be petty, entitled, cowardly, and inferior to the two mice in every respect. It is profoundly hampered by its complex brain and utterly useless beliefs and emotions.

Yet there is a different, more convincing message in this story, too. Most importantly, it encourages us to let go of entitlement thinking and self-pity. It also invites us to let go of old behaviors and beliefs when they no longer serve us. There is something undeniably poignant and inspirational in reading about Haw bravely letting go of his old dwelling place and all his shattered dreams, venturing out of his comfort zone into the unknown. Johnson does not deny how difficult this act of letting go is. Instead, he emphasizes the importance of holding on to our vision of new cheese as a powerfully motivating force—whatever our cheese may be.

In Johnson's parable, then, letting go is represented as a form of basic common sense and instinct-driven entrepreneurial adaptability—even as a strategy for maximizing our financial success. While Haw lets go of a specific supply of cheese, however, he does, of course, not let go of his craving for cheese as such. By contrast, the Eastern versions of letting go entail eliminating our cravings— for cheese and all other things besides, once and for all.

CHAPTER FOUR

Be Good

I N DISNEY'S ANIMATED VERSION of *Aladdin* (1992), the epony-
mous hero finds a magic lamp, rubs it, and unleashes a genie
who grants him three wishes. But rather than using these
three wishes selfishly—say, to enhance his powers or to ask
for vast riches or show-stopping good looks—Aladdin reserves one
of his precious gifts for the spirit who granted them. His third wish
is for the genie's freedom, so that he never has to return to the tight
constraints of his magical lamp and can leave behind forever his life
of abject servitude. At the end of the film, the liberated genie, howl-
ing with pleasure, shoots off into the sky, but Aladdin is happy, too.
No longer a street urchin, but a prince in love with and loved by a
beautiful princess, he never really needed the genie's gifts. He had
everything he required to be happy all along. He is, quite simply, a
good person—charitable, generous, caring, and selfless. We know
this from the start, for although he steals some bread at the beginning of the film, Aladdin ends up giving it to two starving children,
preferring to go hungry himself rather than see them suffer.

Aladdin's act of kindness beautifully illustrates the concept of
altruism. Altruism denotes the desire to ensure the good of others,
and to care for them in a benevolent way. It can come at a personal
cost, in that we may choose to give up something we need ourselves. We might even put our lives at risk to help others, in which

case altruism becomes heroism. Some theorists of altruism argue
that well-meaning intention is what is most important. Others say
that good intentions alone are not sufficient, but must be translated
into actions to be of any value.[1]

Which forms can altruism take? How has it been practiced in
the past, and what does it look like in our times? And are there
other ways of being good besides altruism? Altruism is the highest
moral value in most philosophical and religious systems. In Confucian China, it took the form of a collectivist tradition that always
privileges what is best for the many. But altruism can equally be
manifest in embracing the doctrine of nonharming—a vital precept
in Buddhism. Being good may also be related to an emphasis on
cultivating the classical virtues, which was Aristotle's interpretation
of the ancient injunction. Its Christian form (*agape*) is unconditional love for everyone—for ourselves, our neighbors, and even
our enemies. Buddhists extend their circle of care even further,
wishing for the happiness of all sentient beings.

In stark contrast to the ancient doctrines, which broadly interpret the imperative to be good in social terms, as a genuine concern
for the well-being of others, being good in modern self-help frameworks often takes the form of being good *at* something. Usually,
this involves honing our communication or interpersonal skills, or
becoming more productive and efficient at what we do. But it is not
all selfish news. Some self-help writers still prefer a character ethic
to a personality ethic, and advocate searching for meaning that is
located outside ourselves. And while living virtuously and putting
others first have ceased to be a dominant concern in our current
self-help landscape, some new forms of being good have emerged
in their place. Chief among them is an environment- and future-
generation-oriented mode of caring for others.

But why should we engage in altruistic behaviors to begin
with? The short answer is that practicing altruism satisfies one of
our five basic needs. In addition, as numerous psychologists have
shown, engaging in altruistic acts not only makes others happier; it
also makes the one performing the act feel better.[2] Evolutionary
biologists have established that groups that practice inner-group
altruism have a developmental advantage over groups that do not.
It is, quite simply, an age-old win/win behavior. Without altruism,
and a more general consensus that "goodness" in all its various

forms is a value we cherish and to which we should all aspire, the very foundation upon which our social contracts rest would be in peril.

As we have already seen, the Stoics repeatedly emphasize our pro-social and interdependent nature and consider altruism an essential quality. But the origins of the idea of privileging the needs of others above our own go back even further. The Chinese philosopher Confucius (551–479 BCE) strongly believed that the concern for the wider social good should always trump the fulfillment of our individual desires. The needs of the collective are best served, he argued, when we honor tradition and ritual, for they are the bond that holds together the social fabric. Living during the turbulent Zhou dynasty, Confucius was of the view that China was experiencing a period of cultural decline. He looked back nostalgically to the early centuries of the Zhou era, convinced that it had been a golden age, characterized by harmony and ritual decorum.[3] He felt that the traditions of the past contained the cures for a present with which he was completely disenchanted. Social relations, he believed, had dramatically deteriorated, as warring feudal lords, constantly vying for territory and power, were failing their people. Tried and tested rituals were no longer being honored, and the result was moral degeneration and harmful selfishness. Confucius was convinced that a combination of moral self-cultivation and sage leadership was the panacea for the social ills of his times. Above all, he advocated obeying ancient traditions and virtuous action as key recipes for restoring social harmony.

"The Master taught these four things: culture, conduct, doing one's best, and trustworthiness."[4] This statement from the *Analects*— a collection of Confucius's teachings, compiled and edited by his disciples—concisely sums up Confucian thought and its emphasis on culture, tradition, and learning, on filial devotion, obedience, effort, and constant self-improvement, and on virtuous action. Confucian philosophy focuses both on what constitutes good government and how we can become more virtuous citizens. Crucially, the two aims are interrelated: Confucius holds that a moral vanguard is needed to lead not by force but by example, to govern wisely and honorably, and to inspire others to follow suit. Leaders, in other words, should model the behaviors they advocate. In this way, the principles of virtuous leadership will trickle down and eventually transform the entire empire. But the virtues can also spread horizontally—from the righteous individual, they radiate outward to the family, the village, and across the provinces. In ancient China, then, self-cultivation was understood not as a self-serving pursuit, but rather as an act of civic altruism, a way in which the sociopolitical order could be enhanced. Self-cultivation was seen as a collective duty, the very foundation for a harmonious society.[5]

One of the highest virtues in the Confucian tradition is *ren*, which has been variously translated as benevolence, humanity, humanness, and true goodness. It is related to our notion of empathy—how we perceive, judge, and treat others. Importantly, *ren* is not a state that can be achieved in one fell swoop and then simply possessed. Rather, it is a behavior that requires constant honing.[6] As Confucius writes: "I dare not call myself a sage or a humane man. What could be said of me is that I work toward it without ever feeling sated and I am never tired of teaching."[7]

Above all, true goodness entails respecting the responsibilities of the five relationships that Confucius defines as core: father–son, ruler–subject, husband–wife, older brother–younger brother, and friend–friend. Obeying ritual is so important to Confucius because it provides clear guidance on how we should relate to others. Ritual regulates our social exchanges, and in that way ensures the smooth functioning of all our social interactions. It specifies how to address others appropriately and respectfully, what we should wear and eat, and even how we should celebrate our holy days and honor our dead. By respecting ritual, we signal that we are putting the good of the community above the satisfaction of our individual needs.

Importantly, Confucius believes that rituals are not just empty gestures. If practiced sincerely, they have the potential to transform both the mind and society. By enacting the feeling behind the formal practice, he holds, we really do feel the emotions associated with specific rites.[8] If we were to bow when encountering an elder, for example, we would feel humbly deferential toward them, rather than just engaging in meaningless conformity-signaling. In that sense, following ritual is rather like forcing ourselves to smile when we feel down, which, as psychologists have shown, really does make us happier. The field known as "proprioceptive psychology" is based on precisely this premise. By physically behaving in certain ways, such as smiling or adopting a power pose, our external actions will cause us to feel certain emotions.[9]

Our nature, Confucius believes, is malleable. It can, and indeed must, be constantly improved. It is over this question of how we can improve our nature that two of the most important interpreters of Confucian thought clashed. The final years of the Zhou dynasty, also known as the Warring States period (479–221 BCE), were marked not just, as the name suggests, by political uncertainty and belligerent feudal lords but also by often vastly different schools of thoughts and intellectual agendas competing for dominance. During that period, Mencius (ca. 385–312 BCE) and Xunzi (ca. 310–219 BCE) provided radically different answers to the question of our moral perfectibility and how self-improvement can best be achieved.

Mencius and Xunzi agree on the fact that moral goodness is the ultimate aim of self-cultivation, that morality is the most effective tool for creating a stable and thriving sociopolitical order, and that learning must play an essential part in the progress. However, Mencius believes that we are naturally good, while Xunzi holds that we are naturally evil. Unsurprisingly, their diametrically opposed assessments of human nature shaped their respective approaches to self-improvement.

Mencius believes we must look inward in seeking to improve ourselves, while Xunzi emphasizes the need to turn outward, toward the environment and culture. Mencius trusts that we have innate good tendencies; if we cultivate these virtuous qualities that dwell naturally within us, we can develop them into humaneness, rightness, propriety, and wisdom.[10] Empathy and our capacity to feel shame and guilt feature prominently in Mencius's thinking. "All human beings have a mind that cannot bear to see the sufferings of others," he writes.[11]

Tellingly, the metaphors with which Mencius illustrates our empathetic and naturally good human qualities are drawn from the natural world. It is culture and outside interventions that corrupt us, for by nature we are good: "The goodness of human nature is like the downward course of water. There is no human being lacking in the tendency to do good, just as there is no water lacking in the tendency to flow downward. Now by striking water and splashing it, you may cause it to go over your head, and by damming and channeling it, you can force it to flow uphill. But is this the nature of water? It is the force that makes this happen. While people can be made to do what is not good, what happens to their nature is like this."[12] Many hundreds of years later, the French philosopher Jean-Jacques Rousseau was to present a similar argument.

Xunzi, by contrast, believes that our nature is crooked. As a consequence, he grants culture, ritual, and teachers a key role in our formation. His is thus decidedly not a philosophy of self-improvement. In order to improve, we need the firm guidance of others. We must, he declares, follow the instructions of a teacher, as well as ritual. The "warped wood" that is the human being must, Xunzi writes, "be laid against a straightening board, steamed, and bent into shape before it can become straight; blunt metal must be ground on a whetstone before it can become sharp."[13] Self-cultivation, as Xunzi understands it, is thus part of a socializing process, which depends on formative interactions with others. He believes not in our potential for self-correction, but rather in a thorough reeducation that is conducted by external cultural agents.

As in Confucius's *Analects*, ritual propriety occupies a central place in Xunzi's philosophy. "Not to approve of a teacher and a guide, preferring to do everything your own way, is," he declares, "like relying on a blind man trying to distinguish colors or a deaf man, tones."[14] Here, we find the perfect counterpoint to the notion of Western individualist self-reliance. Since the age of the Romantics in the second half of the eighteenth century, we in the West have tended collectively to cherish originality, authenticity, creativity, and self-realization—all of which contrast starkly with Confucian values.

Unlike many modern forms of self-improvement, then, which serve the purpose of increasing our own personal well-being and enhancing our skills, and which often disregard questions of moral goodness, Confucian self-cultivation primarily serves a social function. We can even understand it as a civic tool, for Confucian doctrine centers on the obligation to better ourselves morally for the benefit of society as a whole.[15] Confucian-style self-improvement is thus a profoundly pro-social act—designed to serve the collective rather than merely the individual.

Being good, then, can take the form of putting what is best for the many first. While Confucius felt that the interests of the many were best served by obedience, following ritual, and respecting rigid social hierarchies, Buddhist thinkers came up with a less conservative, less creativity- and authenticity-stifling solution. Being good in Buddhism entails living according to the doctrine of nonharming, but is also manifest in the call dramatically to widen our circle of care. Buddhists seek to extend their compassion not just to as many other human beings as possible, but to animals and plants as well.

Buddhism is structured around a set of humanistic ethical values, above all the principle of nonharming (*ahimsā*). Based on a sense of our shared suffering and mutual interconnectedness—we can, after all, be reborn as animals—it teaches respect for all life.[16] Buddhism's core aims are the cultivation of insight and compassion, understood to constitute the path to individual enlightenment. Because it advocates concrete techniques that guide us toward achieving a state of spiritual self-realization, the scholar Damian Keown argues that Buddhism regards the religious life as "a course in self-transformation."[17] Crucially, this self-transformation is ethical in spirit. Tenzin Gyatso, the fourteenth Tibetan Dalai Lama, agrees that Buddhism offers a comprehensive framework for ethical self-improvement.[18] Through effort and practice, and by adopting basic Buddhist assumptions about the world, the Dalai Lama believes, we can cultivate happiness, well-being, and compassion. Buddhism, he holds, provides an effective psychological, philosophical, and spiritual framework for transforming the self—above all through practicing compassion.

As we have seen, all Buddhists recognize the Dharma, or law. Central to this law are the Four Noble Truths: life is suffering; suffering is caused by craving; suffering can have an end; and there is a path that leads to the end of suffering. This path is the Noble Eightfold Path, a set of practical guidelines for reaching nirvana. It covers the categories of wisdom (right view and right resolve), morality (right speech, right action, and right livelihood), and meditation (right effort, right mindfulness, and right meditation).[19] The importance of the value of compassion follows naturally from the recognition of the Four Noble Truths: if we recognize the first truth, that life is suffering, we realize that suffering is our shared lot; this insight, in turn, inspires a sense of fellow feeling with all sentient beings.

The Buddha's compassion, then, is based on a heightened and radically extended form of empathy—an acute sensitivity to the sufferings of others. Moreover, if we see the world as it truly is— that is, holistically, and recognizing that our sense of separate selves is an illusion—we will be less likely to differentiate between our own suffering and that of others. The Dalai Lama therefore declares kindness to be the very essence of his religion. "Every sentient being, even my enemy," he states, "fears suffering as I do and wants to be happy. This thought leads us to be profoundly concerned for the happiness of others, be they friends or enemies. That is the basis for true compassion."[20]

The French-born Buddhist monk Matthieu Ricard—reportedly the happiest man on earth—is both a theorist and a practitioner of altruism. In *Altruism: The Science and Psychology of Kindness* (2013), he argues that the more widely our circle of care is extended, and the more unconditional and inclusive it becomes, the more genuine and profound our altruism is. While we all have a biological tendency to care about the well-being of our children, our own kin, and the people who are kind to us, we must cultivate the art of extending our altruism much further. Ricard presents altruism as the panacea for all our problems—social, economic, and environmental. Altruism, he writes, "is the Ariadne's thread allowing us to connect harmoniously the challenges of the economy in the short term, quality of life in the mean term, and our future environment in the long term."[21]

Crucially, Buddhists desire not only that all beings find happiness, but also that they understand the causes of that happiness as well as those of suffering. There is, then, a highly important cognitive and insight-oriented dimension to Buddhist altruism: it is not just a matter of the heart, but also a matter of our rational minds. Insight and compassion belong together, for one without the other is useless. As the Dalai Lama puts it, "In the beginning, meditate on compassion; in the middle, meditate on compassion; in the end, meditate on compassion." And yet compassion always needs to be combined with creativity and courage, with intelligence and action, for "if compassion without wisdom is blind, compassion without action is hypocritical."[22]

To illustrate what compassionate detachment and strict nonviolence look like in action, the Buddha recommends we follow the example of the bee: "As the bee takes the essence of a flower and flies away without destroying its beauty and perfume, so let the sage wander in this life."[23] Buddhism urges us to let go of our egocentric conception of the self and to acknowledge the fundamental interrelatedness of all beings. In fact, the Buddha believes that our notion of selfhood as a discrete psychophysical entity is the root cause of all suffering. Only if we overcome it can we embrace our true compassionate nature, which is the "Buddha nature." Correct insight, too, is an ethical obligation. We all carry the potential for goodness and enlightenment within us, then, but, in order to actualize it, we need radically to restructure our very notion of selfhood.

In many ways, Buddhist ethics resemble Western virtue ethics such as those advocated by the Greek philosopher Aristotle (384–322 BCE). In both frameworks, the emphasis is on our becoming habitually good.[24] Buddhist and virtue ethics similarly promote the long-term transformation of our personalities, encouraging us to retrain ourselves to become genuinely good by cultivating specific virtues. In the case of Buddhism, these are insight and compassion. In ancient Greece, Socrates (470–399 BCE) established the four classical "cardinal virtues" of temperance, courage, justice, and *phronesis*, or practical wisdom. He argued that we should constantly strive to correct our actions if we become aware that they are falling short of these ideals. The prize for this process of continuous self-inspection and self-correction is the *eudaimonic* life, that is, the good and meaningful life.

Many philosophers after Socrates have also placed considerable emphasis on ethical living and on how best to integrate the virtues into our daily lives. Yet Aristotle was the first philosopher to dedicate an entire treatise to the virtues, and they held a prominent place in his general philosophy.[25] He believed that happiness is the ultimate goal of human life, and that happiness is inextricably linked to being good.[26]

Broadly speaking, there are three different categories of virtues: those relating to self-discipline, such as courage and patience; those relating to conscientiousness, such as honesty and fairness; and those relating to altruism, such as kindness and compassion.[27] Virtues are also affiliated with habit. To be truly virtuous, virtuous actions need to become something we are automatically inclined to do. Aristotle believes that in order to be good, we have to internalize virtues and assimilate them into firm habits so that we voluntarily and automatically wish to perform good actions at all times.

In order to be happy, Aristotle writes, we must seek to fulfill our potential and actualize our highest human capacity.[28] The now ubiquitous personal development cliché of unleashing our true potential is thus much older than we may have thought. Our primary function as human beings, Aristotle holds, is rational activity in accordance with virtue.[29] In order to realize our potential, we have to work on our behavior and emotional responses to become the best possible versions of ourselves. Aristotle strongly believes that we can train ourselves to be good by strengthening our virtues and controlling our vices. A happy state of mind, he writes in the *Nicomachean Ethics,* comes from "habitually doing the right thing."[30] Aristotle considers habituation, rather than teaching and intellectual understanding, to be the primary route to moral virtue.[31] Happiness is inextricably linked to repeated virtuous action. The only way to be a good person, he believes, is to train ourselves to do good things, repeatedly and with good intentions. But we need to want to perform these good deeds, too. They must become a natural and automatic habit.

Following Socrates and Plato, Aristotle places the virtues at the center of a well-lived life. Like his teachers, he regards the core virtues (justice, courage, temperance, and practical wisdom) as "complex rational, emotional and social skills."[32] Unlike them, however, his emphasis is less on a theoretical knowledge of goodness than on how we can actually practice virtuous living. Socrates believes that virtue is knowledge; Aristotle disagrees, arguing that *doing,* consistently and virtuously, is much more important than merely *knowing.* He is the original prophet of the power of habit.

Importantly, the Greek word *areté* has two meanings, translating both as "virtue" and as excellence in a more general sense.[33] Aristotle differentiates between intellectual virtues on the one hand, and moral or character virtues on the other. The intellectual virtues include theoretical and practical wisdom, science, intuitive understanding, and craft expertise. Practicing the intellectual virtues can therefore be understood not just as doing good, but also as doing something excellently. Aristotle's core character virtues include justice (treating others fairly), courage (not shying away from doing the right thing out of cowardice or laziness), and temperance, or self-control. Modern psychologists would describe temperance as our ability to control our impulses. In addition, Aristotle advocates magnanimity—a general generosity of spirit, as well as liberality, magnificence, pride (in the positive sense of self-respect), good temper, friendliness, truthfulness, and wittiness.

The philosopher understands these moral virtues as a character disposition, shaped by our habits and our proper emotional responses. We must become comfortable with the virtues as early as possible and learn to derive pleasure from them. Virtuous living therefore needs to be instilled as a habit when we are children. Only in that way will our emotional responses evolve proportionately. The virtues, in that sense, can be compared to a craft, something that can be honed and perfected over time. The earlier we start to learn them, the better.

Aristotle is also famous for the theory of the "Golden Mean," the idea that every virtue is positioned exactly in the middle between states of excess and deficiency. Generosity, for example, is flanked by financial wastefulness and miserliness, while self-respect sits sandwiched between obsequiousness and arrogance.[34] Living virtuously is thus also about balance and avoiding extremes. Unlike the Stoics, however, who argue that strong emotions such as anger and fear are never appropriate, Aristotle believes that they sometimes are. Anger in the face of blatant injustice, for example, is justified. "Anyone can become angry—that is easy," he writes. "But to be angry with the right person, to the right degree, at the right time, for the right purpose, and in the right way—this is not easy."[35] There are, then, situations in which strong emotions can be healthy and entirely apt responses. And as the former lead singer of the punk band the Sex Pistols, John Lydon, knows, anger can also be an energy.[36]

Aristotle divides those who simply cannot live virtuously, or who find it very difficult, into three kinds. First, there are evil people who, driven by a desire for dominance and luxury, deliberately reject the virtues. Then there are the "incontinent" and the "continent." The incontinent sin against reason and goodness because they allow it to be overridden by *pathos*—that is, strong emotions or feelings. Our emotions may defeat our reason either because of weakness or because of impetuousness. The weak person tries to deliberate before acting, but in the end allows passion to have its way. Imagine, for example, that we feel we have been treated unfairly at work. We might not speak up immediately, instead trying to look at the matter rationally and calmly. But our sense of having been wronged may be so strong that, a few hours after the event, and in spite of our efforts to calm ourselves, we find ourselves sending a furious email to the person who we feel has mistreated us. The impetuous person, by contrast, acts in the heat of the moment without deliberating at all, but may afterward regret what they have done. If we fall into this latter category, we might engage in a shouting match at work in the middle of a meeting, and only later feel remorse about our emotional reaction.

Like the incontinent, the continent person also experiences strong feelings that are in conflict with the virtues, but they manage successfully to overrule them. Outwardly, they succeed in living virtuously. But it is extremely hard for them. Because their emotional responses are out of sync with their reason, they constantly have to battle against their instincts.[37] So while they would neither send enraged emails after a period of deliberation, nor publicly blow up at work, they would dearly love to do both. They are simply better at controlling their impulses.

It is noteworthy that Aristotle does not consider the continent—sturdy moral fighters that they are—as being as worthy as those to whom living virtuously comes naturally. Unlike Christians, he does not see the overcoming of temptation as the noblest act of which we are capable.[38] This may seem unfair to the modern reader, but it makes sense within his framework, in which the highest aim is precisely the development of an ethical disposition so that we will not desire bad things or suffer from inappropriate emotional responses in the first place. True moral virtue, in Aristotle's view, is neither a passion, nor a mere capacity, but a matter of character. No brownie points, then, for repression. Immanuel Kant, the most famous proponent of a "duty ethics," by contrast, saw the matter differently, advocating willpower and duty as our highest goods. He defines virtue as "the moral strength of the will in obeying the dictates of duty."

In *Aristotle's Way* (2018), the classical scholar Edith Hall presents a strong and charming case for the relevance of Aristotle's virtue ethics as a timeless self-help framework. Hall highlights that Aristotelian *eudaimonia* emphasizes our own moral responsibility for our actions; we have to actively "do" *eudaimonia*, as, for Aristotle, "happiness is activity (praxis)."[39] She also stresses that the "realize" in "realizing our potential" has two meanings: "becoming conscious of, and turning into reality—and Aristotle's idea involves both."[40]

Aristotle, then, urges us both to be good and to do good—neither is enough on its own. If our good inclinations do not translate into habitually virtuous action, they are worthless. And if our character and emotional responses are not properly honed, doing good against our impulses still falls foul of his lofty ideal. The most famous example of a virtuous act motivated by pure goodness is that of the Good Samaritan, whose name has become shorthand for altruistic selflessness. The parable that recounts the Samaritan's story also illustrates the centrality of altruism in the Christian faith. In the Gospel of Luke, Jesus relates the story of a man who, on his way from Jerusalem to Jericho, was attacked by robbers. They stripped him naked and beat him viciously, leaving him to die like an animal by the roadside. A priest simply walked past the dying man, as did a Levite. But then a Samaritan traveled that way, and when he saw the man, he was overcome with compassion. He stopped and "bound up his wounds, pouring in oil and wine, and set him on his own beast, and brought him to an inn, and took care of him. And on the morrow when he departed, he took out two pence, and gave *them* to the host, and said unto him, Take care of him; and whatsoever thou spendest more, when I come again, I will repay thee" (Luke 10:33–35).[41] Samaritans and Jews, it is important to remember, were sworn enemies back then, who had caused each other much hardship and suffering.

Central to Jesus's teachings is the commandment to love our neighbor as ourselves. But he goes further, urging us to forgive, and even love, our enemies. The Gospels of the New Testament present Jesus's unique vision of goodness, or charity. Teaching that divine love knows no limits, Jesus promises an egalitarian kingdom of love and a radically new order of things. All-powerful savior, rousing teacher, healer, and miracle worker, Jesus lived his life as an example to his followers. His version of *agape*, the highest form of love, is not just selfless but also self-sacrificing—as illustrated by his message of forgiveness (turning the other cheek) and his dramatic end on the cross, accompanied by his cry: "Forgive them, Father, for they know not what they do."

In the Gospel according to Matthew, Jesus states in the clearest possible terms the altruistic commandments at the heart of his teaching: "Thou shalt love the Lord thy God with all thy heart, and with all thy soul, and with all thy mind. This is the first and great commandment. And the second *is* like unto it, Thou shalt love thy neighbour as thyself. On these two commandments hang all the law and the prophets" (Matthew 22:37–40).[42] Yet in the Sermon on the Mount, he makes a much more dramatic request: "Ye have heard that it hath been said, Thou shalt love thy neighbour, and hate thine enemy. But I say unto you, Love your enemies, bless them that curse you, do good to them that hate you, and pray for them which despitefully use you, and persecute you; That ye may be the children of your Father which is in heaven: for he maketh his sun to rise on the evil and on the good, and sendeth rain on the just and on the unjust. For if ye love them which love you, what reward have ye?" (Matthew 5:43–46).[43]

At the core of Jesus's message lies a radically inclusive form of love—not just unconditional, but all-encompassing, with a specific emphasis on the most difficult of tasks: extending our care to those who may have deliberately done us harm. The magnanimity inherent in the act of loving our enemies is illustrated most powerfully by those who are able to forgive the killers of their children, wishing not for revenge but instead seeking to reform them. When all animals embark on a migration south in the film *Ice Age* (2002), fleeing the fast-approaching ice, the melancholic mammoth Manfred walks in the opposite direction. Suicidally depressed following the loss of his family, he seeks permanent relief from his suffering in the permanent chill. His intrinsic goodness and deep-seated care for others, however, eventually propel him out of his self-destructive mode, and he agrees to save a lost human child and to reunite it with his people. We later learn that the human hunters whose child he saved had previously killed his own beloved wife and baby son. The Christian form of radically inclusive love is, then, predicated on a profound capacity for forgiveness, and a deep-seated belief that even the most evil and vicious among us are capable of being cured by love.

What form does the imperative to be good take in twentieth- and twenty-first-century self-help? And does it still matter? While, as we have seen, altruism and the classical virtues, fueled by a more general conception of us as relational and deeply interconnected beings, were central to the philosophies of self-improvement in the past, they have declined in importance in our own day. There can be no doubt that in modern-day self-help, the emphasis is primarily on being good in the sense of being excellent—that is, in terms of enhancing our performance—rather than in an ethical sense. This may include optimizing our efficiency, productivity, and creativity, as well as becoming better at relating to others—romantically, professionally, or as friends—and transforming our finances and careers. Being good, then, is now most frequently understood simply as improving or acquiring specific skills related to confidence, communication, impulse-control, and self-acceptance.

And yet doing good deeds has not entirely disappeared from the current self-help landscape. Various writers, such as Stephen R. Covey, the author of *The 7 Habits of Highly Effective People* (1989), bemoan the shift from a "character ethic" to a "personality ethic" and continue to advocate ancient virtues, emphasizing doing good rather than merely becoming better.[44] Modern virtuous actions can take the form of service, duty, care for the community, subscribing to causes located outside the self, practicing kindness, helping others to grow, and developing a charitable mindset.

The writings of the Austrian psychiatrist Alfred Adler (1870–1937), originally one of the "great three" analysts alongside Freud and Jung, have recently seen a revival in the self-help world. Interestingly, the renewed interest in Adlerian thought started in Japan, from where it spread back to the West. It is not a coincidence that Adler's self-transcendence and community-oriented psychology first captured the imagination of a non-Western society the values of which, historically and culturally speaking, are more pro-social than ours. Adler, who is nowadays primarily known for his theory of the "inferiority complex," was also an important influence on both Dale Carnegie and Stephen Covey. It is easy to see why many of his ideas chime with modern self-help writers and their readers.

The Courage to Be Disliked: How to Free Yourself, Change Your Life, and Achieve Real Happiness (2013), coauthored by the Japanese philosopher and Adler scholar Ichiro Kishimi (b. 1956) and the writer Fumitake Koga (b. 1973), is an international bestseller that has been translated into numerous languages. Written in the form of a highly readable Socratic dialogue between an initially very doubtful student (Koga) and his master (Kishimi), it relays the principles of Adlerian individual psychology. Gradually, and skillfully, the master manages to convince his suspicious student of the wisdom and practical usefulness of Adler's ideas.

Adler believes not only that our worlds are highly subjective but also that our pasts do not matter. His psychology is radically antideterministic and antietiological, with the emphasis instead placed on purpose, goals, and community. Adler believes that we create our symptoms and problems because they fulfill a specific goal in the present (psychologists and neuro-linguistic programming practitioners would refer to "secondary gain"). Low self-esteem and being overweight, for example, might serve the function of protecting us from getting hurt in relationships. *Pace* Freud, Adler argues that trauma does not exist. We make of our experiences whatever suits our present purpose. We are thus determined not by our past experiences, but rather by the meanings we give them. "People are not driven by past causes, but move toward goals that they themselves set," Adler writes.[45] He asks us radically to shift our perspective and see things the other way around: our "problems" are not our problems, but instead fulfill very specific psychological goals.

As the title of this Japanese self-help book indicates, the ancient virtue of courage is central in Adler's work. Often, Adler believes, we simply lack the courage for positive change. He also argues that all of our problems are in essence interpersonal in nature. These include low self-esteem, which is above all a proactive defense mechanism: before somebody else gets the chance to judge us negatively and to hurt us, we preventatively do it ourselves. If we think the worst we can possibly think of ourselves, nobody else can upset us with their own negative conclusions about our character. Low self-esteem is therefore also indicative of a lack of courage, as its core cause is fear—fear of being disliked by others and of being rejected. By disliking ourselves first, and by avoiding openness, intimacy, vulnerability, and sometimes even any meaningful human relationship at all, we basically seek to protect ourselves.

Adler, then, puts courage—in particular the "courage to be disliked"—at the very heart of his psychology. But even more important for our discussion of goodness is Adler's conviction that in order truly to improve ourselves, we need to switch from a concern with self-interest to a concern for others—that is, social interest.[46] Our aim should always be to be self-reliant and to live in harmony with society. The goal of all interpersonal relationships is what Adler terms a "community feeling," which is most strongly manifest in seeing others not as enemies but as comrades.

Adler's pet hate, then, is self-centeredness—into which category our inferiority complexes also fall. If, for example, we are obsessed with a desire for recognition, we appear to care about other people only very superficially. In reality, we completely lack concern for them, for they are nothing but pawns in our own narcissistic game. As the philosopher in *The Courage to Be Disliked* explains to his student, "You want to be thought well of by others, and that is why you worry about the way they look at you. That is not concern for others. It is nothing but attachment to self. . . . You are a part of a community, not its centre."[47] True self-worth has to be based on the feeling that one is beneficial to the community. Our focus on self-affirmation and self-esteem is thus entirely wrongheaded. What we need instead is simple self-acceptance combined with confidence in others, and the courage to make a valuable contribution.

In *Man's Search for Meaning* (1959), the founder of logotherapy and Holocaust survivor Viktor E. Frankl places a similar emphasis on meaning and purpose located outside the self. We should not ask what we expect of life, but rather, what life expects of us. "Life," Frankl argues, "ultimately means taking the responsibility to find the right answer to its problems and to fulfil the tasks which it constantly sets for each individual."[48] Like Adler's model, Frankl's logotherapy differs from Freudian psychoanalysis in a number of crucial ways. Less retrospective and introspective than psychoanalysis, it focuses on the future. Rather than reinforcing "the typical self-centredness of the neurotic," Frankl aims to break it up by confronting and reorienting the patient toward the meaning of their lives.[49] Frankl shifts the focus away from conflicts between drives and instincts toward existential problems. Furthermore, he views our "will to meaning" as our primary motivation in life, rather than, as Freud would have it, a simple act of sublimation.

In order to live good and fulfilling lives, Frankl argues, we need to take full responsibility for actualizing the potential meanings of those lives. Crucially, these meanings cannot simply be self-centered aims such as wishing to become the best possible version of ourselves; rather, they must be located outside our selves. Self-improvement, learning, and growing for their own sake alone would thus not constitute proper meanings in Frankl's sense. Like Adler, he believes we must aim to achieve self-transcendence, for "the true meaning of life is to be discovered in the world rather than within man or his own psyche, as though it were a closed system." Being human, he writes, "always points, and is directed, to something, or someone, other than oneself—be it a meaning to fulfill or another human being to encounter."[50] Our primary tasks, then, lie in being of service to an idea or another person. Like Adler, Frankl considers a focus on the self to be a woefully inadequate purpose, because a truly good purpose must encompass something bigger and more important than our own psyches.

The founding father of positive psychology, Martin Seligman, has some interesting thoughts on the role of goodness in self-improvement, too. He argues that in our age of personal control, we have come to exalt the self, considering our own personal fulfillment a sacred right. As he sees it, we mistakenly take the "pleasures and pains, the successes and failures of the individual with unprecedented seriousness." Unlike our ancestors, who were primarily concerned with duty, we privilege feelings (more precisely, our own) and are excessively concerned with our personal gratifications and losses. "Our society," Seligman writes, "grants power to the self that selves have never had before: to change the self and even to change the way the self thinks."[51] Yet with this exaltation of the self, Seligman argues, comes a diminished sense of community, family, commitment to institutions and the nation, as well as the loss of a higher purpose. We now look inward for meaning, which inevitably implies a "decline in the commitment to the common good."[52] Our current epidemic of depression is in no small part a result of this "overcommitment to the self and an undercommitment to the common good."[53] The self, Seligman concludes, much like Adler and Frankl before him, "is a very poor site for meaning."[54]

Many other recent self-help writers, too, propose regimes that seek to overcome what is often painted as an unbridgeable gulf between "good" forms of social engagement and a selfish and apolitical focus on personal development. As we have seen, some politically left-leaning thinkers consider the self-help industry to play a vital role in a capitalist ideology designed to stifle our instinct to address the social causes of our suffering. By trying to up our productivity and coping mechanisms, they maintain, the industry personalizes what are structural ailments, and aims to produce pliable and faithful servants to the grand neoliberal cause of enhancing efficiency and thus profit.[55] Some of these arguments lack nuance. Moreover, they also understand "being good" very narrowly in social-activist terms. This is a reductive assumption in its own right, for practicing goodness can be realized in a variety of other ways. As we have seen, altruism has many faces, not just a political one, and its multiple manifestations should not be so summarily dismissed. Whether self-improvement is a social or a selfish act, moreover, has much to do with our underlying conceptions of selfhood. If we view ourselves as relational, interdependent members of a community, improving ourselves will inevitably impact positively on this wider sphere. A growing number of philosophers, such as Lene Rachel Andersen, Tomas Björkman, Jonathan Rowson, and Zachary Stein,

seek to revive the eighteenth-century concept of *Bildung*, emphasizing that inner and social transformation are inextricably linked.[56]
Ever more activists, too, consider personal and spiritual development as a precondition for constructing new social imaginaries and
bringing about effective system-change.[57]

In addition, some self-help writers are acutely aware of the social causes of much of our suffering, and suggest very explicit both/
and approaches. They consider the strengthening of our resilience,
self-understanding, and self-awareness merely a first step, designed
to equip us with the courage to take social action and address some
of the structural causes of our discontents. Gloria Steinem's classic
Revolution from Within: A Book of Self-Esteem (1992) is a case in
point, highlighting the social origins of women's lack of self-esteem
and outlining a concrete pathway for combining inner and outer
change. Katty Kay and Claire Shipman's *The Confidence Code: The
Science and Art of Self-Assurance—What Women Should Know* (2014)
also analyzes the correlation between self-esteem and gender, diagnosing the confidence gap between men and women as culturally
produced. Kay and Shipman's therapeutics are more science-based
than Steinem's, but they, too, rest on rectifying the social origins of
the unequal distribution of self-esteem across gender lines.

Even in esoteric self-help such as Deepak Chopra's *The Seven
Spiritual Laws of Success: A Practical Guide to the Fulfillment of Your
Dreams* (1994), we can find the recommendation to give first that
which we seek: "if you want joy, give joy to others; if you want love,
learn to give love; if you want attention and appreciation, learn to
give attention and appreciation; if you want material affluence,
help others to become materially affluent. In fact, the easiest way
to get what you want is to help others get what they want."[58] While
one could argue that these remain vague and apolitical prescrip-
tions, and that micro-kindnesses do not necessarily impact on political structures, we should not forget that social transformation
can occur in many ways, including in the form of changes to social
attitudes.

What other forms may "being good" take today? While classic
modes of altruism remain as important as ever, they are now com-
plemented by novel ones, such as veganism, conscious consumerism, and other forms of caring for other species and the planet. The

notion of being a good ancestor—prominent among the thinkers of Extinction Rebellion and also advocated by Greta Thunberg—is one example of a recent, more inclusive and future-oriented form of goodness.[59] In *Lanterns: A Memoir of Mentors* (1999), the American civil rights activist Marian Wright Edelman asks her readers to "be a good ancestor. Stand for something bigger than yourself. Add value to the Earth during your sojourn."[60] Our ancestral responsibility dictates above all that we create a world that remains fit for future generations. The notion of being a good ancestor is thus a radically future-oriented form of altruism, based on the conviction that being good should include caring not only for the people and creatures who are alive now, or for our immediate descendants, but also for more distant and hypothetical generations to come. It is a temporal extension of our circle of care. Returning to the example of Aladdin, who spared one of his wishes for the genie who granted them, being a good ancestor entails sparing a wish for all of those who are not yet born.

CHAPTER FIVE

Be Humble

AT FIRST GLANCE, THE injunction to be humble does not sound particularly appealing. It appears to be in conflict with our current valorization of self-esteem and self-worth, and to contradict one of the core messages of almost all self-help literature, namely that we should celebrate our achievements and take pride in ourselves. But humility does not mean meekness, and neither does it equate to weakness. This ancient virtue has nothing to do with adopting a self-effacing, submissive doormat mentality, and is not to be mistaken simply for low self-esteem. Rather, humility is a form of spiritual modesty that is triggered by an understanding of our place in the order of things. We can practice it by taking a step back from our own desires and fears, and by looking outward at that larger world of which we are a part. It has to do with changing our perspective and realizing our own limited significance in that bigger picture. It means stepping out of our bubble and understanding ourselves as members of a community, a particular historical moment, or even a profoundly flawed species. Humility is also intimately related to gratitude—to appreciating what we have rather than focusing on what we lack. Finally, as Socrates knew well, it has to do with recognizing just how much we don't know and acknowledging our blind spots.

Saint Augustine called humility the foundation of all other virtues. Many other writers, past and present, have reflected on humility, including, as we have seen, Confucius. The ancient Chinese philosopher believed that knowing our place in a larger social world, as well as obeying social rituals and traditions, was the antidote to the evils of his time. In his philosophy, our individual needs and desires are always secondary to what is deemed best for society at large. The Confucian form of humility is profoundly pro-social in spirit, valuing the collective good more highly than the satisfaction of our personal aspirations and ambitions.

Humility is also a core value in Christianity, where it takes the form of self-renunciation and complete submission to God. The German-born medieval theologian Thomas à Kempis, for example, believed there is but one way of leading a godly life—by imitating Christ, and in particular, by emulating his humility, which is manifest in his patient suffering. While the Christian version of humility—associated, as it is, with guilt, shame, sin, and self-abnegation—may not be to everyone's taste, there is still something important to be learned from the theologians. For they teach us to avoid arrogance and pretentiousness, to see ourselves as belonging to a species that is far from perfect, and to remind ourselves of the very limited role we each have to play in the fate of humanity as a whole.

We all have much to learn, not only from each other but also from other species. If we could live more like plants, for example, we might discover how to exist in harmony with nature and not recklessly seek to exploit its resources. If we could live more like cats—Zen masters all—we could learn to privilege well-being and self-care over ceaseless activity, and stop our pointless striving for attention and approval. If we could live more like wolves, we could learn a lesson or two about intuition and loyalty. Wolves can show us how to develop more sophisticated family and parenting arrangements, benefit from the wisdom of our elders, exercise more pro-social behaviors, and learn to cherish the value of play.

Humility, then, is also about admitting our own shortcomings and seeking to overcome them. It is about a readiness to learn best practice from others. At the opposite end of the spectrum from those who advocate nature and animals as our best teachers are those who argue we should learn to be more like machines. The theorists of transhumanism believe that humans are physically frail and imperfect beings, and that our bodies can and should be technologically enhanced. But is transhumanism really a sign of humility, an admission that we are, if compared to smooth-functioning machines, less than perfect? Or might it instead be the opposite—a project driven by unbounded hubris?

Humility involves teachability, a mindset that embraces constant self-correction and self-improvement. But why should we care about humility in the first place? The reason is that it is not just an ancient virtue with a long and rich history, but also a distinctive psychological trait. Recent psychological research has shown that the more humble among us possess a large number of advantages.[1] A humble mindset has significant positive effects on our cognitive, interpersonal, and decision-making skills. Humble people are better learners and problem solvers. Humble students who are genuinely open to feedback often overtake their naturally more talented peers who think so highly of their own abilities that they reject all advice. Studies have found that humility is more important as a predictive performance indicator than IQ.[2] Humility in our leaders, moreover, fosters trust, engagement, and creative strategic thinking, and generally boosts performance.[3] Humility is thus vital for our ability to learn and an essential prerequisite for improving ourselves. For if we cannot admit to gaps in our knowledge, or flaws in our character, we will never be able to take the steps necessary to address them.

Humility is also the only effective antidote to narcissism. In many respects the predominant bane of our age, narcissism is a challenge that we have to address at both an individual and a wider social level. It is a condition frequently associated with selfie-snapping millennials and with the forty-fifth American president, who has normalized what was only a few years ago considered self-aggrandizing behavior that was simply beyond the pale. However, these are merely symptoms of a wider shift. In 2009, the American psychologist Jean Twenge diagnosed a narcissism epidemic in the US, defining it as a pervasive and measurable pattern of dramatically increased feelings of grandiosity, need for admiration, and lack of empathy in younger generations.[4] Many students who were confronted with the research simply defended their attitudes, ironically confirming Twenge's findings further: "This extremely high opinion of oneself is justified, since this generation will be remembered as the best ever," one of them wrote to a newspaper. Another countered, "But we are special. There is nothing wrong with knowing this. It is not vanity that this generation exhibits—it's pride."[5]

The dramatic increase in narcissistic traits in younger people has been traced to the self-esteem movement, and a more general focus on self-worth and self-admiration in the West. The concept of self-esteem first gained traction in the mid-1960s, when the social psychologist Morris Rosenberg equated it with self-worth and developed the Rosenberg self-esteem scale.[6] In the 1970s, proponents of the ever more influential self-esteem movement in America argued that low self-esteem was the root cause of a wide range of personal and social problems, including academic underachievement, crime, drug use, and teenage pregnancy. The ideas of the self-esteem movement have dramatically impacted on teaching and parenting styles. Their doctrine suggests that any form of criticism is detrimental to children's well-being, who should instead be showered with unconditional praise and positivity—regardless of their actual skills or performance. This took absurd forms such as children being taught to sing, "I am special! Look at me!" in kindergarten and awarded trophies for coming last in competitions.[7] Today, it is not unusual for managers being trained in appraisal techniques to be told to remember that the middle word in "appraisal" is "praise."

A growing number of psychologists now view the focus on self-esteem much more critically. They relate it not only to the steep increase in narcissism but also to low resilience for coping with failure and a growing lack of pro-social behaviors. The psychologist Roy Baumeister, who has analyzed a large number of self-esteem studies, takes a dim view of the concept. "After all these years," he writes, "I'm sorry to say, my recommendation is this: forget about self-esteem and concentrate more on self-control and self-discipline."[8] All things considered, then, it seems that reviving the ancient art of humility is a pressing necessity. With that in mind, let us turn to the early Christian theologians to find out what they may have to teach us.

Humbleness looms large in Christian thought, and is based on the notion of original sin. The bishop Augustine of Hippo

(354–430 CE) believed that we are a flawed and fallen species, for the original sin committed by Adam and Eve has corrupted all of their descendants. Willfully tasting of the forbidden fruit from the Tree of Knowledge in the Garden of Eden, they put an eternal curse on our kind. According to the harsh logic of kin liability, we are thus responsible for our own suffering. The great fall is the primal cause of all our problems, the human condition and all its sufferings being the punishment for this ancient transgression.

Just like the first human couple, Augustine believes, we are all pitiful creatures. Ruled by our appetites and passions, we allow them constantly to overwhelm our reason and self-control.[9] He maintains that we are entirely powerless to help ourselves, for we can never be saved by our own efforts; God's grace alone must be our salvation. Augustine's pessimistic account of original sin and of human beings as profoundly damaged goods, his preoccupation with corruption, sin, guilt, and shame, his vilification of sexual desire, and the twisted implications for human agency that result from his beliefs, have substantially shaped the self-understanding of the Christian self. The soul's weakness, then, is the cause of all the evil that afflicts us.

Augustine is the author of one of the greatest autobiographies in Western literature, *Confessions*, a psychologically astute text that has provided a blueprint for confessionary literature ever since. The *Confessions* establish a key pattern that continues to shape modern self-improvement literature, namely, the personal salvation narrative, which chronicles the journey from a state of depravity and unhappiness toward redemption. Following the "once I was lost but now I am found" trajectory, such narratives echo the parable of the Prodigal Son. They also reenact the broader biblical narrative of mankind evolving from a fallen species to one receptive of divine grace. Both of those narratives, in their turn, trace the allegorical journey of the soul from the vale of tears into the light.[10]

Augustine's key insight is profoundly humble, and in essence an anti-self-help thought, for he argues that helping ourselves is impossible because only God can help us, by exercising divine grace. Will and reason cannot cure us, only faith can. Christian self-help, then, can only work as a form of humble surrender, an act of submission based on the realization that all genuine agency belongs to

God. Salvation, moreover, is a gift available only to the humble—namely, those who acknowledge their own helplessness.

Like Augustine, Thomas à Kempis promoted complete submission to God's will. A German-born priest who lived from ca. 1380 to 1471, Kempis was a member of a religious movement called Modern Devout.[11] Devotion, too, is a close cousin of humility. In his highly influential devotional text *The Imitation of Christ* (1424–27), he presents practical maxims adapted from the Bible that are applicable in everyday situations. The *Imitation* is essentially a spiritual self-help book that shows the path to the godly life. Kempis's emphasis is on our private inner religious experience and the spiritual salvation that we can achieve by the strength of our own devotion and by living a humble, simple, secluded, and virtuous life.

As the title of his work announces, in Kempis's view there is but one way of being good, and that is by imitating Christ, by emulating his humility, his patient suffering, and his virtues. Christ declares: "Apart from Me, there can be no help, no advice and no lasting cure."[12] Kempis takes this to heart. His is a message of self-renunciation. Like the Buddhists, he advocates that we quench our desires. The Christian version of self-renunciation is, however, very different from the Buddhist doctrine. No middle way is promoted here. Instead, the prescription is radical self-denial, the complete rooting out of desire. The passions are recast as temptations devised by the Devil to ensnare us, dragging us down into eternal damnation.[13]

Kempis asks us to disdain, even to despise, ourselves. He advocates what can best be described as a radical doctrine of anti-self-esteem. Preaching an extreme form of self-abasing humility, he goes far beyond the usual Christian preference for spirit over matter, and contempt for the flesh, by including the human spirit in his detestation of the human. His doctrine is based on a misanthropic assessment of human nature. He deems us weak, corrupt, frail, and evil, and asks us constantly to debase ourselves. We are only "dust and ashes," he writes; "ascribe nothing good to yourself or anyone else, but attribute everything to God, without whom you have nothing."[14] Indeed, Kempis believes that we are such lowly and wanting creatures that we do not even deserve God's grace. Our only pathway to salvation is constantly to remind ourselves of our weakness and wickedness. As he puts it:

But if I humble myself and admit my nothingness; if I reject all my self-esteem and reduce myself to the dust that I really am, then Your grace will come to me, and Your light will come into my heart. So the last trace of self-esteem will be swallowed up in the depth of my own nothingness, and vanish for ever. . . . By myself, I am nothing and am all weakness. But if, for a moment, You look on me, I become strong once again and am filled with new joy. . . . Since, by pernicious self-love, I had lost myself, now by seeking to love You alone I have found both You and myself. . . . Sweetest Lord, You treat me much better than I deserve, and above all that I dare to hope or pray for.[15]

There is little emphasis on kindness and charity in *The Imitation of Christ*. This is in part because Kempis deems others irrelevant. The exclusive focus of his attention is the despicable self. He stresses that while we should not judge our neighbors, we should always judge ourselves as harshly as we can. In addition, he advocates a withdrawal from the world and a retreat into the inner life. He finds little good to say about community and company. The saints, he reminds us, "avoided society and preferred to serve God in solitude." Kempis also quotes one of Seneca's most misanthropic utterances: "As often as I have been among men, I have returned home a lesser man."[16] We should, then, not waste our energies on human relationships, but seek to invest all our love in God.

If we truly desire goodness, we must privilege the salvation of our souls in the afterlife over the here and now, considering ourselves to be no more than "a stranger and pilgrim on this earth."[17] A good death is more important than a long life. Unlike Confucius, Kempis is also no fan of learning as a pathway to self-improvement. "A humble peasant who serves God is," he declares, "more pleasing to God than a conceited intellectual who knows the course of the stars but ignores the things of the spirit. Those with real self-knowledge realize their own worthlessness, and do not enjoy public approbation."[18] Kempis's recipe for practicing humility, then, is constantly to debase ourselves, to embrace devotion, diligence, and suffering, and, of course, to imitate inspiring examples (that of Christ above all, but also the saints). Most importantly, however, we can be humble by completely and utterly surrendering our will to God's, abandoning all personal agency. "It is a good thing to live under obedience to a Superior and not to be one's own master," Kempis writes. "It is much safer to obey than to rule. . . . [People] will never find freedom of mind, unless they are totally submissive in their hearts and in their love of God. . . . So do not have confidence in your own views, but listen to the ideas of others."[19]

Kempis's contempt for the human and his emphasis on self-debasement may seem relentless and cruel to the modern reader. The notion of self-contempt as a tool for self-improvement could not contrast more starkly with our present-day emphasis on healthy self-esteem. The radical self-loathing that Kempis champions as a redemptive practice goes far beyond the bounds of classical humility. Nowadays, such a negative attitude toward ourselves would be considered pathological, as a mental health issue requiring urgent treatment. It might be interpreted as a symptom of depression, or as the consequence of mental or physical childhood abuse. But the very fact that we find Kempis's approach so alien, perhaps even disturbing, shows us how far the pendulum has swung. It is almost impossible for us to imagine now how so many readers could have found solace in pouring scorn on themselves. Yet astoundingly, the *Imitation* is the second most widely read Christian text after the Bible. Perhaps the fact that the self-loathing Kempis advocates has nothing to do with our personal qualities, but addresses a collective problem shared by all humankind, has sweetened the pill.

Equally disturbing to the modern reader is the idea of submission as a self-improvement strategy. Just as we believe in healthy self-esteem, we tend to cherish our agency and autonomy. Nowadays, serving and obeying, surrendering all agency, is seen as the preserve of masochists. Moreover, the notion of submission raises a philosophical conundrum. If we submit our agency—be that to another person, a supernatural being, fate, or more nebulous cosmic forces—can we still talk about self-improvement? Do we then not grant someone or something else all power over us, including over our potential perfectibility? Kempis's recommendation that we should passively endure our own shortcomings and simply hope for grace suggests such a reading. As Kempis puts it: "If we are unable to correct ourselves, or others, we should wait patiently until God decides otherwise."[20]

But we could also see the matter differently. The original act of voluntary submission involves a considerable degree of agency. In some cases, submission can be sweet, as the author of the erotic novel *Venus in Furs* (1870), Leopold von Sacher-Masoch, knew well. Actively choosing to be relieved of agency we do not want may well be experienced as a liberation. We may see it as relieving ourselves of a terrible kind of freedom, and of a responsibility for our fate that is as oppressive. Some of us may well feel happier without it.

Of course, these potentially well-being–enhancing side effects of Kempis's hard-core humility run counter to the spirit of his work. Christian self-improvement, then, leaves us with a problem. Kempis ultimately seeks to better our soul and its chances of a happy afterlife, very much at the cost of seeking to enhance our experience in the here and now. In fact, the more the self suffers on earth, the happier it is thought to be in the afterlife. Can such future-oriented and, ultimately, speculative soul enhancement count as true self-improvement? Perhaps it can, if it provides us with solace, purpose, and a strong sense of belonging. If we deem these factors more important than other available modes of well-being and meaning, then Kempis and Augustine can still be valuable guides. And yet, it is hard not to find the self-flagellating nastiness directed at the self that Kempis preaches troubling. While it puts into perspective our own, perhaps equally crass, practices of exalting the self, Kempis's model could not contrast more starkly with the Buddhist message of self-compassion and loving-kindness. It is therefore time to turn our attention to less self-harming forms of humility. For what we need is a middle way, one that steers clear of both the Scylla of narcissism and the Charybdis of self-loathing.

As we have seen, humility has many faces. Christian humility can take the form of self-abasement, a fetishization of suffering, and the abdication of our agency to a supernatural creature. A revival of this eerie version of humility is unlikely. Aspects of Confucius's prescription to tackle arrogant self-centeredness, by contrast, seem more appealing. The idea that we need to look beyond the boundaries of the self, to care more about the communities of which we are a part and not be led exclusively by selfish desires, is slowly gaining purchase again in the West. Another interpretation of the injunction to be humble can be seen in a more recent self-help trend. It centers on the idea that we have much to learn from other species. Self-help that encourages us to learn from animals or even from plants suggests that our problems can be seen as species-specific. In order to improve ourselves, animal self-help proposes, we need to study nonhuman life-forms. This is a mode of humility that freely acknowledges our limitations as a species and that seeks to learn from role models that are truly other than ourselves.

A quotation that is widely (and probably also falsely) attributed to Sigmund Freud is "Time spent with cats is never wasted." Eckhart Tolle memorably describes his cats as "Zen masters."[21] Gloria Steinem writes that "animals are professors of self-esteem: unselfconscious, confident, and utterly themselves."[22] And they are far from the only people advising us to turn animals into our teachers: numerous self-help books, some serious, some more tongue-in-cheek, tell us we have much to learn from our non-anthropoid friends. This idea is by no means new—many cultures believe in spirit and totem animals that can serve as our guides. Shamanism asks us to identify with such a guiding animal. The Web is teeming with neo-shaman "What's Your Spirit Animal" quizzes (rather disappointingly, a number of them seem to suggest that my own spirit animal is the turtle, and not, as I was hoping, a more graceful lupine or feline creature).

In the self-help literature of the last three decades, the list of animals whose behavior we are encouraged to emulate is topped by wolves, followed closely by cats, while the sloth is a noteworthy recent addition. Naturally, the animal most revered in the business sector is the shark. Clarissa Pinkola Estés's bestselling *Women Who Run with the Wolves: Contacting the Power of the Wild Woman* (1992) is one of the first and most successful animal-inspired self-help books. A poet, storyteller, and Jungian psychoanalyst, Pinkola Estés urges women to get back in touch with their wild and intuitive natures. Traditional psychology, she argues, does not cater to the issues that really matter to women. These include the "archetypal, the intuitive, the sexual and cyclical, the ages of women, a woman's way, a woman's knowing, her creative fire."[23]

Her entire book, she writes, was inspired by the study of wolves. Above all, the wolf is a symbol of wildness—untamed, free-spirited, intuitive, sometimes ferocious, sometimes loving. By reconnecting with our inner wolf, we humbly acknowledge the limits of the human, as well as the demand of our civilized societies that we repress or even kill off an important part of ourselves. Estés thinks of wolves as teachers who can guide us back to our instinctive psyches: they can help us to relearn how to trust our instincts, establish our territory, find our pack, and inhabit our body with confidence and pride; they can also show us how to be aware and alert, how to rely more on our intuition, and, when we fall, how to rise again with dignity. From wolves we can also learn precious lessons about loyalty and relationships, for they know how to forge strong bonds. Their mates are frequently for life, and they fiercely defend their young. Wolves, finally, can also educate us about endurance, resilience, the strength of the pack, and the art of self-preservation.

A more recent, and less sprawling, book, *The Wisdom of Wolves* (2017) by the German lawyer and wolf enthusiast Elli H. Radinger, is built on similar premises. Radinger is not interested in deep psychology, and hers is a much more sober and also less lyrically evocative presentation of what we can learn from wolves. Radinger's mission is vaguely feminist—female wolves, we are told, make all the decisions that really matter. But the thrust of her argument is traditionalist, in that wolves are celebrated as creatures that honor ritual, family, and firm hierarchies. Everything in the world of wolves revolves around the family. Wolves not only parent as a pack, but also cherish older family members, whom they would never think of abandoning. In fact, packs with older family members tend to hunt and survive more effectively than those without, because they benefit from the wisdom of their elders. Wolves are models of constancy, loyalty, and dependability. In Radinger's words, they are "bourgeois par excellence," and she means that as a compliment.[24]

Wolves naturally respect hierarchies and strong but fair leadership, but not the clichéd "alpha male" type of leadership we might expect. Tyrannical and unfair leaders are not tolerated. Radinger debunks the alpha-wolf myths that have such traction in the business world to justify ruthless and exploitative behavior. The "Wolf of Wall Street" Jordan Belfort's self-help book for salesmen, *Way of the Wolf: Straight Line Selling—Master the Art of Persuasion, Influence, and Success* (2017), is a well-known and misinformed example. Contrary to their reputation, the best of the lupine leaders display mental strength and social intelligence, and practice a silent, wise form of authority that requires no domination or aggression. Wolves are also masters of clear and effective communication, speaking with their entire bodies. Their excellent communication skills, Radinger suggests, are the reason why they rarely fight one another.[25]

Most surprising of all is the fact that wolves are not at all well equipped for the type of hunting in which they engage. Their jaws are not ideal for attacking large animals; they do not have a killing bite; and with age, their canines and incisors wear down.[26] They also do not have retractable claws, nor powerful front legs with which to hold down their prey. Although we tend to think of them as the epitome of effective hunters, Radinger suggests that wolf packs generally succeed by sheer resilience, teamwork, and by playing a numbers game. An astonishing 80 percent of their attacks are unsuccessful. In most cases, they simply wear down their prey. Clever planning also plays a key role, for they are highly adept at cornering and leading their prey into traps. Wolves are also extremely patient and persistent, but will sensibly count their losses and withdraw when the risks entailed by pursuing their original plans prove to be too high. Finally, hunting is always a team effort, with clearly assigned roles and a strict division of labor. The lessons Radinger invites us to draw from this are obvious.

Wolves also cherish play. Yet for them, play is not just fun, for it also constitutes an important form of social learning. It teaches skills such as self-control and communication, constitutes a physical workout, and strengthens social bonds. It allows wolf cubs to learn about different social roles. Finally, wolves teach us about our own insignificance in the grand scheme of nature, and remind us that there is a wildness within us. Studying the complex social systems of wolf packs, Radinger writes, has taught her the most valuable lessons about morality, responsibility, and love. Her mantra is thus not "What Would Jesus Do" (WWJD), but "What Would Wolves Do" (WWWD).[27]

While wolves remind us of our lost wild nature, and model the advantages of strong social bonds, cats have long been envied by humans for very different reasons. The French writer Stéphane Garnier's international bestseller *How to Live Like Your Cat* (2017) tries to explain our age-old fascination with felines, and to translate the lessons into advice about how we should live. Although he fails to provide any scientific details on feline behavior, Garnier rightly points out that the lives of cats revolve around their own well-being, and that they spend a large proportion of their time seeking comfort and pleasure. Masters of self-care, they love grooming their physical appearance, sleeping, stretching, sunbathing, and playing. At heart, they are hedonists who know how to demand and take their pleasures. They are also creatures of habit who dislike changes to their treasured routines. Fiercely independent, they are nevertheless loyal. Most importantly, they are self-contained, knowing their worth and preferences, gracing others with their attention only on their own terms. Garnier does not explore this further, but this non-neediness—a form of self-sufficient sovereignty—is also the core quality that attracts us to cat-like people.

It is precisely the autonomy of the self-reliant that makes them so attractive to us, their very cat-like indifference to winning the approval of others. But, Garnier writes, "We love cats first and foremost because they love themselves. Why not do as they do, without asking too many questions?"[28] His conclusions, then, do not capture the feline enigma; rather, Garnier makes cats sound like pleasure-seeking paragons of narcissism. Even if presented in this reductive manner, however, we can see why a cat-like way of being would appeal in our age, in which concepts such as autonomy, self-care, well-being, and self-worth are so highly valued. For masters in humility cats are not.

A perhaps at first sight surprising addition to the list of animals from which we are asked to learn in the recent self-help literature is the sloth. Having displaced unicorns as a cutesy gift-print creature, the shaggy arboreal mammal has a considerable online presence, starring in popular memes and viral videos.[29] Most importantly, there are also a growing number of self-help books, albeit mostly of the light-hearted and humorous kind, that advocate the "way of the sloth."[30]

The sloth craze does in fact make sense in our age of accelera-
tion and rapid technological change, in which productivity, activity,
achievement, competitiveness, and efficiency enhancement are some
of our most prized collective values. Sloths have been cast as cute
symbols of resistance to the capitalist rat race in which work dominates much of our time. Chillaxed antiheroes, they are the Oblomovs
of the animal kingdom. Sloths are the slowest mammals on earth. If
they move at top speed, they can master about 4.5 meters per minute. They spend most of their time in trees, floppily clinging to a
branch, like tired hammocks. They sleep between ten and eighteen
hours a day. Happy introverts, they prefer to hang out alone. Their
grip is so strong that, on occasion, they remain dangling in the trees
in their native Central and South American rainforests even after
they die. Herbivores with an exceptionally slow metabolism, they can
take up to a month to digest a meal. Their tousled coats tend to host
green algae and other parasites with which they form friendly and
mutually beneficial relationships. Thanks to their tiny ears and very
poor hearing, they remain largely undisturbed by the clamor of the
jungle. When predators approach, they stay completely still. Although one would think that all these features combined would not
make these creatures very likely to survive for long, they have in fact
been around for millions of years. In part that is because they have
fully mastered the art of energy conservation.[31]

In *The Little Book of Sloth Philosophy: How to Live Your Best Sloth
Life* (2018), Jennifer McCarthy writes that sloths are "mindfulness
in action," and that they are "contemplative, deliberate, relaxed and
focused."[32] They are natural yogis, she suggests, because they
breathe slowly and deeply. Fully aware of the benefits of moving
unhurriedly, they engage in low-impact exercise only. The celebration of the sloth as a self-help role model, then, taps into anxieties
similar to those that led to the cults around minimalist living
and mindfulness. It testifies to a profound longing for deceleration,
unwinding, and slowing things down to enjoy the here and
now. Moreover, sloth-inspired self-help actively seeks to redeem
laziness—one of the most vilified characteristics of our age, running counter, as it does, to many of our core capitalist principles,
not to mention it having been one of the Seven Deadly Sins in the
Middle Ages.

We may find some of these tales of how things are done in the animal kingdom inspiring, or else be troubled by the occasionally crude anthropomorphizations that are at work here. But what does animal-inspired self-help have to do with humility? Animals can be seen as a metaphor for our instinctual or unconscious nature. Following this line of thought, animal self-help can be understood as a call to rewild ourselves, to get back in touch with our nonrational and intuitive being, and to stop living in our heads all the time. The way of the animal offers a corrective to our fetishization of reason. Those works that champion the wolf also suggest a return to a different kind of social organization, the extended family pack. Given that many of our own communal structures have become so obviously deficient, these alternatives tap into our nostalgia for a lost way of communal life. In our increasingly atomized and loneliness-plagued societies, the notion of the pack animal, rather than the lone wolf, is particularly appealing.

Yet at a deeper level, books of this school of self-help suggest something much more radical. They imply that we may, after all, not be the crown of creation, as we tend to think. They dispute our built-in (and decidedly unhumble) sense of superiority, challenging the very core of our anthropocentric assumptions. They call into question our belief in humanity's God-given dominion over the animal kingdom. Many philosophers, anthropologists, and zoologists have of course wrestled with the question of our difference from animals. We do, after all, share about 99 percent of our DNA with chimpanzees, and a fair amount with pigs. Exactly which qualities and abilities set us apart from our furry ancestors? Is it our capacity to reason, to control our instincts, and to shape the world around us? Or is it that we can make things, construct symbolic meaning, or, most importantly in our context, that we possess the ability to improve ourselves?

The French philosopher Jacques Derrida, author of *The Animal That Therefore I Am* (2008), questions the very principles upon which we base the essential distinction between humans and animals. How, and why, he asks, can we be so confident about "othering" the animal? In *Being a Beast* (2016), Charles Foster recounts his attempt to live like various wild animals, including a badger, a fox, a deer, and an otter. "Species boundaries are, if not illusory, certainly vague and sometimes porous," Foster concludes. "Ask any evolutionary biologist or shaman."[33]

An even more extreme version of humble openness to learning from nonhuman experience is the idea that we should look toward the botanical realm for inspiration—that even plants can be our teachers. We should not automatically deem ourselves superior to trees or even vegetables. There is much they master better than we do, including living in harmony with other life-forms and not exploiting and destroying one's habitat. This idea features centrally in, for example, *Think Like a Tree: The Natural Principles Guide to Life* (2019) by Sarah Spencer, and Annie Davidson's *How to Be More Tree: Essential Life Lessons for Perennial Happiness* (2019). Davidson argues that trees are amazing, and not just because they change carbon dioxide into oxygen. Trees, she observes, "build networks with other trees, can take action when they are being threatened and have all sorts of clever ways to carry on growing even when they are knocked flat." They have been around for nearly 400 million years, which, she notes, is "a good amount of time to accumulate some serious wisdom." According to Davidson, trees are "masters at adapting, surviving and thriving."[34] They can teach us valuable life lessons such as how to exercise patience, weather storms, and cooperate peacefully with other forms of life.

The philosopher Michael Marder, too, suggests that we should aspire to be more like plants, living cleanly on sunlight and water, drawing what we need from the soil, and then giving it back again when our lives have drawn to a close. Above all, we should not obsess so much about the boundaries between ourselves and our environment, but rather adopt a more fluid conception of identity. We should also espouse "vegetal ethics" and embrace more floral ways of being in the world. We need to stop considering plants as lower life-forms, which we may choose to consume if they are tasty or put in vases if they look pretty. Plants are conscientious objectors to our possessive and violent approach to exploiting our habitats. Unlike us, plants naturally respect other species and do not believe in ego-boundaries. Marder provides a powerful counterargument to our anthropocentrism: "Plants are the weeds of metaphysics," he writes, "devalued, unwanted in its carefully cultivated garden, yet growing in-between the classical categories of the thing, the animal, and the human."³⁵

It is no coincidence that the literature of self-improvement is teeming with botanical metaphors. From the very beginning of the genre, its authors have urged us to cultivate the better parts of our nature, to strengthen our roots, to harvest rewards, to nurture and nourish ourselves, to seed change, to turn our faces and branches toward the sun, and to weed out our bad habits and negative thoughts.

As members of the human species—troubled and dangerous as we are, busy torturing our own kind, as well as other life-forms, and destroying nature at an unprecedented speed—we should not lazily assume that our alleged superiority is a simple fact. We do indeed have much to learn from nonhuman teachers, which can suggest surprising and new ways of tackling our challenges. Serious plant and animal self-help reminds us that we are flawed and problematic, predisposed to suffering and to inflicting mental and physical pain, and that we need to address our in-built limitations by looking across the species barrier. By urging us humbly to admit that we may, after all, not be the pinnacle of creation, such books powerfully challenge our arrogant anthropocentrism.

Situated at the opposite end of the philosophical spectrum from those who tell us to learn from our furred and foliaged friends are those who see our bodies as imperfect vessels that are in dire need of technological enhancement. The proponents of transhumanism advocate the use of technology to improve the human, ultimately with the aim of transcending the human body altogether. Is transhumanist thought an example of humility, nature admitting its own imperfection when confronted with the perfection of the artificial? Are its advocates simply objective about the frailties and flaws of our species, humbly accepting that we can improve ourselves only by mobilizing outside technological help? Or might it be more fitting to view the transhumanists as deeply hubristic in nature, aspiring, as they do, to the status of superhumans?

In *To Be a Machine: Adventures among Cyborgs, Utopians, Hackers, and the Futurists Solving the Modest Problem of Death* (2017), the Irish journalist Mark O'Connell relates in vivid detail the stories of a number of visionary individuals who have sought, with the help of technological means, to overcome their animal natures. The subjects of his investigation are perhaps the most extreme kind of self-improvers of our age, rattling against the cages of what they consider our "suboptimal" human condition. We are seriously hampered by our sickness-prone, aging, and death-bound bodies, they argue, as well as by our inadequate minds, our notoriously poor impulse control, and our perpetually self-sabotaging psyches. With the aid of various biotechnological devices, transhumanists wish radically to enhance our cognitive powers, our senses, and our vitality and, ultimately, to remove or at least postpone our expiry dates.

O'Connell focuses on human "biology and its discontents"—that is, people who are deeply dissatisfied with their limited physical and intellectual abilities and their carbon-based biological form.[36] Rather than learning from animals, the transhumanists believe, we should instead emulate, if not become, machines. Driven by a radical form of techno-optimism, they dream of life extension, cryopreservation, genetic selection, brain implant technologies, mind uploading, and mind-driven avatars. Even if the price is total enslavement to technology, complete emancipation from our biology is the goal.[37] Transhumanists view our minds and bodies as "obsolete technologies, outmoded formats in need of complete overhaul."[38] Wishing to reprogram biases and mistakes in our reasoning that are determined by our biological inheritance, some resort to smart drugs. Others opt for neuroprosthetic replacements of parts of our brains. Theirs is a utopian endeavor, in that they hope to increase not just the intelligence of the individual but that of our species as a whole.

Transhumanists subscribe to a view of human life that is both mechanistic and instrumentalizing, viewing our bodies as mere vessels of mind. Their metaphors and rhetoric are often disturbing. AI (artificial intelligence) pioneer Marvin Minsky, for example, writes that because the brain is, unfortunately, a "meat machine," we should upgrade it to something with a higher degree of functionality.[39] Another futurist thinker, Ray Kurzweil, describes our bodies as "version 1.0 biological bodies . . . frail and subject to a myriad of failure modes, not to mention the cumbersome maintenance rituals they require."[40] And Tim Cannon, chief information officer for the biohacking conglomerate Grindhouse, argues that "there is no amount of optimization of this barely evolved chimp that is worthwhile. We just don't have the hardware to be ethical, to be the things we say we want to be. The hardware we do have is really great for, you know, cracking open skulls on the African savannah, but not much use for the world we live in now. We need to change the hardware." Conceiving of humans as "deterministic mechanisms," he advises us not to make the mistake of anthropomorphizing ourselves, and claims that we need to get out of the "biology game."[41]

O'Connell observes that the transhumanist ethos is, in essence, a radical version of the classic American belief in self-betterment, but driven to such extremes that it is in danger of obliterating the very idea of the self. As we have seen, self-betterment is of course not a uniquely American idea. Transhumanists such as the philosopher and futurist Max More explicitly link their project to the wider and much older human project of self-improvement. More (who deliberately chose his unhumble surname) defines his aim as overcoming "constraints on our progress and possibilities as individuals, as organizations, and as a species." His goal is "to get better at everything, become smarter, fitter, and healthier."[42] The radical technology-driven enhancement of the human, then, is the ultimate aim of all transhumanists.

The transhumanist metaphor par excellence is the human as a computer—or more specifically, the mind as software that is trapped in obsolete hardware (our bodies are, after all, made of biomatter and prone to perishing and malfunctioning). The mind-as-computer metaphor is ubiquitous in our age. But the transhumanists take it literally, blurring the boundaries between vehicle and tenor. Past metaphors of the human body were modeled on the water technologies of antiquity, such as pumps and fountains, which inspired the Greek and Roman notions of pneuma and the humors. During the Renaissance, the human body was frequently thought of as a mechanical operation, much like clockwork, while the Industrial Revolution, which saw the advent of steam and pressurized energies, inspired Freud's notion of the unconscious and precarious inner-psychological pressure economies.[43] Now the human mind is, as O'Connell observes, primarily envisaged as a device "for the storing and processing of data, as neural code running on the wetware of the central nervous system."[44]

The metaphors we use to describe the relationship between the mind and the body, it is worth remembering, have wide-ranging real-life consequences. Metaphors are not just a question of more or less appealing imagery. They reflect deep cultural assumptions and shape how we think about our inner life. Perhaps most importantly, they determine the therapeutics we develop to cure our ailments, including the models of self-help with which we engage. Transhumanism suggests that if "we want to be more than mere animals, we need to embrace technology's potential to make us machines."[45]

It is possible, then, to see the transhumanist endeavor as humble in spirit. Transhumanists simply acknowledge how flawed a species we are—weak meat-machines, faulty dying animals. They argue that we need technological help to optimize our various failing functionalities, and, in essence, learn to be more like machines. It is, however, equally possible, and perhaps more apt, to view the entire transhumanist venture as an act of astounding hubris. Transhumanists want more than they were naturally given. They are convinced that they should be exempted from death, that they should be able to rise above the laws of biology, and that they can and should play God, tinkering with the basic code of creation in an attempt to optimize it. What does and does not constitute human optimization is, of course, very much open to question. Finally, there are some, especially in the biohacking community, who quite simply wish to become superhuman.

Biohacking (another computer metaphor) refers to the practice of augmenting our sensory and information-processing abilities by means of subdermal implants or other interventions.[46] Seeking to merge their flesh with technology, biohackers essentially wish to become cyborgs. The Silicon Valley entrepreneur Serge Faguet is a telling case study—and nobody could ever make the mistake of calling him humble. Faguet practices a form of "extreme biohacking," which combines high-tech, wellness, nutrition, drugs, anti-aging, and various other approaches to enhance the functionality of mind and body. He wears expensive hearing aids, for example, although his hearing is, by human standards, perfect. Extreme biohackers may also attempt to increase their intelligence by micro-dosing

MDMA or LSD, or enlist the help of endocrinologists to alter their hormone economy—for example, to become less introverted.

Faguet takes sixty pills a day, prescribed by his medical team of top neurologists, cardiologists, endocrinologists, and psychotherapists. They have been tasked with finding data-driven solutions to his "challenges," which he describes as "anxieties, insecurities, introversion, weight, focus, anger management and procrastination issues." Faguet takes an estrogen blocker to boost his testosterone, so that he can perform better (that is, more aggressively) in business. He also takes daily injections of somatropin, a muscle growth–promoting hormone, to slow down the aging process. Because he feels it is "better to have mental clarity and not be bothered by emotions, et cetera," he takes antidepression medication. Not being a short-termist, he works with fifty-year goals in mind, aiming for "good mood, confidence, focus, energy, willpower, stress resilience, brainpower, calm, health, longevity, removal of social anxieties and inhibitions. All the time. With minimal investment and minimal risk."[47] This statement nicely sums up the self-improvement spirit of our age: he wants it all, now, and without effort. But he is willing to pay for it. As of 2018, his self-improvement quest had already cost him $250,000.

Because he aims to preserve an optimal cognitive and physical state of functioning, there is a small but sensible preventative dimension to Faguet's self-optimization endeavor. Overall, his list of desired qualities neatly captures the core aspirations explored in most twenty-first-century self-help. Health, intelligence, and longevity, as well as stable mood, confidence, extroversion, focus, energy, reasonable aggressiveness, high productivity, resilience, and the absence of social anxieties and inhibitions are all culturally valorized states of being. In one way or another, they would probably feature on most of our wish lists, too. The difference is that Faguet and his ilk consider these desires human engineering problems that can be solved with a techno-medical mindset (and considerable amounts of money).

What is most remarkable, however, is that Faguet seems to be completely unable to articulate why being in possession of all these qualities is a desirable state. Like many transhumanists, he perfunctorily mentions the idea of wishing to live long enough to colonize space. Other than that, his logic is circular, indicating that such self-improvement is a valuable objective in its own right. "Ulti-mately," he states, "the real value is being able to upgrade yourself and become something much better and smarter, and live for mil-lions of years."[48] Moreover, telling basic needs are missing from Faguet's list: social relations and altruism. There is simply no room for "emotions, et cetera" in his life. It is perhaps precisely for that reason that he does not have a single convincing idea of what he would actually do with his artificially pumped-up mind and body and his extended life span. His, then, is a telling case of extreme ef-ficiency enhancement without higher purpose. But efficiency for efficiency's sake simply does not cut it as a blueprint for a truly meaningful existence.

The sociologist Greta Wagner has recently shown just how widespread drug-induced cognitive enhancement is, particularly among students. But neuro-enhancement with methylphenidate-, modafinil-, and amphetamine-based medication raises complex ethical questions.[49] Just like doping in sports, this kind of "brain doping," as well as the many other modes of transhumanist self-op-timization, quite simply seems like cheating. It is a kind of self-help without the inner work. Strictly speaking, it does not even count as self-help, as it involves the use of mind-altering products and medi-cal interventions, many of which need to be administered by others. Personally, I still desire to master my problems on my own terms, with my own uniquely biased cognitive capacities, my entirely inad-equate psychological skills, and my flawed human hardware in the form of my aging body—however imperfect and slow in coming the result may be. Perhaps I lack vision and ambition, but, all things considered, I prefer being a faulty dying animal to being a machine. Rather than being acquired as a result of effort, hard work, and trial and error, the results of techno-optimization, as a product that can simply be purchased, are unearned. The stern old Protestant in me believes that putting in your hours actually matters, that rewards should come to those who have tried hard to achieve them. Pop-ping pills or implanting gadgets can never qualify as self-improve-ment in the old-fashioned sense, for it entails no learning process and leaves our psyches, spirits, and ethical dispositions unchanged.

Faguet's case illustrates the dangers of heedlessly unleashed neoliberal performance enhancement. Here as elsewhere, efficiency is considered a worthy end in itself, if not the sole good. But much more important than achieving efficiency for efficiency's sake is the question of what we actually do with it in our lives. What purpose may it serve and how can we best put it to use? True, it may buy us time, but if we do not know how to fill that time with meaning to begin with, why bother? Email and various other technological inventions that speed up our processes of communication and transportation are further examples that illustrate this problem. Once upon a time they were meant to save us time— time, it was optimistically assumed, that we would spend on more important things. And yet we now waste much of our newly liberated time by pointlessly killing it online. Besides, we still work as much as we used to, if not more—paradoxically precisely because of email and our nonstop connectivity. We have not yet seen the wider introduction of shorter workdays or four-day weeks, and I doubt we will anytime soon. We do not engage in more recreational leisure activities. Many studies suggest that our mental health is worse than ever before. We do not learn more and spend more time in nature, with our friends or children, or being creative. Quite the opposite. If anything, our relationships with others have become ever more fraught and complicated.

The following parable neatly illustrates why relentless efficiency enhancement (be it on the individual or a wider economic level) may be an empty, circular aim, detached from a deeper purpose:

An American investment banker went on a much-needed holiday to Thailand. Having worked hard all year, he was exhausted, dying for a proper break. He booked himself into a luxury hotel, drank cocktails at the bar in the evenings, and spent his days fishing in the calm emerald-green waters that caressed the resort's sandy beach and gently rocked the colorful small boats moored at the ramshackle pier of a nearby fishing village. On his first afternoon, the banker struck a deal with one of the local fishermen, who sat idly on the pier in the sunshine. The man agreed to take the investment banker to a good fishing spot in his little boat for a few hours each day. On the third day, as he sat in the boat fishing, the banker began to question the fisherman about his life.

"How many fish do you catch on a good day?" he asked.

"I never catch more than five."

"Why?" the banker asked, astounded. He had been able to catch seven on his second day, and was hoping to break his record that day.

"Why not?" the fisherman replied. "We only need five. My family and I, we couldn't eat more than that, and fish don't keep."

"Why don't you sell the additional ones at the market, or to the hotel?"

"Why should I?" the fisherman shrugged.

"To make a profit, of course! In just a few weeks, you could earn enough to buy a second boat and hire an employee. Together, you could catch even more fish and earn even more money. You could soon afford an entire flotilla of boats, build warehouses for storage, and sell your fish at more distant markets."

"But why would I want to do this?" The fisherman was genuinely puzzled.

"You would grow rich!"

"And then? What would I do with my money?"

The banker laughed. He thought the fisherman was joking. But when the latter remained silent, the banker tried to explain further: "You could buy Porsches, live in a big house with air conditioning and a pool, wear fancy clothes, buy the latest technological equipment. You could drink champagne instead of water. You could eat oysters every day. You could buy your wife designer handbags and shoes. You could send your children to Harvard!"

The fisherman was not impressed. These things did not mean anything to him.

The banker was becoming exasperated. But then he had an idea: "You could go on holidays to great places like this one, and spend all day enjoying the sun and fishing!"

"But I'm already doing that," the fisherman said, smiling. And then he rowed the banker back to the shore.[50]

Adopting a humbler mindset, then, could have wide-ranging social consequences. It could keep in check our, for the most part purposeless, pursuit of efficiency enhancement (both economically speaking and in relation to transhumanist tinkering with human functionalities). It could remind us of our own cognitive and emotional limitations, and make us more willing openly to acknowledge our flaws. By piercing our anthropocentric fantasies of supremacy, it could encourage us to treat not just other species but the very planet more respectfully. Human reason is not the only good worth celebrating. After all, many animals are better than we are at something: they may be faster or fiercer; they can hear, see, or smell better; they may be better at self-care, relaxing, and bonding; and many have more stable and supportive social structures than we do. While we may want to avoid becoming misanthropic preachers of self-loathing à la Kempis, we could certainly do with bringing our self-regard down a notch, or ten. For humility is also the only effective antidote to narcissism, and all its associated evils. It is, in essence, a readiness to admit our shortcomings coupled with a willingness to learn, be that from people, animals, plants, or even machines—whoever masters something we do not. The opportunities are infinite.

CHAPTER SIX

Simplify

A GROWING NUMBER OF THINKERS argue that we are currently experiencing not just a "meaning crisis" but a "sensemaking crisis" as our world has become too complex for our own good. System and integral thinking—ways of wrestling with this rapid increase in complexity—are experiencing a notable revival.[1] At the same time, the interest in simpler ways of living, working, and being has surged in recent years. The more complex our geopolitical and economic structures become, the more we seem to crave a return to simplicity. Many of us feel that the digital communication technologies that have wormed their ways deeply into our daily routines have not streamlined but rather complicated our lives. Similarly, our consumerist lifestyles have led to a growing concern that we are losing control over our ever more cluttered living spaces. The more we are pushed to acquire stuff we do not need, the more we dream of minimalist living and a return to basics. Our increasingly urban, greenery-deprived, and sedentary indoor lifestyles, moreover, have reawakened curiosity about nature's restorative powers. Our longing for simplicity is evident even in current furnishing and clothing trends that celebrate functional designs and more restrained Scandinavian and Japanese aesthetics. It is not surprising, then, that we are currently witnessing a sharp rise in self-help regimes that promise to uncomplicate our existence. They range from decluttering advice à la Marie Kondo, return-to-nature therapeutics, and life-cost calculations, to digital detoxing cures.

The desire to simplify our lives is not, however, a new phenomenon. In the form of asceticism, it has been with us for millennia. Many philosophers and religious thinkers have preached the art of ascetic living, including the Stoics and various Buddhist, Jain, Hindu, Sufi, Christian, and Jewish sects. Those who have made it their sole mission to pursue higher spiritual aims—hermits, fakirs, and yogis chief among them—frequently adopt extremely austere lifestyles. They renounce not just material possessions and worldly relations, but all sensual pleasures, too. Ascetic practices can include fasting, celibacy, sleeping in bare cells, and voluntary poverty. In the most extreme cases, those practices may involve sitting on a pillar for hours or even days at a time, abandoning personal hygiene, and various forms of mortifying the flesh. We know of self-flagellating monks, devout Christians wearing scratchy hair shirts on their naked skin, and spiritual seekers sleeping on beds of needles.

Whether mild or extreme, all of these forms of asceticism are based on the assumption of a strong link between simplicity and spirituality. Only by controlling our worldly desires can we purify our souls and fully focus on spiritual matters. For if we remain slaves to the demands of our flesh, we remain chained to the material world. Extreme asceticism is a bid for control. It is grounded in a rigorously dualistic view of body and spirit in which the former is held in very low esteem. Some of these practices, it is fair to say, amount to out-and-out physical self-abuse. The most extreme forms of asceticism tend to be driven by a deeply hostile attitude to the body and its basic needs.

Moreover, there is of course no guarantee that renouncing material possessions, worldly relations, and sensual pleasures actually leads to spiritual enlightenment. The Buddha famously gave up on his extreme ascetic lifestyle after just a few years, when he realized that it had not brought him any closer to his goal. He subsequently explored a much more livable "middle way," seeking to avoid the extremes of both asceticism and excessive consumption. The art of simple living is now particularly central to Zen Buddhism, and is reflected in its clean and plain aesthetics.[2]

The ancient Spartans, too, knew a thing or two about simplicity, with their emphasis on physical development, stark living, and military training. The word "spartan" has become a synonym for a particularly rigorous version of minimalism. Associated with joyless austerity, however, spartan is not a compliment. It is the eighteenth-century philosopher Jean-Jacques Rousseau and the nineteenth-century American transcendentalist Henry David Thoreau whom we must credit with having reglamorized simplicity. Like many of us today, they longed to simplify their lives in order to escape from the growing complexities of their worlds. In search of authenticity, they wished to reconnect with nature. It is to their examples that we shall turn first.

The Renaissance humanist Italian scholar Marsilio Ficino (1433–1499) already knew about the healing powers of nature. He therefore prescribed to the melancholic and energy-deprived readers of his self-help manual *Three Books on Life* (1489) "the frequent viewing of shining water and of green or red color, the haunting of gardens and groves and pleasant walks along rivers and through lovely meadows."[3] But it was Rousseau in the second half of the eighteenth century who was one of the first Western philosophers to propose a return to nature as an antidote to the complexities and pitfalls of modern life. To counter the growing sense of alienation in modern urban society, he suggested, we must reembrace nature, seek solitude, and let both our feet and our minds wander.

His final, unfinished work, *Reveries of the Solitary Walker* (1782), chronicles Rousseau's attempt to find solace and meaning in the simple things of life, and most importantly, in nature. His search for peace away from society was not just prompted by his belief in the goodness of all things natural, including human nature; it was also a reaction to an ongoing campaign of public mockery. His contemporaries had turned against him and his ideas, a state of affairs that troubled him greatly. Wounded by the social ostracism to which he had been subjected, he tried hard to reestablish a sense of equilibrium and purpose.

The essays contained in *Reveries*, written between September 1776 and April 1778, are loosely structured around ten walks. During these walks, Rousseau escapes from the city, Parisian society, and his many perceived tormentors. While perambulating freely through woods and fields, Rousseau reconnects with his authentic self, finally able to forget his painful social situation and simply *be*. "These hours of solitude and meditation are the only time of the day when I am completely myself, without distraction or hindrance, and when I can truly say that I am what nature intended me to be," he writes.[4] His detailed description of the inner torment of someone who feels himself completely at odds with the values and collective judgments of society was a new phenomenon. His struggle appears strikingly modern: Rousseau's is a conflict that very much chimes with our own preoccupation with self-realization and authentic living.

What, then, are Rousseau's key strategies for rebuilding his injured sense of selfhood? First and foremost, he relied on the healing powers of nature. In particular, he worshiped its awe-inspiring beauty and its ability to remind us that we are but a tiny part of a larger whole. As many other Romantic thinkers have also emphasized, when we are confronted with the sublimity of nature, we realize our own insignificance. Nature, in other words, is a powerfully humbling force. It puts our often petty concerns into perspective.

Rousseau also recommended solitude. This stance contrasts with the Enlightenment notion that we are social animals, born to be communal. But Rousseau prizes alone time. He feels that it allows him to commune with his own thoughts, entirely liberated from any requirement to conform to social conventions. By walking unobserved, surrounded only by plants and animals, he feels the lifting of a burden—that of the critical and potentially hostile gaze of his fellow men. Is it any surprise I love solitude so, Rousseau asks himself, when "I see only animosity on men's faces, and nature always smiles at me."[5] He is, of course, far from alone in cherishing solitude as a cure for our ailments. The early Christian desert fathers, as well as numerous other hermits before and after them, believed that our true spiritual self only reveals itself in retreat from the world. Many other Romantic thinkers, including William Wordsworth, advocated a solitary withdrawal into nature. They, too, considered it to be a way to reconnect with their authentic selves, to restore their health and their sanity, and to boost their creativity.[6]

Yet it is not just the natural setting, but also the act of walking itself that is deemed to be restorative. Physical movement allows the mind to move as well. "Solitude, I'll walk with thee," writes John Clare, while Wordsworth has immortalized the idea of wandering "lonely as a cloud." And Wordsworth practiced what he preached: it is estimated that the poet walked 180,000 miles during his lifetime. Walking through nature makes it possible for the Romantics to let their minds wander, too, by allowing them to indulge in a similar kind of non-goal-orientated ambulating. Walking in nature, Rousseau writes, he can stop thinking—thinking having become an instrument of self-harm.

These Romantic strategies for regaining our peace of mind are currently experiencing a major revival.[7] A whole raft of "nature cure" self-help has been published in the last two decades, urging us to rewild ourselves, to go forest bathing, cold-water swimming, and bird-watching, to haunt urban parks, or simply potter around more in our gardens.[8] Walking, too, has been rediscovered as a potentially healing activity. It was already enjoying a comeback (with an urban spin) in the late nineteenth century, when the distinctly Parisian art of *flânerie* was born. Much in line with Romantic thinking on the matter, Jonathan Hoban, in *Walk with Your Wolf: Unlock Your Intuition, Confidence, and Power* (2019), for example, urges us to start walking, to rediscover the curative power of nature, and to reclaim the wildness inside us. Walking, Hoban argues, allows us to destress, to reenergize, and properly to process our feelings.[9]

The Romantics' emphasis on solitude and on countering mental stress by daydreaming, meditating, and allowing the mind to ramble has proven to be equally influential. Numerous recent self-help books, such as Sara Maitland's *How to Be Alone* (2014), emphasize the dangers of a "solitude deficit" and the importance of silence and spending time alone in order to recharge and reconnect with ourselves.[10] Because of nonstop digital connectivity, we find ourselves in a new twilight zone, neither properly connected to others nor ever really alone.

Both Rousseau's and his more recent followers' strategies, then, are designed to serve as an antidote to a specifically modern experience of alienation. A more simple way of being frees us from ever more complex and draining social dynamics. Reconnecting with nature, seeking silence and solitude, and letting both our feet and our minds drift remain readily available simplicity-based tools for providing some respite. It is not in the least surprising that self-help has recently rediscovered the benefits of these activities. We are spending less time than ever in nature, are constantly connected to others through social media, and have largely lost the habit of walking for walking's sake. But there are also critical voices who take issue with the neo-Romantic vision of nature as a giant repository of "green Prozac."[11] They problematize the medicalization of nature, and our instrumental attitude toward it.[12] We should not merely seek to extract well-being from our meadows, moors, seascapes, and woodlands, but should think more about how we can preserve them. Critics also point out that nature's healing powers should not be so crudely overestimated: nature cannot guarantee our mental well-being—after all, depression and other mental health issues exist among those living in the countryside, too.[13]

The healing powers of nature and solitude are also of pivotal importance to the American philosopher Henry David Thoreau (1817–1862). In the mid-nineteenth century, he famously withdrew to a cabin on the banks of Walden Pond, in Concord, Massachusetts. It was there that he sought to live deeply and "deliberately," by the labor of his own hands, for two years and two months. Thoreau wished dramatically to simplify his existence, to live in a way that was reliant only on the "necessary of life."[14] His list of essential needs is short and sharp, including only food, shelter, clothing, and warmth. By contrast, he felt that most "of the luxuries, and many of the so called comforts of life, are not only dispensable, but positive hindrances to the elevation of mankind."[15] His aim was to live a life of complete simplicity and independence.

Above all, Thoreau wished to avoid living a life of "quiet desperation," which, he maintained, was the sad fate of the vast majority of people.[16] "Simplify, simplify" being his central mantra, he valued his freedom over luxurious carpets, fine furniture, and haute cuisine.[17] "I went to the woods because I wished to live deliberately, to front only the essential facts of life," he famously writes, "and see if I could not learn what it had to teach, and not, when I came to die, discover that I had not lived. . . . I wanted to live deep and suck out all the marrow of life, to live so sturdily and Spartan-like as to put to rout all that was not life, to cut a broad swath and shave close, to drive life into a corner, and reduce it to its lowest terms. . . ."[18] These were not just catchy minimalist slogans. Thoreau took the economics of simple living extremely seriously. In the first chapter of *Walden* (1854), he introduces the captivating notion of "life cost." Many of us unthinkingly seek to acquire as much money as possible, and to accumulate as many possessions as our salaries allow. Thoreau assesses the question of work from a radically pragmatic perspective. In fact, he turns it upside down. First determining his essential basic needs, he then proceeds to calculate the exact amount of money he needs in order to pay for these. His aim was not to work a single hour more than was necessary to cover his basic living expenses. He valued time and freedom over the luxuries of life. Thoreau established that he needed to work only six weeks of the year in order to cover his minimum expenses. He also chose to earn his money as a day laborer, which allowed him the freedom to be flexible with his hours. Moreover, he was able to detach completely from his work the second it ended.

For the remainder of the year, he was free to do what he really desired and valued: philosophizing and spending time in nature. The normative values of wealth and social esteem simply had no purchase in his personal system. His programmatically simple, nonmaterialistic lifestyle allowed him to be the sole master of his own time. Thoreau anticipated the modern debate about work-life balance, but decidedly privileged the latter. He viewed paid work as a necessary evil to which we should dedicate as little time as possible. His attitude could not contrast more starkly with the Protestant work ethic once described by the German sociologist Max Weber as the spiritual engine of capitalism. To this day, this particular work ethic continues to shape many of our core values and work-related mindsets.

A modern version of Thoreau-inspired simple and self-sufficient living is manifest in the "voluntary simplicity" and the "financial independence" lifestyle movements.[19] Voluntary simplicity adherents reject materialism in favor of downsizing. They believe that our high-consumption lifestyles degrade the planet and are unethical in a world defined by severe shortages of essential goods. Moreover, acquisitiveness neither provides meaning nor enhances happiness. Very little is needed to live well, for abundance is a state of mind.[20] The members of the Simplicity Collective, for example, voluntarily choose lower incomes and a much lower level of consumption in order to have more time and energy to pursue "non-materialistic sources of satisfaction and meaning." They seek to dedicate the lion's share of their time to goals other than buying and displaying things. These include "community or social engagements, more time with family, artistic or intellectual projects, more fulfilling employment, political participation, sustainable living, spiritual exploration, reading, contemplation, relaxation, pleasure-seeking, love, and so on."[21]

The American social activist Duane Elgin defines voluntary simplicity, much in the spirit of Thoreau, as "a way of life that is outwardly simple and inwardly rich ... a deliberate choice to live with less in the belief that more life will be returned to us in the process."[22] The historian David Shi understands voluntary simplicity as a form of "enlightened material restraint."[23] Lifestyle movements that pursue the simple life tend generally to value frugality, nature, and self-sufficiency. They privilege creativity and contemplation over conspicuous consumption. In addition, they care about long-term sustainability and social justice.[24] Unlike austerity, then, which is based on scarcity-thinking, voluntary simplicity is a choice based on a deep understanding of what we really need.

Many psychological studies show that such an approach is more likely to make us happy than the materialist lifestyles that the majority of us lead by default. In *The High Price of Materialism* (2002), for example, the psychosociologist Tim Kasser shows what materialism does to our psyches. The most ardent consumers, he found, tend to be those who are least satisfied with their lives. Avarice and acquisitiveness are not royal roads to happiness, for meaning matters more than money, and connections always trump consumption. While materialists tend to overvalue objects and status, they undervalue friendships, the quality of their experiences, and altruism. They feel fewer positive emotions and are more anxious and depressed than their nonmaterialist peers. Materialism,

Kasser concludes, is in fact seriously detrimental to our psychological well-being.

Also of interest in this context is the Financial Independence, Retire Early (FIRE) movement, which gained traction among millennials in the 2010s and was popularized, among others, by the Frugal Guru lifestyle blogger Peter Adeney, aka Mr. Money Mustache.[25] FIRE philosophy promotes aggressive saving (ideally 70 percent of our income) and radically decreasing expenses. Followers also seek to make sensible long-term investments so that the income from these assets eventually allows them to live independently. They aspire to live by the "4 percent rule," withdrawing no more than 4 percent per year of their capital (which is invested in stocks and shares), so that it never diminishes. Their money-saving tactics are truly hard-core, ranging from walking everywhere, renting out their bedrooms, and sleeping on sofas, to living on sale-priced supermarket items only. Their ultimate aim is to retire as early as possible— ideally decades before the standard retirement age.

These ideas were first popularized by Vicki Robin and Joe Dominguez in their bestseller *Your Money or Your Life* (1992), and again, almost two decades later, in Jacob Lund Fisker's *Early Retirement Extreme* (2010) and Grant Sabatier's *Financial Freedom: A Proven Path to All the Money You Will Ever Need* (2019). Like Thoreau, Robin and Dominguez ask us to reflect on how much of our "life energy" we spend at work and whether what we get out of it in return is worth the price. Do we gain sufficient happiness for our investment of life-time into work? Are our salaries commensurate with the many sacrifices they require? They, too, encourage us to live more deliberately and meaningfully, but throw hard economics (in the form of extremely high saving rates) into the mix.

Their project differs from Thoreau's and the voluntary simplicity movements' approach in one key respect: time. FIRE is all about making more money in significantly less time, so that we can spend more time, sooner, doing the things we love to do. The FIRE version of simple living is radically future-driven: the hope is that frugality in the present will result in freedom from work in the future. Simplicity or downsizing is not the aim, but rather a means to an end. The true aim here is gaining as much free time as possible, as fast as possible. While Thoreau based his "life cost" calculations on a single calendar year, FIRE adherents take our entire life span into consideration. The FIRE philosophy, then, is future- rather than present-oriented—even if its adherents wish to accelerate the arrival of a better future.

The idea of simplifying our lives, and prioritizing what really matters, remains attractive. In fact, this desire has grown stronger than ever in our own time, as the ongoing vogue for self-help books centering on minimalist living, digital detoxing, and decluttering suggests. The Japanese tidying expert Marie Kondo is the most prominent representative of this trend, but there are numerous others who tap into the desire to shed our possessions and regain control of both our physical and our mental space.[26]

Consumer capitalism rests on creating artificial desires for objects we do not really need. Many of us find ourselves drowning in pointless stuff that clutters up our living spaces. The trend forecaster James Wallman argues that we suffer from collective "stuffocation," losing ourselves amid unnecessary objects which render us increasingly anxious.[27] Yet a growing number of us, Wallman maintains, are turning our back on consumerism. What the American economist and sociologist Thorstein Veblen, in his book *The Theory of the Leisure Class* (1899), described as conspicuous consumption has not made us happier but instead more depressed. In response, ever more of us are turning our back on consumerism. This may involve abandoning our city jobs in search of the simple life—moving into cabins and cottages in the countryside, for example—or practicing "medium chilling"—forgoing promotion, say, in order to spend more time with friends and family. But the best way to counter stuffocation, Wallman suggests, is simply to focus on experiences. We should all become experientialists, he argues, pursuing fulfilling activities rather than continuing to accumulate inane objects.

Marie Kondo's considerable global appeal is no doubt a symptom of a rapidly growing fatigue with materialism. However, capitalism exhaustion explains only in part why an unassuming tidying expert who does not speak English managed to secure her own Netflix show. Her house-decluttering methodology also touches on some of our deeper spiritual desires. In *The Life-Changing Magic of*

Tidying (first published in Japan in 2010 and translated into English in 2011), Kondo asks us to keep our house in order—not just literally but also metaphorically. Drawing on basic feng shui ideas, she argues that all things have energy. The organization of our living spaces impacts on the free circulation of positive energy. Clutter and overcrowding create blockages. Moreover, our external spaces reflect our inner space, because our ownership patterns reveal deeper values. The possessions we accumulate and hoard expose our psychological states. All the useless, ugly, or ill-fitting things to which we hold on signify an unhealthy attachment to the past, or else our fear of the future. "If we acknowledge our attachment to the past and our fears for the future by honestly looking at our possessions," Kondo writes, "we will be able to see what is really important to us. This process in turn helps us to identify our values and reduces doubt and confusion when making life decisions."[28]

In more practical terms, Kondo recommends that we tidy by category rather than location. She urges us to start with clothes, then move on to books, papers, *komono* (that is, miscellaneous items), and to finish with sentimental items. Each item within these categories is to be taken out and placed in the middle of the room. Next, we need to touch every single item and determine whether or not it "sparks joy." If not, we must discard it. The element of touch is important, as we need to listen to our heart and gut in this process, not just our head. We should keep only what makes us truly happy, not what we think we may need in the future, or what merely connects us to the past. The entire exercise serves the purpose of identifying our true needs, as they manifest themselves now, in the present. It involves letting go of baggage and outdated ideas of ourselves. Kondo is also fervently opposed to piling things into vertical towers. Horizontal storage is key in her system, because only in that way can we see what we own at a glance. If we do not see what we have, we will keep on buying or wearing the same things over and over again.

While Kondo's mantra of keeping only those items that spark joy may be easy to mock, hers is in fact a much more radical proposal than it might at first seem. For it entails thinking about our true needs and desires, and about what has become superfluous in our lives. It forces us to reflect on what makes us genuinely happy.

Equally importantly, once we have reduced our possessions accord-ing to these principles, we will be much more reluctant to make bad, shortsighted purchases and to clutter up our living spaces again. The ideal result is that we will think more carefully about what we buy, and stop purchasing useless things altogether. Kondoing our living spaces can thus lead to a shift in perspective, away from the material toward the experiential and spiritual. If the Kondo method is prac-ticed correctly, we may realize that we already have what we need; we might start using the items in our possession that make us happy, rather than saving them for special occasions or craving an endless array of new stuff. Serious Kondoism could even have serious eco-nomic consequences. Entire industries would die out if we all stopped purchasing products that do not truly fulfill our needs.

Even before Kondo, Japan was firmly associated with all things minimalist in the popular imagination. When we think of Japan, we think of traditional Zen principles and its deliberately simple aes-thetics, but also of Shintoism and the concept of *wabi-sabi*. *Wabi-sabi* acknowledges the transience of all phenomena, and finds beauty in impermanence and imperfection. Another theory for the preva-lence of minimalism in Japan relates it to its geographical unique-ness. Only about a tenth of its forbidding mountainous landscapes are arable; it is susceptible to earthquakes, tsunamis, and volcanic eruptions. In the past, the Japanese often had to take flight at a mo-ment's notice on account of fires, fighting, bandits, and natural di-sasters, carrying all of their most precious possessions with them. They have thus learned to reduce those possessions to the bare es-sentials.[29] For many centuries, Japan was a closed culture, static and isolated, which has allowed many of its older aesthetic traditions to be preserved. A perhaps more pragmatic explanation for the domi-nance of minimalist principles in Japan is that it is also a highly populous nation distributed over a few smallish islands. Especially in big cities, living space is extremely limited.[30]

French culture, by contrast, tends to be associated with a rigor-ous quality-oriented approach, in particular with regard to clothes, food, and cosmetics. In *L'art de la simplicité: How to Live More with Less* (published in French in 2011, English translation 2016), the bestselling French writer Dominique Loreau, who has lived in Japan for decades, brings these two cultural traditions into a productive dialogue. The result is distinctly Franco-Japanese lifestyle advice. Perhaps unsurprisingly, Loreau's core mantras are "less is more" and "quality tops quantity." Instead of buying twenty bargain-basement, soon-to-be-discarded outfits, she suggests that we invest in one good-quality cashmere garment. Fashion-wise we ought generally to shun all things cheap and of mediocre or poor craftsmanship, and instead seek to invest in a few luxurious, classic essentials. The same quality-driven approach applies to all other spheres of our lives as well: to our beauty care, our mental space, friendships, and furniture. It also holds for food: we should aim to eat little and only highly nutritious and healthy foods.

However, Loreau is a tad too obsessed with slimming in the literal sense. "Remember, weight is your enemy," she warns, "weight is not good for objects, nor is it good for your health."[31] "Every time we put on weight," she writes, "we die a little."[32] While her fixation on slimness and her occasional snobbism can be irksome, Loreau does make an important point about self-care. In Judeo-Christian cultures, she argues, taking good care of our bodies has traditionally been disregarded and discouraged, being associated with sin, taboo, and selfish indulgence.[33] In many Asian cultures, by contrast, what we now refer to as "self-care" has been practiced seriously for millennia, related to a strong tradition of preventative medicine. Indeed, it makes a lot of sense to take good care of our bodies, minds, and energy before they become ill or depleted.

Carefully curating our possessions is a potent way of simplifying our lives. But as Kondo shows, this process is merely symbolic of others that reach much deeper. Keeping it simple is about prioritizing needs, showing gratitude for what we have, and understanding what makes us truly happy. It can entail eating good, simple, unprocessed food—"not too much" and "mainly plants," as Michael Pollan put it so memorably.[34] It can mean curating our social networks, investing our time and energy only in the relationships that really matter. It involves focusing on one task at a time, whether working or playing. It is, in sum, about allowing the principle of "less is more" genuinely to transform our life.

Keeping it simple in the twenty-first century involves yet another set of important tasks. These include decluttering our minds by switching off our devices and disconnecting from digital distractions. In *Digital Minimalism: On Living Better with Less Technology* (2019), Cal Newport argues that information technology has turned us all into behavioral addicts. Having become screen slaves, we no longer use technology in a self-determined way. Instead, technology is using us. The technologies that were supposed to make our lives easier, by saving time and energy and rendering communication more instantaneous, have in fact created a host of very serious problems. They endanger both our mental health and our physical well-being. Paradoxically, we also spend most of the time that smartphones and other devices save us by pointlessly wasting it online.

Because we never switch off, and are always connected and reachable, the boundaries between our working and our private lives have become ever more blurred. This has resulted in a dramatic increase in stress-related ailments. Because we are always elsewhere in our thoughts, our attention vaguely focused on the exploits of faraway people and places, we neglect to pay attention to those around us—friends, partners, children. Our presence is constantly seeping away, through all kinds of digital holes, for we are always distracted. We suffer from exhaustion and display core signs of behavioral addiction, spending hours each day checking our smartphones, binge-watching Netflix series, shopping online, gaming, or even consuming online pornography.

The picture Newport paints of our condition is bleak. Our digitalized lifestyles have reduced our concentration spans from 12 seconds to 8—shorter than that of the infamously ill-focused goldfish, who manages to concentrate for 9 seconds.[35] Our ability to empathize has also dramatically diminished.[36] We constantly compare our own lives to carefully curated snippets of other people's lives, as presented, heavily filtered, on platforms such as Instagram. As a result, we find our existence wanting and deficient. Perhaps most worryingly, we are hardly ever alone with our own thoughts. This permanent "solitude deprivation" renders us increasingly unable to engage in deep thinking, and complicates getting in touch with our feelings. Our nonstop connectedness has rendered us lonelier than ever, for the quantity of our online social relations cannot replace the quality of real-life contact. Online living, moreover, stokes our darkest instincts, encouraging rage, hate, cruelty, trolling, and bullying. And because being online takes up so much of our time, it distracts us from activities that might be more beneficial for our well-being.

Even something as innocuous as constantly checking our email and text messages has far-reaching consequences. It can take up to twenty-five minutes to refocus on a task after an interruption. Office workers tend to spend a quarter of their days dealing with emails, and check their accounts, on average, thirty-six times per hour, or every two minutes.[37] This kind of behavior cannot be good for tasks that require sustained concentration. Average smartphone users spend around three hours a day on their devices, picking them up thirty-nine times in the course of a twenty-four-hour period.[38] "Nomophobia"—the fear of being without our mobile phone—is now a widespread condition.

It gets worse. For even more concerning is what these technologies have done to the younger generations. Those born between 1995 and 2012 have basically grown up on social media. Their device usage is constant as, on average, they spend nine hours per day on their smartphones.[39] Some alarming studies have shown that this generation, nicknamed "iGen," is struggling with an unprecedented rise in mental health issues, in particular with depression and anxiety. It is not a coincidence that what has been described as a "teen anxiety epidemic," and as the worst mental health crisis in decades, corresponds exactly to the moment when in America smartphone ownership became universal.[40] The American psychologist Jean Twenge believes that smartphones have essentially destroyed an entire generation.[41] iGeners are never alone with their thoughts, and they have so little face-to-face contact that they have unlearned how to make sense of their own and others' emotions. "Much in the same way that the 'innovation' of highly processed foods in the mid-twentieth century led to a global health crisis," Newport writes, "the unintended side effects of digital communication tools—a sort of social fast food—are proving to be similarly worrisome."[42]

What is perhaps most troubling is that the technologies responsible for this new mental health crisis are specifically *designed* to be as addictive as possible, as the term "attention economy" makes clear. The more attention we dedicate to our gadgets, the more someone somewhere profits from keeping us spellbound. It is very telling, for example, that Steve Jobs refused to let his own children use iPads.[43] The political commentator Bill Maher goes so far as to claim that the tycoons of social media are "tobacco farmers in T-shirts selling an addictive product to children. Because, let's face it, checking your 'likes' is the new smoking." Yet while Philip Morris "just wanted your lungs," Maher concludes, "the App Store wants your soul."[44]

This may sound like an exaggeration—after all, technology is neither good nor bad in its own right. Its value depends on how we use it and to what purpose. But as Adam Alter demonstrates in *Irresistible: The Rise of Addictive Technology and the Business of Keeping us Hooked* (2017), tech companies do indeed aim to generate addictive behaviors in various subtle and not so subtle ways. As the chilling Netflix docudrama *The Social Dilemma* (2020) has shown, Facebook, Instagram, and shopping platforms are all designed to ensnare us. Interfaces, background colors, fonts, layout, and audio features are cannily optimized to hold our attention as long as possible. The strategy of systematic user-hooking is most apparent in the world of gaming. Games operate with carefully calibrated, compelling goals that are just beyond reach and tasks that become slowly more difficult over time. The psychologically highly rewarding sense of incremental progress is what keeps us playing.[45]

But attention-hooking is also manifest in the shrewdly calculated cliff-hanger endings to episodes in Netflix series, or in deliberately engineered positive feedback mechanisms. The latter exploit our strong drive for social approval. Social validation creates a dopamine rush in our brains. The rush is even stronger when it is delivered unpredictably, such as in the case of "likes." Alter argues that our behavioral addictions to tech activate the same brain regions as substance addictions. They also feed on the same unfulfilled psychological needs, including "social engagement and social support, mental stimulation, and a sense of effectiveness."[46] For all of these reasons, our compulsive usage of such technologies, Newport concludes, is "not the result of a character flaw, but instead the realization of a massively profitable business plan." We have been engaging "in a lopsided arms race in which the technologies encroaching on our autonomy were preying with increasing precision on deep-seated vulnerabilities in our brains, while we still naively believed that we were just fiddling with fun gifts handed down from the nerd gods."[47]

What, then, are we to do? For many of us, it is impossible to go cold turkey on technologies such as email or text messaging, as we need them for work and to coordinate our social lives. Newport's solution is a philosophy of technology usage that is rooted in our deeper values. To unhook ourselves from our devices he suggests a thirty-day digital detox, followed by a sober and thorough cost-benefit analysis of the technologies we wish to use in the long run. He, too, mobilizes Thoreau's idea of life cost here. He reminds us that the cost of a thing "is the amount of what I will call life which is required to be exchanged for it, immediately or in the long run."[48] If the technologies we use provide only bland diversion or negligible convenience, their mental and physical costs might simply not be worth it. Working backward from our deeper values, Newport invites us to make deliberate choices about the technologies we wish to include in our lives. They need to fulfill only one key function: they must be tools to support our deeply held values.

According to Newport, we all need to become digital minimalists and join the "attention resistance." We should aim to use tech in strictly delimited ways only, with the aim of extracting maximum value from products "while avoiding falling victim to compulsive use."[49] In more concrete terms, this means having strict personal rules about how, when, and to what purpose we use digital technologies. It also means reconnecting with leisure activities that are meaningful and productive, and which we may have neglected. These can include spending time alone, taking long walks (leaving our smartphones at home), and engaging in real-life face-to-face conversations, pandemics permitting. It means stopping our mindless tapping, swiping, and checking, and simply letting go of all those low-quality digital distractions. It may mean making or joining something, and returning to slow media for a deeper and more productive kind of intellectual stimulation.

During the COVID-19 pandemic in 2020–21, everything changed, including our relation to technology. When the world slowed and many of us went into lockdown, much of our usual activity and face-to-face socializing ceased. The status of communication technology changed dramatically once again, from distraction and mental-health risk to life-saver. It enabled many knowledge-workers to continue to work from home. Most importantly, it became our primary means of staying socially connected while the species-jumping virus forced us to remain physically apart. We zoomed, teamed, and streamed en masse, almost bringing down the Internet. We shared virtual Quarantinis, started dressing only from the waist up, rearranged our virtual backgrounds, and touched up our Zoom faces. Nobody was thinking of digitally detoxing.

But since working from home has become the new normal for many of us, our old tech-related itches have flared up again, and with a renewed urgency. The global pandemic has dramatically accelerated the future of work. Many transactions are bound to stay online in the long run. Virtual meetings, online learning and shopping, and home office culture have already started to reshape our social fabric. If anything, the need to draw up our own philosophy of technology use has become even more pressing. For if we work and shop and even socialize from home, the boundaries between work and leisure are bound to get ever blurrier. If a large part of our working life now happens online, it is even more important to steer the focus of our private lives firmly back into the nonvirtual realm.

The rapid growth in minimalism- and back-to-basics-inspired self-help in recent years suggests that the more complex our social, economic, and technological environments become, the more we crave simplicity in our lives. It is likely that the trend will continue, perhaps even intensify, in the post-COVID-19 world. Simplicity in the form of ascetic practices was once firmly aligned with spirituality. Keeping it simple in our time, by contrast, is primarily a means to de-stress and, crucially, to regain control—be that over our physical living spaces, our time, the things we consume, or our attention spans. Twenty-first-century modes of simplicity-seeking, then, appear to be predominantly secular rather than saintly in nature.

And yet elements of the ancient link between simplicity and spirituality persist. They lurk under the surface of seemingly more worldly regimes. The KonMari method, for example, draws not only on feng shui but also on devotional rituals of Shinto, encouraging us to pay respect to our possessions and the spaces in which we dwell. Our general desire to live with less is also an attempt to shed material baggage so that we can refocus our energies on lighter and loftier matters. Finally, because distraction—the most toxic effect of the digital technologies that now rule our lives—prevents present-moment awareness, our growing unease about technology indicates a desire to reintroduce more mindful ways of being back into our lives.

In the pre-COVID-19 world, technology's promise to simplify our lives had backfired. It did not just introduce significant new stressors, but reshaped our cognitive patterns, diminished our capability to be present in the here and now, and impoverished our ability deeply to connect with people. Above all, it made us lonelier than ever before, while also, paradoxically, wiping out our restorative moments of solitude. The full story of the role of technology in the post-COVID-19 world still remains to be written. It is, however, very likely that many of these challenges will only be exacerbated. Moreover, what was, to a certain extent at least, a choice might soon become our only option. Face-to-face interactions—which we so cavalierly took for granted and perhaps even neglected before the pandemic—now come with serious health risks. Our social choices have wide-ranging ethical implications. Our opportunities for socializing, traveling, and leisure activities may well shrink for good, or else take another form. The more we are forced to conduct our public and private lives online, the more complex a task it will become to control our interactions with technology. Our quest for simplicity, then, may well have been rendered much more difficult by the events of 2020–21.

CHAPTER SEVEN

Use Your Imagination

W HILE THE STOICS ADVOCATE reason as our primary tool for self-improvement, others emphasize the vital role of our imagination in the
process. Purely intellectual techniques and in-
sights, they feel, cannot bring about lasting emotional and behavioral change. We are not just rational animals; there is a large part
of us that is emotion-driven and of which we are not fully conscious. If rational knowledge were able to solve all our problems,
we could simply read an insightful book and be transformed by the
author's knowledge. And we would be able to change long-standing
bad habits and self-destructive patterns of behavior after just one
consultation with a psychologist. But naked facts and accurate di-
agnoses alone cannot impact on our more deep-seated beliefs and
habits. For knowledge to become insight—that is, something that
we practice repeatedly and even unconsciously, and that truly
changes the way we see ourselves and the world—the imagination
needs to be involved.

Our imagination is crucial in the process of self-improvement
in many ways. First and foremost, if we want to change the status
quo, we need to be able to imagine what could be rather than
merely what is. We need to have the ability to generate a positive
vision of our future selves that differs from our present condition.[1]

We will only ever take action to improve both ourselves and our situation if we have clearly imagined the benefits and rewards of those improvements. If we cannot envisage a better future for ourselves, we are very unlikely to embark on the process of change. This is also the case if we do not believe in the power of our own efforts, and think of ourselves as helpless, or if we are prone to catastrophizing, regularly imagining that the future holds nothing but horrors.[2] Whether our vision of the future is positive or negative, then, is absolutely crucial to the realization of any desire to achieve self-improvement.

The Romantics were the first to put the imagination on a pedestal as the greatest of our mental faculties, contrasting it with the instrumental reason so valued by Enlightenment thinkers. Daydreaming, reverie, and mind-wandering were central to their conception of the self, as were folktales, fairy tales, and medieval lore, which the Romantics considered precious repositories of nonrational forms of knowledge. Perhaps most importantly, the Romantics, like Lao-tzu before them, treasured originality, creativity, and authenticity—values that are closely aligned with the imagination. These new Romantic values marked an important turning point in the history of self-improvement, for they formed the basis for our current valorization of the self-realizing individual.

Using our imagination in the form of creative visualizations is also a crucial self-improvement technique in its own right. Again, visualization is a tool with a much longer history than we may think, having already been used as a self-improvement aid in the ancient world. It is an important element in both Buddhist and Hindu insight meditation. The Stoics, moreover, practiced what can perhaps most aptly be described as the opposite of positive thinking: that is, negative visualizations, or *premeditatio malorum*. In order to prepare themselves mentally for the worst-case scenario, they deliberately imagined bad circumstances and outcomes. This kind of resilience-enhancing catastrophizing was also supposed to produce a sense of gratitude when the worst did not happen.[3]

Nowadays, we are encouraged to do the exact opposite: to imagine positive outcomes, in as vivid detail as possible. At the beginning of the twentieth century, the French apothecary Émile Coué de la Châtaigneraie (1857–1926) developed the theory of autosuggestion.

A form of self-hypnosis, it is based on the idea that our imagination has to be on board if we want to change behaviors or take action. We have to convince our unconscious mind of the benefits of what we wish to do, for it is much more powerful than our conscious mind. Visualizing desired results and how we can achieve them is also a staple technique in sports psychology. In many respects, it is the essence of "positive thinking." Neuro-linguistic programming (NLP) practitioners in particular use visualization exercises in a highly strategic way: they encourage us to imagine positive outcomes, in as much sensory detail as possible, or they ask us to picture ourselves in the act of performing tasks at the height of our powers.

The imagination, then, has always played a crucial role in self-improvement. It is broadly understood as our ability to form new ideas, images, or concepts of external objects that are not present. It can also relate to forming experiences in our minds, either re-creations of past experiences or completely invented ones. More generally, being imaginative can be understood as our capacity to be creative and to solve problems. Understood in that way, the imagination is closely linked to learning and our ability to integrate experiences. It is often cast as reason's big other, when in fact it can work very closely alongside our rational faculties. Crucially, it is also related to our capacity for mental projection. Our imagination enables us to project ourselves from the present moment into the future, or back into our pasts. Daydreaming, we can project ourselves into the realm of fantasy, or else into other people's heads, imagining what the world might look like from their point of view. Last but by no means least, our imagination is, of course, also the underlying driving force for all creative acts. And it is the products of others' imaginations, such as paintings, films, music, and stories, that are some of the most powerful tools for activating our own imagination. With this in mind, we can first turn our attention to the crucial role played by stories in both the art and the science of self-improvement.

Willpower is a limited resource, and reason's powers are not as wide-ranging as we like to think. On their own, willpower and reason are not potent enough to generate sustainable changes in our habits. What St. Augustine knew intuitively is now widely accepted by psychologists: "What is the cause of this monstrous situation?"

Augustine wondered. "The mind commands the body and is instantly obeyed. The mind commands itself and meets resistance."[4] Many writers on self-improvement, past and present, also understand this conundrum. They have therefore come up with ingenious ways to harness the power of our imagination. For the imagination can be a powerful bridging force, helping us to transform information into insights that we can put into practice. Some also like to think of it as a direct road into our unconscious mind.

Imagery and metaphor remain essential and timeless devices for rendering theories of self-improvement more relatable and memorable. Think of the many metaphors used to describe our minds— for instance, as computers, chimps, or black boxes. Think how often you have come across descriptions of us as enterprises, machines, soldiers in a war zone, competitors in a race, uncarved blocks, bricks in a stone arch, or delicate flowers in challenging soil. All of these metaphors invite us to make imaginative connections between different domains of knowledge. But by far the most obvious way in which self-improvement writers appeal to our imagination is via stories. These can be personal anecdotes, or case studies from clients, or even examples from books, films, or the lives of famous people. Parables, too, have long been used by advocates of self-improvement. They feature prominently in the *Tao*, the Buddha's speeches, and the Christian Gospels, and are still central devices in self-help literature today. Spencer Johnson's bestselling booklet *Who Moved My Cheese?* (1998) is an extended parable, and it is highly effective.

Stories have special powers. Consider, for example, an old Cherokee tale that is often used in coaching. It goes like this: One day, an old Cherokee sat down with his grandson and gave him some advice. "A fight is going on inside me," he said to the boy. "'It's a terrible fight between two wolves. One is evil—he is hatred, anger, greed, envy, arrogance, grudge, resentment, miserliness, and cowardliness. The other is good—he is happiness, joy, serenity, love, kindness, compassion, hope, humility, generosity, truthfulness, and confidence. They are also fighting inside you and inside every other person, too.' The child thought about it for a minute and then asked his grandfather, 'Which wolf will win?' The old Cherokee simply replied, 'The one you feed.' "[5] This story dramatizes inner conflict. It furnishes our less attractive qualities with a memorable shape and

a name. It provides us with a vivid image for the ongoing battle between the better and the less good parts of our nature. The image of
the two wolves fighting within us can be a powerful tool not just for
raising awareness of our behavior and emotions, but for actively trying to control the more wolfish ones. A friend of mine regularly
opens his coaching sessions with the question: "So, which wolf have
you been feeding this week?"[6] His clients really relate to that. The
battle of these inner wolves has become a key metaphor through
which they understand themselves.

Other stories that tend regularly to be used in self-help contexts are those that follow the journey of a hero. In stories of that
kind, the hero leaves home to answer a calling or confront a challenge. That can be slaying monsters, fighting evil tyrants, or un-
earthing a treasure. The hero ventures deeply into unknown
territory, such as dark forests, caves, the bottom of the sea, or other
mysterious realms. He or she is usually aided by helper figures, and
often has wise guides who mentor them so that they can make it
through their challenges with integrity. Often, there is a crucial
moment of temptation. Sometimes they give in to that temptation,
and the success of their mission is endangered or delayed. But in
the end, they master their challenges and return home victorious
and much wiser, sharing with their people the knowledge they have
gained during their adventures or else a boon, such as an elixir of
life. When we hear stories of that kind, we cannot help but identify
with the hero. We are inspired by their courage and feel hopeful
and heartened by their success.

It was Samuel Smiles (1812–1904), the Victorian founding father of the self-help genre as we know it today, who pioneered the
systematic use of inspiring mini-biographies of great men to moti-
vate his readers. All of the many aspirational tales in *Self-Help*
(1859) follow the same narrative pattern, which resembles that of
the hero's journey. Smiles's stories recount the development of
men, mainly from modest backgrounds, who managed to overcome
enormous adversity and achieve greatness through a combination
of perseverance, hard work, and virtuous living. Crucially, these
motivational stories are not just examples of what other men have
done, but illustrations of what each of us might, "in a greater or
less degree, do for himself."[7]

Smiles's formula is alluring, and has become a self-help blueprint. Many self-help books today continue to be peppered with stories of miraculous makeovers and superhuman achievements in the face of adversity. Or else they contain rousing autobiographical anecdotes, rags-to-riches tales, and examples of marvelous transformations drawn from the lives of both ordinary and famous people. Appealing to our imagination, these tales illuminate and illustrate; by adding narrative flesh, they render abstract theory relatable, and they activate our emotions. Moreover, the biographical vignettes impose order on the chaos of existence, distilling it into lives with purpose and direction. One of the most successful self-help publishing franchises is built on nothing but such inspirational tales. *Chicken Soup for the Soul,* created by Jack Canfield and Mark Victor Hansen, has made it its mission to inspire its readers with timeless stories "about everyday miracles that illuminate the best of the human spirit." The *Chicken Soup* stories, the authors promise, provide a form of comforting spiritual nourishment and "will inspire you to be a better person, reach for your highest potential, overcome your challenges, and embrace the world around you."[8]

It is the prerogative of stories to educate and to amuse, to provide solace and inspiration, and to appeal simultaneously to our emotions and to our intellect. One of the primary psychological mechanisms triggered by stories is identification. When reading the life stories of great self-transformers, we cannot help but identify with them, projecting upon them our own hopes and desires. Smiles, it seems, was acutely aware of this. As he observes, "Biographies of great, but especially of good men, are . . . most instructive and useful, as helps, guides, and incentives to others. Some of the best are almost equivalent to gospels—teaching high living, high thinking, and energetic action for their own and the world's good. The valuable examples which they furnish of the power of self-help, of patient purpose, resolute working, and stead-fast integrity . . . exhibit in language not to be misunderstood, what it is in the power of each to accomplish for himself."[9]

Stories, examples, imagery, and anecdotes add what Aristotle terms "pathos" to "ethos"—our credibility—and "logos"—persuasion through logic. Both ethos and logos, Aristotle believes, remain powerless if they are not supplemented by pathos, or the art of appealing to our emotions. By activating our faculty of what-if thinking, moreover, stories encourage us to believe that we, too, could succeed in transforming ourselves, just like the heroes and heroines of inspirational tales. They invite us to put ourselves in their shoes, fantasizing about what it would be like if we were them.

As Aristotle also knew well, stories have the power both to evoke and to purge us of strong emotions. The American philosopher Martha Nussbaum argues that they can be powerful tools for improving ourselves, by turning us into more ethical and more humane beings.[10] They do so above all by inviting us to project ourselves into the minds of others, thereby fostering our ability to experience empathy. In addition, they make us more tolerant, hone our capacity to deal with ambiguity, nuance, and uncertainty, and sharpen our powers of attention.

The famous TED talker Brené Brown considers stories to be "data with a soul."[11] Like many other successful TED talkers, Brown knows that stories can reach not just our minds, but also our hearts, and as such are a highly effective means for building a connection with others. Moreover, they switch on specific areas in our brains. Merely factual information tends to activate our language-processing centers. Stories, by contrast, stimulate much larger areas in our brains, including not just the language center but also those parts that are responsible for visual and motor processing, as well as our sensory cortex.[12] Stories can activate our mirror neurons, allowing us to imagine ourselves in a particular situation, doing something specific. They can also trigger hormonal responses in our brains: our adrenalin and cortisol production might be stimulated by narratives that evoke fear, for example, whereas stories appealing to our compassion and empathy can result in higher emissions of dopamine and oxytocin. All of this matters. Via this kind of imaginary experiential immersion, stories can prompt strong emotional states. These, in turn, can affect our moral responses and even alter our attitudes. And it is, after all, this shift in how we see ourselves and others that is required for changing how we behave.

As mentioned above, the celebration of the powers of our imagination was the central concern of the Romantics in the late eighteenth and early nineteenth centuries. They wished to address what they perceived as a damaging cultural bias in favor of our rational faculties cultivated during the Age of Enlightenment. Enlightenment thinkers believed in the absolute supremacy of reason. Championed by philosophers such as Voltaire, Denis Diderot, and Immanuel Kant, the triad reason, science, and progress constituted the crown of Enlightenment values. Empirical inquiry and the scientific method, based on experiment and observation, were considered the only legitimate pathways to knowledge. Most Enlightenment thinkers also believed that we can improve ourselves by purely rational means. In his celebrated essay "What Is Enlightenment?" (1784), Kant argues that "enlightenment is man's emergence from his self-incurred immaturity." If human beings remain unenlightened, he writes, it is on account of their "laziness and cowardice."[13] Kant thus saw it as a moral imperative for us to improve ourselves, to pass from ignorance to knowledge, and the way to do so was through the power of reason.

Together with intuition, sensibility, creativity, and interiority, the Romantics championed the transformative power of the imagination. The poets William Wordsworth and Samuel Taylor Coleridge reflected extensively on the wonders of the imagination, pitting it against reason and arguing that it should be our primary guide. Our imaginative faculties, they held, are responsible for acts of memory, perception, and projection. On the wings of our imaginations, we can travel to the past and the future, and to places that do not exist. Wordsworth writes that the Romantic poet has the "disposition to be affected more than other men by absent things as if they were present, an ability of conjuring up in himself passions."[14] Unsurprisingly, the Romantics thought of themselves as particularly imaginative, as more firmly aligned with the imagination than their ancestors.

The imagination also had a crucial moral function. The poet Percy Bysshe Shelley called the imagination the "great instrument of moral good." He specified further: "A man to be greatly good, must imagine intensely and comprehensively; he must put himself in the place of another and of many others; the pains and pleasures of his species must become his own."[15] In other words, by putting ourselves into somebody else's shoes and imagining what the world may look like from their perspective, our imaginations allow us to mentalize and to empathize.

Many Romantics proposed simplicity, nature, and reverie as the best cures to the mental maladies brought about by their sworn enemy, soulless mechanical reason. Letting their minds off their leashes, they sought to let them wander freely, allowing them to stroll, sniff, explore, and dawdle as they pleased, and at their own pace. They wished to let their souls take flight through the universe "on the wings of the imagination in ecstasies that exceed all other pleasures."[16] By connecting deeply with nature, beauty, and the sublime, the Romantics sought a sense of fusion with a greater whole, an oceanic feeling of being at one with the world.

As a result of the Romantic exaltation of the imagination, there was a new emphasis on originality, authenticity, uniqueness, self-reliance, and self-realization. All of these values still very much dominate our current self-help discourse. But how exactly are they related to the imagination? By valuing originality and uniqueness, the Romantics devalued tradition and convention. They developed a horror of the ordinary and the normal, to the point where madness was sometimes seen as a kind of wisdom. By constantly seeking newness and authenticity, they equipped our inner lives and subjective beliefs with new powers. It is up to us, they felt, to create and live by our own authentic values, rather than just accepting established wisdom or social conventions. Living in accordance with Romantic principles is therefore in itself a creative act, for establishing our own original values is an imaginative undertaking.

If we seek to be driven by our own inner values rather than external norms, we also have to become ever more self-reliant. If we no longer wish to allow culture to dictate its norms to us, we have to rely increasingly on our own moral compass. We have to become the captains of our own ships. Self-reliance is a principal aim of most current self-help guides. But the most famous philosophical articulation of self-reliance can already be found in an essay published in 1841 by the American philosopher Ralph Waldo Emerson (1803–1882). In "Self-Reliance," the prophet of transcendentalism and American individualism introduces two new ideas that were substantially to shape all modern self-help. The first is that the individual is more important than society. The second is that our independent judgment tops social conventions.

While he drew on European Romantic thought, Emerson was the founder of a uniquely American brand of idealist individualism. He believed that we can and indeed must rise above our circumstances. "Man is his own star" is the most telling of his essay's epigraphs.[17] Indeed, it neatly sums up his argument. Emerson not only elevates nonconformity to an art form, but declares it our ethical duty. We must always trust our own judgment, listen to our intuition and our instincts, and rediscover our spontaneity. Society, Emerson believes, is like a "joint stock company," in which members agree, for the sake of security and comfort, to surrender their liberty. It is for this reason that society values conformity above all else. But the integrity of our mind must at all times be our primary aim. We should insist on ourselves, and never imitate. We should "affront and reprimand the smooth mediocrity and squalid contentment of the times" by not being afraid to defy customs, trade, and offices.[18]

Emerson thus preaches the complete opposite of Confucius's doctrine, which advocates the importance of honoring rituals, rites, and social hierarchies. He holds that we should accept nothing uncritically—a mantra that applies to religion as well as to any other principle or belief. Above all, it is essential to be true to ourselves, and not to be swayed by the views of others.[19] While he hopes that his fellow men will love and respect him, Emerson declares that he will not hide his tastes and aversions, and will follow his principles even when society whips him with displeasure, for "nothing can bring you peace but yourself."[20]

Romantic thought and Emerson's ideas, then, are important turning points in our history of self-improvement. Both equip the imagination with absolute powers—above all, the power confidently to create and pursue our own values and to critique traditional ones. By promoting authenticity and self-reliance, the Romantics position the needs, desires, and judgments of the individual above a concern for social cohesion. This shift had far-ranging consequences, for these ideas helped usher in the age of the atomized self. The philosopher Julian Baggini argues that the atomized self privileges integrity—individual identity and authenticity—over intimacy.[21] The relational self, by contrast, perceives itself as intricately connected with other selves. It does not think of itself as a discrete unit.

While self-improvement in Confucius's sense, for example, was in-extricably bound up with the improvement of society as a whole, the Romantic self emphasizes its uniqueness and separateness from the masses. It elevates our own personal values over those of society. As a consequence, it begins to feel a more acute sense of loneliness and separation. It is perhaps for this reason that it seeks closer ties with nature—which is another way of feeling part of a larger order of things.

Another influential nineteenth-century thinker who privileged the imagination is the German philosopher Friedrich Nietzsche (1844–1900). "I tell you: one must have chaos in one, to give birth to a dancing star," he famously declared.[22] It is only by activating our imagination and creativity that we can make a unique contribution to this world, Nietzsche believes. Moreover, he furnishes the products of our imagination with nothing less than redemptive powers, holding that art and creativity are the only sources of meaning and salvation in our Godless universe.[23]

Nietzsche is perhaps best known for his claim that God is dead, and that it is we who have killed him. Faced with the death of God, and with the spiritual vacuum left in his absence, we need to adopt the role of Godlike creators ourselves. Like Emerson, Nietzsche advocates a total reliance on the self and a deep distrust of institutions, authorities, and, above all, established morality. In the secular age, religion can no longer deliver on its promise of redemption. Art, philosophy, literature, and music must take its place. Culture must take over the sense-making work of Scripture. It is only the products of our imagination that can save us from the specter of nihilism and anomie, he argues.

Nietzsche's ideas have substantially shaped many self-help books in the twentieth and twenty-first centuries. He also coined the influential notion of "self-overcoming," which still resonates with many. It features centrally in *Thus Spoke Zarathustra*, written between 1883 and 1885. *Thus Spoke Zarathustra* is a work that can be read as a self-help parable. Its protagonist, a prophet called Zarathustra, having lived as a hermit and in complete seclusion for many years, decides to descend from his mountain and to teach the people his doctrine of the *Übermensch*, or superhuman. He tells us to strive to rise above our human limitations, to aim higher, and to dream bigger.

He defines the superman in the following terms:

> *I teach you the Superman.* Man is something that should be overcome. What have you done to overcome him?
>
> All creatures hitherto have created something beyond themselves: and do you want to be the ebb of this great tide, and return to the animals rather than overcome man?
>
> What is the ape to men? A laughing-stock or a painful embarrassment. And just so shall man be to the Superman: a laughing-stock or a painful embarrassment. . . .
>
> Man is a rope, fastened between animal and Superman—a rope over an abyss.[24]

Although only nebulously outlined, the superman is a creature of the future, full of potential. Nietzsche asks us to imagine a what-if scenario: What if we could overcome our present limitations? Who and what could we become? Supermen must above all transcend their own epistemic boundaries, constantly aiming to self-improve. They have to break courageously with existing values and the common morality of the "herd." As supermen, we must expose the hypocritical foundations of society's moral frameworks and create new values. Demolishing uncritically accepted habits of mind and ancient prejudices, we should seek to become "aeronauts of the spirit."[25] In other words, we must be guided by our imagination and bold visions for a better future, bravely embracing our own original beliefs rather than accepting established wisdom. This belief is one that Nietzsche shares with the Romantics and Emerson. But like Zarathustra, Nietzsche warns his readers, the creative, value-overturning supermen of the future will be lonely and despised: "Behold the good and the just!" he declares. "Whom do they hate most? Him who smashes their tables of values, the breaker, the law-breaker—but he is the creator."[26]

Above all, then, Nietzsche believes that we should become what we are by following our inner laws and creating our own sets of values, beyond established notions of good and evil. Celebrating our uniqueness and our talents, we should have the courage to reject a restrictive morality that prevents us from flourishing. But how exactly are we to "overcome" ourselves? And how does creating our own values work? While these are grand, evocative phrases, Nietzsche gives very little practical advice on how we could translate them into action. Many contemporary self-help books, by contrast, go into considerable detail on how we can identify our own core values and live "value-based" lives. In *Awaken the Giant Within* (1991), for instance, Anthony Robbins argues that the only way to achieve long-term happiness is to "get clear about what is most important in our lives and decide that we will live by these values, no matter what happens." He urges us always to remember that our values, whatever they are, are "the compass" that is guiding us to our "ultimate destiny."[27]

Another important thinker who put the imagination center stage is the French pharmacist Émile Coué, mentioned above. In 1922, he wrote a self-help book entitled *Self-Mastery through Conscious Auto-suggestion: A Classic Self-Help Book.* An instant success, it was translated into numerous languages. Coué's principal contribution to the history of self-improvement is the idea that in order to change for the better, we need to involve our imagination, rather than relying on willpower alone. He was the first explicitly to state that naked willpower will get us nowhere in our quest for improvement. For, he argued, if we do not also appeal to our imagination, and convince it that change is a good idea, our unconscious is bound to boycott all attempts to alter our ways.

In his work as an apothecary, Coué became acutely aware of what was later called the placebo effect. He made a point of always reassuring his customers and emphasizing the efficacy of the remedies he was dispensing to them, and found that medicines accompanied by such positive messages tended to have a much more potent effect than those dispensed without them—even if they happened to be pills made from bread.[28] Then, in 1886–87, Coué learned the art of hypnotism from Ambroise-Auguste Liébeault and Hyppolite Bernheim. In contrast to the hypnotists, however, Coué was interested in the self-cure potential of this method. He wished to equip his patients with the tools to cure themselves, so that they did not remain dependent on someone else. Crucially, he saw himself as an educator, not as a healer.

In 1910, Coué retired from his profession as a pharmacist and opened free clinics in Nancy, where he saw a very large number of patients until his death in 1926. Many of them were shell-shocked World War I veterans. By the 1920s, word of his method had spread as far as Russia and the United States. Coué was particularly popular in the latter, where his optimistic message of self-reliance resonated strongly. When he visited New York City in 1923, he was feted as a celebrity. Combining secular individualism with pragmatic optimism, Couéism also emphasizes the wider impor-tance of moral and psychological self-care for society as a whole.[29]

Coué argues that we are divided into a conscious and an un-conscious self, and that of the two, the latter is infinitely more powerful—a belief he shared with the founder of psychoanalysis, Sigmund Freud. Unlike Freud, however, Coué does not distinguish clearly between the unconscious and the imagination; indeed, he often uses the two terms interchangeably. What is most remarkable about his theory is that it is among the first in the modern period to push willpower from its pedestal. This was nothing short of rev-olutionary. Like Freud, Coué challenges the idea that we are pri-marily reason-driven creatures able at all times freely to determine our behavior. He even describes us as "wretched puppets" of our imagination, arguing that "we only cease to be puppets when we have learned to guide our imagination." He compares the imagina-tion to a torrent that, when left uncontrolled, "fatally sweeps away the poor wretch who has fallen into it." Properly channeled, how-ever, this torrent can generate movement, heat, and electricity. Elsewhere, he describes our imagination as "an unbroken horse which has neither bridle nor reins."[30] But if the rider succeeds in breaking in this horse, the dynamic is reversed.

Coué advocates autosuggestion for controlling our imagination. He understands autosuggestion as a form of self-hypnosis, which he defines as the *"influence of the imagination upon the moral and physical being of mankind."*[31] Everyone is capable of autosuggestion. Indeed, Coué holds that all effective suggestion is autosuggestion, for sug-gestions by others cannot be implanted in our minds unless our un-conscious allows it to happen. If we resist suggestion, consciously or unconsciously, it will have no effect whatsoever. In our daily lives, we constantly make unconscious autosuggestions, some of which are extremely damaging. If, for example, we tell ourselves that we are worthless and incapable of achieving our dreams, we will very likely never do so. If we tell ourselves that we are unlovable, we will project this message to others and turn it into a reality. Such thoughts become self-fulfilling prophecies. But if we learn the art of mastering conscious autosuggestions, Coué believes, we can reverse the dynamic. What is absolutely imperative, however, is that when we seek to cure our physical and moral ills, we do not involve our wills. Instead, what is required is the *"training of the imagination,"* for "when the will and the imagination are antagonistic, it is always the imagination which wins, *without any exception.*"[32]

Coué's theory of autosuggestion clearly draws on the psycho-analytical idea of the unconscious. But Coué shares with late-nineteenth-century mind-cure thinkers such as Phineas Quimby and Mary Baker Eddy the conviction that illness can be the result of a belief, or in his terms, an act of the imagination. Certain ill-nesses are, he believes, entirely in our head. Conversely, if we accept that our unconscious is the source of many of our troubles, it follows that it can also cure our physical and mental ailments.[33] Nobody needs to be ill, in Coué's view. Recent reprints of his *Self-Mastery* include a lengthy list of serious physical and mental ail-ments, from paralysis and tumors, that his followers have reported being cured through his techniques.

The self-helping Couéist must adopt a strict regime. Every morning before rising, and every night before getting into bed, they must shut their eyes. Then they must repeat twenty times, in a monotone, and counting with the aid of a string with twenty knots in it, the mantra "EVERY DAY, IN EVERY RESPECT, I AM GETTING BET-TER AND BETTER."[34] Coué's *Self-Mastery* also includes numerous re-flections on self-confidence and self-belief. At the time, these were relatively new terms, which were to become ever more important in the course of the twentieth century. Coué writes that it is abso-lutely essential for every human being to have self-confidence: "Without it one can accomplish nothing," he declares; "with it one can accomplish whatever one likes, (within reason of course)."[35]

Coué's method is an important contribution to the psychology of belief, a creed that features at the heart of positive psychology and many recent self-help books. Simply by believing in our own competency, Coué and his many modern successors argue, we can realize our desires. "ALL THAT WE THINK BECOMES TRUE FOR US. WE MUST NOT THEN ALLOW OURSELVES TO THINK WRONGLY."[36] Research by the founder of positive psychology, Martin Seligman, and many others since has confirmed that being an optimist and having a positive view of ourselves does indeed impact on our motivation, performance, and health.[37] However, Coué's claim, taken literally, amounts to magical thinking. Owing to its incantatory quality, Coué's famous formula, too, has the air of a magical spell. Modern psychology acknowledges the importance of visualization and imagining positive outcomes. And yet unjustifiable positive thinking, detached from our physical and socioeconomic reality, can also be damaging. Everything, then, hinges on the word "reasonable" in relation to autosuggestion and positive thinking—which, to be fair, Coué emphasizes repeatedly in his text.

The self-help school that harnesses the powers of our imagination most systematically, and that provides the most detailed instructions as to how exactly we can benefit from it, is without doubt neuro-linguistic programming. NLP is very influential in the world of life coaches, consultants, and motivational speakers, and many of the most successful self-help books of recent decades draw heavily on NLP-based ideas and techniques, including Robbins's *Awaken the Giant Within* and the works of the bestselling British hypnotist Paul McKenna. NLP was created by Richard Bandler and John Grinder in California in the 1970s.[38] They drew on thinkers associated with the Human Potential movement and the Esalen Institute, such as Fritz Perls, Virginia Satir, and Gregory Bateson, as well as the hypnotist Milton H. Erickson.

Peppering their discourses with neurological jargon, Bandler and Grinder emphasize what they see as the scientific underpinnings of NLP (though these have been questioned).[39] NLP has been described as "the study of the structure of subjective experience." It is based on the idea that we all have a preferred way of thinking about the world. If we want to learn from or influence someone, we have to pay close attention to how that person views reality. NLP assumes that there is a connection between neurological processes, language patterns, and our behavior. Just like a computer, our brains can therefore be reset with the aid of various fast and simple reprogramming techniques, which blend approaches from hypnosis, transformational grammar, and personal development. Practitioners claim that NLP can not only turn us into more effective communicators, but also cure phobias, depression, and other long-standing psychological problems in just one or two sessions.

NLP is based on the study of successful behaviors, including thought patterns and the way we inhabit our bodies. By studying and then modeling high-achieving people, we can learn their skills. This involves targeted acts of projection. If we want to model someone, we have to imagine that we are that person and view the world from their point of view. By mentally stepping into the shoes of our role models and visualizing the way they stand, speak, behave, think, and move, our unconscious can integrate these patterns of behaviors and copy their "code of excellence." In the words of the NLP coaches Romilla Ready and Kate Burton, "NLP modelling is the ability to replicate fully the desirable competence of another person by getting to the unconscious behaviours beneath that skill and coding those behaviours into a model that you could teach to other people, in order to replicate the result."[40]

In order to "reprogram" us for success, NLP also uses very precise and strategically deployed visualizations—a technique that relies heavily on our imagination. NLP pays great attention to our own and other people's internal representations of the world, or "maps." These inner maps impact on the ways in which we filter information. Sensory awareness plays a key role in this process. We all have sensory preferences, and these are reflected in our language usage. We may be a visual person, for example, and regularly use expressions such as "I see" or "That is much clearer now." If we privilege hearing, we are likely to say things like "That sounds good," "That chimes with me," or "That rings true." NLP uses the acronym VAKOG (visual, auditory, kinesthetic, olfactory, and gustatory) to refer to our senses and preferred modes. Also important are "submodalities," which are defined as the "characteristics of each representational system, such as colour and brightness (visual), pitch and tone (auditory) and pressure and temperature (kinaesthetic)."[41] We can think of submodalities as the features of a picture or a film clip that we could edit: we could use a filter, for example, or change the brightness, zoom in or out, add a soundtrack, or intensify or tune down voices and other sounds.

The bestselling self-help writer Paul McKenna combines hypnosis with NLP techniques to help his readers to feel more confident, lose weight, sleep more soundly, stop smoking, or become more charismatic. McKenna's books come with audio trances. Once he has lulled us into a state of deep relaxation, McKenna delivers a blend of positive mantras, vague metaphors, parables, and visualization exercises. All of these are designed to fire up our imagination, which McKenna, too, recognizes as our core transformative force. In order to lose weight, for example, we are asked to visualize ourselves as thinner, at our ideal weight, seeing exactly what our slimmer body would look like. We are to imagine stepping into the body of our thinner self, really experiencing what it feels like to be thin, how we would stand, what we would see, what we would hear, and what physical sensations we would have.

In NLP terms, McKenna asks us to "ramp up" the VAKOG detail in this exercise so that we fashion a vivid and powerfully motivating image of our desired goal, one that is rich in sensory detail. The aim is for our imagination to influence our unconscious—our imagination being infinitely more powerful than our will when it comes to instigating behavioral change. McKenna's basic formula remains the same for a wide range of common self-help aims, such as enhancing our ability to influence others or our confidence. In each case, we are asked to imagine ourselves as highly charismatic or powerfully confident in a specific situation in which we want to shine. We are invited to see ourselves from the outside and then to step into our more charismatic or confident selves, thus creating an imaginary vision and experience of our aspirational state that is hyper-real.[42]

McKenna also recommends very similar visualization exercises for taking the edge off bad memories, troubling thoughts, and unproductive beliefs. In these cases, we are asked to manipulate disturbing images by changing their submodalities—a bit like engaging in imaginary photoshopping. We may, for example, shrink a mental picture of a moment in our lives when we felt humiliated or unloved down to the size of a postage stamp. Or we might wish to drain the color out of it, make it disappear into the distance, or shatter it into a thousand pieces. We may also wish to give a person who has caused us upset a pig's nose or donkey ears, or furnish them with a preposterous mustache. If we have a tendency to engage in negative self-talk, McKenna recommends that we use a ridiculous Mickey Mouse voice for our disempowering interior monologue. Our negative self-talk may include sentences such as "Nobody likes me," "I am a fat, unlovable loser," or "I mess everything up"—whatever unkind things we tend habitually to tell ourselves. If we simply change the pitch and speed of that critical inner voice, McKenna maintains, it will lose its power and authority, and thus its malign influence over us.

We can also use similar techniques for the film clips of bad events that keep playing in our heads, changing the speed, sound track, frame, brightness, volume, and setting, until that scene becomes less troubling. Humor, too, is a precious tool for disempowering threatening voices and memories. Finally, regularly imagining ourselves, in as much detail as possible, in the future, having achieved what we really want to achieve, is another classic NLP technique for harnessing the powers of our imagination.

The way in which the imagination is used in NLP is a far cry from the non-goal-oriented daydreaming and mind wandering advocated by the Romantics. The Romantic imagination ambled freely across both the inner and outer landscape, whereas the imagination in NLP is highly instrumentalized. Strategically deployed for achieving our rational goals, our imagination becomes in fact simply a means to an end: a mere tool to serve reason. On the bright side, Coué's insight is now an accepted fact in most (but by no means all) modern self-help frameworks: we simply cannot achieve sustainable change if our imagination is not on board. As a powerful stakeholder that can block any action or reform, we need to convince it of the merits of our plans for change. We also need to speak its language, for it does not deal in facts and figures. We can best reach it via stories, art, and metaphor.

It is impossible to overstate the importance of the Romantic shift in values for the history of self-improvement. The British philosopher Alain de Botton holds Romantic philosophy responsible for many of our current problems. Because the Romantics celebrated the "untrained intuition," they refused to apply any reason to our emotional life. Instead, they allowed themselves to be driven by spontaneous and unmediated feelings. According to de Botton, it is for this reason that progress in the education of our emotions has stagnated.[43] He believes that in order to counterbalance the Romantics' harmful influence on Western culture, we need to return to Classical ideals. Instead of intuition, we should cherish rational analysis; instead of obscurity, we should reinstate an appreciation of clarity. Education is to be privileged over dilettante spontaneity, realism over idealism, politeness over honesty, and irony over earnestness. But de Botton arguably goes too far in praising Romanticism's others—for there can be no question that Enlightenment rationality, in particular mechanical reason, has caused much damage, too. As so often, the truth lies in the middle, in a balance between reason and imagination, between the privileging of the social and the individual. The challenge is to achieve that balance.

There is no doubt that Emerson's and Nietzsche's ideas resonate particularly loudly through the self-help literature of the twentieth and twenty-first centuries. "Self-reliance" is a basic aim of all self-help, while "becoming who we are" has become a personal-development cliché. It is a mantra embraced by many psychological schools and self-help practitioners, especially by humanist psychologists and the Human Potential movement. All of them emphasize our in-built drive toward self-actualization, and our existential duty fully to express our capabilities and creativity. Their shared, and Rousseau-inspired, assumption is that we are born good, and that malign external influences have prevented us from achieving our true potential. They urge us to disentangle our own values from social expectations and rediscover who we truly are.

Partly because of the Romantic heritage, and partly as a result of Western bourgeois individualism, we now think of values as personal choices rather than culturally dictated. Individual values may differ dramatically from person to person, and can be selected from a large menu. And yet there remain many values that are culturally imposed and that we may merely have internalized. Our seemingly personal sets of values are, in fact, often far less personal and unique than we like to think. They tend to be shaped by numerous factors beyond our control, such as upbringing, class, and wider culturally validated beliefs.

My own core values are creativity (in the sense of creating something meaningful and using my time productively), authenticity, lifelong learning, and humility. The first two in particular are closely related to my background. Of Protestant German stock, I have a real problem with waste—wasted time, wasted words, wasted talent, wasted money, wasted opportunity. I highly value productivity and efficiency, and always feel I need to be making or doing something. I almost never use a credit card, and tend to plan assiduously for the future. I am extremely risk-averse. I get angry about all forms of mismanagement. I expect people to mean what they say and say what they mean. Even after having lived in the United Kingdom for almost two decades, I find it hard to gauge what people here really mean and think, other than that they all seem to value endless witty and self-deprecating banter, at which I remain staunchly hopeless. Only a very narrow and specific kind of humor makes me laugh, and I find most comedy baffling. In other words, I am a living stereotype.

Nietzsche wrote about the "tables of values" that he wished to see smashed by the supermen. Today, "ideology" is perhaps a more fitting term to capture what Nietzsche meant. There are numerous ways in which we are shaped by the dominant ideological narratives of our age—some subtle, some blatantly obvious. My appreciation of efficiency is not just the result of a deep-rooted Protestant work ethic, but is also in line with current neoliberal values—much as I like to criticize those values. It is, in fact, very hard to step out of the frameworks that dictate legitimate meanings and commonly sanctioned values. The imagination is now taken seriously as a force that can enable us to change for the better. Moreover, both its products and its functions are widely valued. In fact, it is fair to say that creativity is one of our highest goods. It is a core skill that can be monetized on the marketplace, being particularly highly prized in the so-called creative industries. Earning a living through creative activities such as blogging, making something arty out of waste products, baking artisanal breads, or putting together eye-catching shelf arrangements is a sign of cool.

But there is a final twist to this saga of the rise of the imagination. In the West today, hyperindividualism reigns supreme. "Self-realization" is one of our most cherished aspirations, and creativity and uniqueness are exalted. In other words, they are now firmly inscribed in our own tables of values. Therefore, the old tables of values can technically no longer be smashed by embracing these now commonly accepted, indeed mainstream, values. Cherishing the imagination and its products today is neither rebellious nor countercultural. Ironically, to be truly original and imaginative today, we would have to challenge these very values.

CHAPTER EIGHT

Persevere

ONE OF THE BEST-KNOWN fables of the ancient Greek writer Aesop (ca. 620–564 BC) concerns a race between a hare and a tortoise. When the swift-footed hare ridicules the slow-moving tortoise one time too many, the tortoise challenges him to a race. The hare speeds ahead. Supremely confident in his ability to win, he takes a nap midway through the race. When he awakes, he finds that his steadfast competitor has already passed the finish line. The story has been read in many ways, but the most common interpretation is that the hare is punished for his foolish arrogance. On account of his trust in his own superiority, his natural talent goes to waste. The tortoise, by contrast, who is far less well equipped to succeed, wins because of her doggedness. The fable illustrates that slow and steady wins the race.

We can take this further. Mindset matters here, as do attitude and effort. Wishing to teach her bully a lesson, the tortoise is highly motivated. In spite of a lack of natural ability, she triumphs thanks to her stronger work ethic. Or does it all boil down to a question of character? Is haughtiness put in its place by a humble master of endurance? It is usually the clever tricksters who triumph in Aesop's animal fables, by outwitting their physically stronger opponents. But here, the brain-tops-brawn moral is replaced by a celebration of a less glamorous ancient virtue: fortitude. Fortitude entails a steadfastness of purpose combined with courage—more precisely, the courage not to allow adversity to turn us away from our goals.

We might now describe this quality as perseverance. Perseverance denotes our ability to continue with a task even in the face of obstacles or setbacks. We might also speak of resilience, tenacity, drive, and resolve. Grit and growth mindsets are other more recent framings that capture our capacity to keep going in spite of repeated disappointments.[1] But perseverance is also connected to two ethically more complex notions: willpower and effort. These qualities are often seen in moral terms. Either tacitly or explicitly, it is frequently assumed that willpower's opposites are laziness, weakness of character, and lack of discipline.

According to the Values in Action (VIA) Inventory of Strengths, perseverance happens to be my own forte. The character test tactfully defines perseverance as "finishing what one starts; persevering in a course of action in spite of obstacles; 'getting it out the door'; taking pleasure in completing tasks."[2] Admittedly, it is not the most glittering of strengths. It is a trait one might associate not only with tortoises, but also with camels, bees, or ants. Dogged toilers, who just keep going.

Perseverance is, however, an undervalued quality. Although I am quite spectacularly untalented at most sporting activities, my long-distance running is tolerable. The sole reason is that running for a lengthy period requires above all tenacity. I do get pleasure from achieving things, however long it takes, and I do not tend to give up on my aims. When I was ten, for example, I announced to my parents that I would never eat anything with a face again. They said they would support me. But later that day, I overheard my mother saying to my father, "Just let her, she'll give it up in a week." I remained a vegetarian for fifteen long years, and only started to eat meat again in my mid-twenties, when I realized that I had probably made my point. Perseverance, then, also involves a healthy dose of stubbornness.

In her book *Grit* (2017), the psychologist Angela Duckworth has recently shown that goal-oriented doggedness is an essential prerequisite for success in life. She argues that although natural talent matters, perseverance always tops aptitude as a predictor of achievement. Her findings neatly tally with the moral of Aesop's fable: although the hare is obviously far more gifted than the tortoise at running, it is the gritty reptilian underdog who ends up winning the race. Culturally speaking, however, we are in thrall to the hare, and tend to value talent over perseverance. This is an ancient prejudice, traceable all the way back to Greek antiquity, and is closely related to the myth of genius. Our overemphasis on genius, however, is problematic, because it devalues the importance of striving, effort, and sheer hard work.

In *Human, All Too Human* (1878), the German philosopher Friedrich Nietzsche offers an incisive critique of the cult of genius. If we think of genius as something magical, he writes, "we are not obliged to compare ourselves and find ourselves lacking."[3] The very notion of genius tends to be weaponized by the lazy and complacent, Nietzsche believes, because it frees us from the necessity of having to up our own game, to aspire to higher standards. Moreover, we dislike gritty strivers because they make us feel bad about our own lack of achievement and commitment.

The publication of Duckworth's book on grit did much to shift the emphasis from easy quick-fix solutions to a revaluation of the importance of persistent effort in the self-help sector. Yet this ancient virtue was already very much center stage in the Victorian era, in Samuel Smiles's *Self-Help* (1859). Given the increased opportunities for social mobility, it is no coincidence that discipline and diligence became core values in the nineteenth century, as personal effort suddenly carried much more weight, being able positively, or negatively, to influence our fate. In theory at least, social mobility frees us from the shackles of rigid class structures that determine our place in life. But it also brings with it new anxieties that can result in guilt and shame. In the nineteenth century, a tension arose between possibility, optimism, and an empowering belief in the individual's own agency, on the one hand, and the idea that we are also personally responsible if we do not prosper, on the other. As a consequence, the art of persevering, even in the face of great difficulties, became ever more existentially important. It still is today, although we have also grown more impatient, and are less prepared to commit ourselves to working for goals that lie in the more distant future.

The belief in the importance of individual effort is also a core pillar of capitalism. It drives the myth of the dishwasher who, through sheer grit, becomes a millionaire. It is the engine of numerous rags-to-riches tales, real and imagined, which encourage us to believe that we can pull ourselves up by our own bootstraps. It is for that reason that the politics of perseverance are full of ethical pitfalls. Especially in discussions of willpower, there is often a moralistic tendency to blame those who appear to lack it. But determining the boundaries between what falls within the remit of our personal agency and what is shaped by circumstances beyond our control is an age-old conundrum: Are some of us simply born with stronger wills than others? Or is our ability to will ourselves out of our problems determined by our upbringing and experiences? And what role is played by our social position, our economic background, and our genetic inheritance?

Perseverance, finally, is also connected with learning and self-improvement. All acts of learning require persistent effort. The psychologist Carol S. Dweck has coined the notion of the "growth mindset"—the belief in our ability to learn and to develop our skills. This mindset, she argues, has a crucial impact on our capacity to evolve. It entails stretching ourselves, seeking challenges, persevering, and learning from failure. Many other psychologists emphasize the importance of learning from failure as a key determiner of persistent improvement.[4]

Self-improvement, too, requires perseverance, for the fantasy of fast and flashy magical transformation is just that—a fantasy. The older notion of self-cultivation, which entails a slow and steady approach to growing and nourishing our finer qualities, acknowledges the importance of persevering in this process. So does the Japanese concept of *kaizen*, meaning "good improvement," which perfectly encapsulates the idea of gradual and incremental long-term change for the better.[5] *Kaizen* rose to prominence in the context of the Toyota car production process. The factory management deemed no improvement too small to be analyzed or implemented, regardless of how trivial it seemed. Whenever anyone in the factory noted an error in the production line, everything was halted, and the entire team would analyze the error. All improvements were then implemented immediately. A measured and continual approach to sustainable habit change, *kaizen* is a philosophy of improvement that focuses on small details. The emphasis is on meticulous reform, rather than flamboyant revolution. True perseverance, then, is flanked by two ancient virtues: courage and patience.

Although both the ancients and medieval theologians sang the praises of fortitude, a more modern notion of perseverance rose to prominence in the Victorian era. Perseverance is the core transformative quality advocated, as we have seen, in the first modern self-help book, Samuel Smiles's aptly named *Self-Help*. The book became an immediate international bestseller, and established the key characteristics of the genre as we know it today. *Self-Help* was published in 1859—the same year as Charles Darwin's *The Origin of Species.* Many have come to think of *Self-Help* as one of the defining documents of the era, no less important in its way than Darwin's work. It clearly hit a nerve, and gave voice to some of the Victorians' most pressing aspirations and anxieties.[6]

Why did the concept of self-help resonate with so many in the second half of the nineteenth century? And why has it continued to resonate with us up to the present day? Self-help promises enhanced agency and control. It holds out the promise that we can take matters into our own hands and assume charge of our destiny. Many features of the Victorian era continue to shape our appetite for self-help today. First and foremost, there was the rapid expansion of the middle classes and the enhanced possibility of social mobility. Queen Victoria's reign (1837–1901) was marked by relative political stability, increased economic activity, and growing prosperity. Between 1851 and 1871 alone, the middle classes tripled in size.[7] As a result of the Industrial Revolution, moreover, the importance of land as the primary source of wealth began to diminish, and consequently of the old system of inherited privilege. It now became easier to make one's fortune in other ways—including in manufacturing, finance, and trade.

But this new age of social mobility had a dark side.[8] The sudden theoretical possibility of social improvement was fraught with ambivalence. Although it was the source of great excitement and optimism, it also gave cause for anxiety and confusion. Most notably, upward social mobility brought in its wake greatly amplified concerns about social status and correct etiquette. Those who had acquired their status only recently were afraid of making embarrassing faux pas, while those from established middle-class families were keen to demarcate themselves from the arrivistes, by trying ever harder to emulate the mores of the aristocracy.[9]

To alleviate their anxieties about correct conduct and the more elusive signifiers of status, the socially aspiring consulted manuals such as *Etiquette for Gentlemen, Being a Manual of Minor Social Ethics and Customary Observances* (1857) and *How to Behave: A Pocket Manual of Etiquette* (1865). These handbooks provided crash courses in middle-class mores, dispensing advice on how to master dinner parties, how to sit and stand gracefully, what "RSVP" means, and how to avoid dirty nails and bad breath.[10] *Mrs. Beeton's Book of Household Management* (1859–61), now primarily known as a cookbook, also offers numerous recommendations on appropriate middle-class conduct.[11]

The sudden surge in appetite for self-help in the Victorian era is also related to a strong belief in progress and improvement, both of the self and of society as a whole. These new ideals are evident in the many reformist initiatives that blossomed in the nineteenth century. They include the Chartist movement, lobbying for universal male suffrage, and later the Suffragettes, who campaigned for women's inclusion in the electorate. In addition, there were the trade unions fighting for better working conditions; the many temperance societies that believed that alcohol consumption and lax morals were the root of all evil; and the education and social welfare reformers who pushed for expanding education to all and for improving economic conditions for the poor. The Victorian vogue for improvement also encompassed the inner life, including character, values, and behaviors. This pervasive belief in progress quickly began to fill the hole left by the diminishing importance of religion.

Smiles was born in 1812 into an industrious middle-class family in Scotland. The son of a papermaker and general merchant, he studied medicine and eventually set up a practice in his hometown. But he, too, was a restless self-improver. He subsequently worked as a newspaper editor, for the railways, and in the insurance business. Owing to the unprecedented success of *Self-Help*, he was eventually able to focus exclusively on his writing career. And a highly prolific writer he was, with hundreds of newspaper articles and twenty-five books to his name.

The primary aim of *Self-Help*, Smiles writes, is "to stimulate youths to apply themselves diligently to right pursuits,—sparing neither labour, pains, nor self-denial in prosecuting them,—and to rely upon their own efforts in life, rather than depend upon the help or patronage of others."[12] Smiles repeatedly urges his readers to embrace the virtues of industry, diligence, and perseverance. He never tires of emphasizing that self-improvement is hard work: "Nothing creditable can be accomplished without application and diligence." We must not be daunted by difficulties, "but conquer them by patience and perseverance." Above all, we must seek to achieve "elevation of character."[13] According to Smiles, the key drivers for social and economic success are focused willpower, cheerful drudgery, diligent application, and a hefty dose of tenacity. Essentially, *Self-Help* is a hymn to grit and perseverance.

Smiles's book is peppered with inspiring minibiographies of self-made men, all of whom achieved success through a combination of doggedness, hard work, and virtuous living. We learn, among many others, of the lives of Sir Robert Peel, creator of the Metropolitan Police, the explorer David Livingstone, the novelist Sir Walter Scott, and the politician Benjamin Disraeli, as well as numerous inventors, engineers, businessmen, and captains of industry. The brief biography of James Watt, inventor of "the king of machines," the steam engine, is a typical example. His achievements powerfully illustrate Smiles's central message regarding the importance of perseverance. "Watt was one of the most industrious of men," Smiles writes, "and the story of his life proves, what all experience confirms, that it is not the man of the greatest natural vigour and capacity who achieves the highest results, but he who employs his powers with the greatest industry and the most carefully disciplined skill—the skill that comes by labour, application, and experience."[14] It is those who simply work hard who are destined for great things, not the geniuses who are born with extraordinary gifts. Just like the philosopher Friedrich Nietzsche and the psychologists Angela Duckworth and Carol Dweck, Smiles believes that genius is overrated: toil and the capacity for long-term commitment are much more valuable assets. This would, of course, have been a reassuring message for his readers, since most of us are not blessed with extraordinary gifts and talents. At the same time, his argument challenges excuses for not trying as hard as we can, in spite of our perhaps only average abilities.

Significantly, Smiles does not consider self-help a selfish pursuit. Indeed, he considers it to be both altruistic and patriotic. "The duty of helping one's self in the highest sense," he writes, "involves the helping of one's neighbours."[15] For we are profoundly relational creatures, firmly embedded in our communities. It follows that all activities of self-improvement therefore also contribute to national progress. Indeed, much like Confucius, Smiles believes that national advancement cannot be separated from self-help, because the nation is nothing but the sum total of its individual parts. It is not its institutions but the character of its citizens that defines the true worth of a nation. According to Smiles, "the nation is only an aggregate of individual conditions, and civilization itself is but a question of the personal improvement of the men, women, and children of whom society is composed."[16]

Unlike many other advocates of perseverance, Smiles does not dodge the broader philosophical questions relating to energy and willpower. He considers the "energy of will" to be "the Man himself" in that it gives "impulse to his every action, and soul to every effort."[17] The idea of the will lies at the heart of much nineteenth-century philosophy—from Arthur Schopenhauer's magnum opus *The World as Will and Representation* (1818) to Nietzsche's concept of the "will to power." It continues to play a central role in modern self-help. According to Smiles, we owe our growth "chiefly to that active striving of the will, that encounter with difficulty, which we call effort."[18] Defined by Smiles as force of purpose, will enables us to do or be whatever we set our mind to. But willpower is a problematic and contested concept, for it puts the responsibility for our failures as well as our successes firmly in our court, and implies that, if we fail in our battles with adversity, we do so on account of our own moral weakness. In this regard, it may well overestimate our agency and the power of our desires. A deficiency of willpower, and by implication, weakness of character, is a common explanation for why we may lack the ability to pursue our aims. It is still much used, and it is a narrative that allows those who rely upon it simply to dismiss the more complex factors that determine our ability to persevere.

Another, no less judgmental explanation is laziness, which features at the heart of M. Scott Peck's bestselling *The Road Less Traveled: A New Psychology of Love, Traditional Values, and Spiritual Growth* (1978). Peck's is one of only a few truly perennial classics in the modern self-help literature, found still, alongside other works of timeless appeal such as Dale Carnegie's *How to Win Friends and In-fluence People* and Napoleon Hill's *Think and Grow Rich!* (both pub-lished in 1937), on the shelves of most personal development sections in bookshops today. Peck (1936–2005) was an American psychiatrist who worked for the army and then became a born-again Christian. *The Road Less Traveled* is a strange book, blending conservative values, psychiatric and psychoanalytical insights, and religious thought. Although he personally struggled with alcohol and drug addiction, as well as infidelity, Peck advocates discipline and the taking of responsibility as the core ingredients for spiritual growth. Sloth is the cardinal sin in Peck's world, for he believes that it is quite simply our laziness that keeps us from facing and resolving our most pressing problems.

The Road Less Traveled famously opens with the words "Life is difficult."[19] Our collective belief that life should be easy, Peck writes, is a dangerous misconception, for "life is a series of prob-lems." What we need in order to overcome those problems is disci-pline. Only discipline can turn our problems into opportunities that will enable us to grow mentally and spiritually, and that will give our lives meaning. The things that hurt us most therefore also have the capacity to instruct us most. What prevents us from learn-ing valuable life lessons, Peck argues, is our tendency to avoid pain and short-term suffering, which we do out of sheer laziness. He holds this proclivity for idleness as responsible for all our suffering and for most forms of mental illness.[20]

The meaning of life, Peck writes, is to grow spiritually. To achieve this aim, two strategies are crucial: we have to delay gratifi-cation and accept responsibility. Delaying gratification is "a process of scheduling the pain and pleasure of life in such a way as to enhance the pleasure by meeting and experiencing the pain first and getting it over with. It is the only decent way to live."[21] Peck, then, would not be impressed if we ate the icing on the cake first. The ability to delay gratification is another facet of perseverance. It entails sticking with our long-term higher aims and resisting the temptation to stray from our path in search of pleasure. It also involves enduring temporary discomfort. The reality, however, is that the vast majority of us embrace a lifestyle characterized by impulsiveness. We do not persevere in pursuing our highest aims because we lack the discipline to do so.

As important as learning to delay gratification is accepting responsibility for our problems. Here, healthy balance is of the essence. If we are on the neurotic side of the spectrum, we will assume too much responsibility for our problems, automatically concluding that everything is our own fault. If we have narcissistic tendencies, we will accept no responsibility at all but automatically assume that "the world is at fault."[22] Both extremes are problems of responsibility. Sane and measured responsibility-taking, again, needs to be combined with discipline. For discipline, Peck believes, is the primary "means of human spiritual evolution."[23]

Crucially, the energy for discipline is provided by love. In Peck's rather unromantic conception, love is a form of work that takes the shape of ongoing attention and commitment. The opposite of love, unsurprisingly, is not hate but laziness. For Peck, laziness is the one true impediment to our spiritual growth. This is a view he shares with the medieval theologian Thomas Aquinas and the Italian poet Dante Alighieri, who also deemed sloth the most dangerous of the Seven Deadly Sins. "If we overcome laziness," Peck writes, "all the other impediments will be overcome."[24] In the part of his book where he switches from a psychoanalytical to a religious perspective, Peck even goes as far as to suggest that laziness is "original sin." Laziness, he declares, "might even be the devil."[25]

Throughout *The Road Less Traveled*, there is a tension between Peck's more sympathetic psychoanalytical arguments and his moralism. On the one hand, he argues that our capacity for discipline is shaped by our parents. If we grow up in a house without love and good role models, it will be so much harder for us to acquire and practice discipline in our adult life. If we think of the world as an

unstable and dangerous place, we will be unwilling to delay gratification, and take our pleasures quickly when and where we can. On
the other hand, Peck labels those who lack the capacity to persevere as lazy. Although he sometimes gestures toward a gentler,
more empathetic understanding of the origins of our troubles,
Peck's is ultimately a highly moralistic character-weakness approach to self-improvement. All things considered, his is a decidedly unforgiving stance. It is surprising that Peck's stern message
has resonated with so many readers, and continues to do so.

In the course of the twentieth century, the language of character
weakness and sin has to a large extent been replaced by the language of damage and trauma. The former entails judgment, while
the latter comes with connotations of innocent victimhood. Most
present-day psychologists acknowledge that our ability to persevere and grow is shaped by many factors, some of which may be
beyond our control. Yet much like Peck, the Canadian psychologist
Jordan B. Peterson has recently revived the character-weakness
school of thought. In order to live a meaningful life, Peterson
writes in his bestselling *12 Rules for Life: An Antidote to Chaos*
(2018), we must take responsibility for our actions and our experiences, work hard on improving our character, embrace traditional
values, and let go of any sense of aggrieved victimhood.

Adopting a deliberately messianic tone, Peterson offers his
readers a seductive concoction of ancient wisdom, philosophy, religion, and selective factoids about human nature. All of this is inter-
spersed with anecdotes from the lives of his friends and family, as
well as diatribes against equality legislation and the decline of traditional values. Peterson first made the headlines in 2016 when he
launched a campaign against political correctness on YouTube. He
believes in a conspiracy of postmodern neo-Marxists and feminist
academics, who preach the gospel of identity politics, demonize
young white men, and ultimately seek to undermine traditional
Western values.[26] Perhaps unsurprisingly, Peterson's primary fan
base is young white men.

His self-help philosophy boils down to the idea that we can
change for the better if only we want to, irrespective of the conditions in which we find ourselves. All we need is willpower and per-

severance. We just have to straighten our backs, reason ourselves out of our misery, accept responsibility for our lot and our actions, stop whining, and grow up.

It was one thing to propagate the absolute power of reason and willpower two millennia ago, or even in the Victorian age. It is quite a different matter, however, to present these ideas in the twenty-first century, when a large body of research has illuminated the complex relation between the mind, the body, and social context. It is particularly surprising that a clinical psychologist who has suffered from depression himself would dismiss out of hand all the evidence that suggests that our ability to change our behaviors and modes of thinking is influenced by many factors—not just willpower or a lack thereof. Our genetic inheritance, social structures, and upbringing have a powerful role to play, too, and may make it far more difficult for some of us to mobilize our willpower. Most modern psychologists, indeed, consider willpower a limited resource, and point out that we cannot live and achieve on the back of willpower alone.

What Peterson fails to consider is the mechanics of *how* we can change our behaviors in the long run. If we could all just stand up straight with our shoulders back, why don't we do it already? In *12 Rules for Life*, our frequent failure to improve our lot is brushed aside cavalierly with phrases such as "Down is a lot easier than up."[27] Just like Peck, Peterson dismisses those of us who struggle to self-improve as lazy shirkers: "It is far more likely that a given individual has just decided to reject the path upward, because of its difficulty. . . . Vice is easy. Failure is easy, too. It's easier not to shoulder a burden. It's easier not to think, and not to do, and not to care. It's easier to put off until tomorrow what needs to be done today, and drown the upcoming months and years in today's cheap pleasures."[28] Both Peterson and Peck, then, believe firmly in willpower and discipline as our path to salvation. If we struggle, nothing but our own laziness and weakness are to blame. In this, respect their work resembles nothing so much as a moral treatise from the Middle Ages.

Others adopt a less hard-nosed, more forgiving stance, homing in on yet another dimension of perseverance: the cultivation of sustainable good habits. Consider, for example, Stephen R. Covey's *The 7 Habits of Highly Effective People* (1989), which, published ten years after *The Road Less Traveled*, is an equally successful classic of the genre. Covey takes issue with the quick-fix "outside-in" solutions offered in many twentieth-century self-help works. He describes his own method as a "principle-centered, character-based, 'inside-out' approach to personal and interpersonal effectiveness."[29] Three of his core habits concern self-mastery, while the others are to ensure "public victory." Above all, he advocates value-based living, integrity, control, and inner-directedness.

Quoting Aristotle, Covey emphasizes that "we are what we repeatedly do. Excellence, then, is not an act, but a habit." As his title indicates, habits are powerful routines that determine how successful we are in our lives. Because habits are "consistent, often unconscious patterns, they constantly, daily, express our character and produce our effectiveness . . . or ineffectiveness." Covey understands habit as the "intersection of *knowledge, skill*, and *desire*."[30] In other words, habits determine what we do, how we do it, and our basic motives.

Challenging ideas of determinism—be they genetic, psychoanalytical, or environmental—Covey argues that we can always decide how to react. There is a crucial gap between stimulus and response, he maintains, and it is up to us to determine how to fill it. This argument is based on the idea of responsibility, understood quite literally here as our ability to choose how we respond, our "response-ability." He, too, then, embraces the classic free-will character-ethic doctrine that is so popular in the self-help literature located on the right of the political spectrum. "Highly proactive people recognize that responsibility," Covey writes. "They do not blame circumstances, conditions, or conditioning for their behavior. Their behavior is a product of their own conscious choice, based on values, rather than a product of their conditions, based on feeling."[31] Our responses, he concludes, are not only entirely within our power, but should always be value-based.

Like Peck and Peterson, Covey, too, believes in discipline. Discipline, he reminds us, "comes from *disciple*—disciple to a philosophy, disciple to a set of principles, disciple to a set of values, disciple to an overriding purpose, to a superordinate goal or a person who represents that goal." If we are an "effective manager" of our selves, our discipline will come from within.[32] Covey understands the self as an entrepreneurial entity. We can optimize ourselves by using good self-management technologies. He recommends that we take good care of the "greatest asset" we possess, namely ourselves. Self-care is "the single most powerful investment we can ever make in life—investment in ourselves, in the only instrument we have with which to deal with life and to contribute. We are the instruments of our own performance, and to be effective, we need to recognize the importance of taking time regularly to sharpen the saw in all four ways."[33] Of note here are the many financial and business metaphors, which liken our selves to assets and compare self-care to a form of investment. Covey's description of the self as an "instrument" also clearly views our main purpose as effective performance.

Efficiency enhancement, which Covey promises in his title, is of course the holy grail of the neoliberal concern with the optimization of performance. While inefficiency is obviously not a desirable attribute, the overvaluation of efficiency carries its own dangers. If we consider pure efficiency as our greatest good, we are in danger of viewing ourselves as little more than machines that function more or less well, and that might be in need of tuning and tweaking, or else replacing with newer models. Covey's "character ethic" approach, then, only appears to be about embracing deeper values. He promotes coherent, authentic, and principle-driven ways of being and interacting with others, not, however, for the sake of these values, but in order to become more efficient. But then again, even Aristotle tried to sell us virtuous living with the promise of *eudaimonia* as carrot.

While Covey tells us which habits to adopt, and to what purpose, he does not go into much detail on the *how*. For something to become a habit, we need routinely to practice a specific action or behavior. But as many of us know from bitter personal experience, nothing is more difficult than breaking habits or introducing new ones into our lives. Anyone who has ever tried to give up alcohol, to curb their consumption of chocolate, chips, or cigarettes, or to go regularly to the gym will be able to confirm that. The journalist

Charles Duhigg has looked more closely into the matter of how we can change our habits, whether as individuals, organizations, or societies.

An efficient brain, Duhigg argues in *The Power of Habit* (2012), needs to automatize as many decisions as possible. If we do not think about certain things and they become nonnegotiable, something we simply practice no matter how we feel, they qualify as habits. Brushing your teeth, for example: it would simply not occur to most of us not to do so first thing in the morning. If, say, going for a run every morning at six a.m. becomes as natural to us as brushing our teeth—regardless of the weather, our mood, or our consumption of alcoholic beverages the night before—we have successfully created a habit.

If we want to break a bad habit and replace it with a good one, we need to understand what Duhigg calls the "habit loop." Every habit can be broken down into three parts. First, there is a cue or trigger, which tells our brains to go into automatic mode and which habits to activate. This is followed by a routine, which can be physical, mental, or emotional. Finally, there is the reward, which helps our brain "to figure out if this particular loop is worth remembering for the future."[34] Over time, this loop becomes ever more automatic. Fortunately, according to Duhigg, we all have the capacity to learn new neurological routines.

Duhigg's recipe for changing our habits centers on the notion of replacement. Life is little more than a series of habits; it is impossible to eradicate them. And so, the bad habits must be replaced by good habits. And the golden rule of habit change is that we need to keep the same cue and the same reward and simply insert a new routine.[35] First of all, we must become aware of what all of these components are. We may, for example, always give in to a craving to buy and eat cake around three p.m. Possible triggers might be low blood sugar, a lack of energy, a need to get some fresh air, or a desire for a chat with others. If it transpires that our true need is fresh air or a chat rather than sugar, we could simply replace the cake with a chat or a walk. Or we might regularly drink too much in the evenings because of our emotional state (exhaustion, anxiety, depression, stress, or boredom). Once we know what our cue is (time of day and emotional state), we could experiment with a different kind of routine, such as doing yoga, writing, or going for a walk, which would give us the same reward as alcohol. The reward could be relaxation, stimulation, or respite from thinking too much.

If we truly want to change our habits, Duhigg also recommends that we focus our energies on our "keystone habit." That keystone habit is the one that, if changed, might have a domino effect on the entire system of habits that make up our life. It is likely to be something like smoking, drinking, overeating, or procrastinating. If we can master our keystone habit, many of our other nonproductive subhabits will fall away. If we stop drinking too much alcohol, for example, we might well be more likely to exercise regularly. We might eat more greens and so have energy for activities that are more rewarding than collapsing on the sofa and falling asleep to Netflix.

Unlike Covey, then, who advocates persistent value-based living as a means to heighten our productivity and interpersonal effectiveness, Duhigg simply presents us with a formula for perseverance. For forming a good habit is the most advanced version of perseverance: habits are persistent and regular repetitions of actions that become a nonnegotiable part of our daily lives. And whatever it is we practice habitually we will inevitably get better at.

The psychologist Angela Duckworth argues—much like Samuel Smiles before her—that grit—by which she means a drive to improve our skills and performance by consistent effort—is more important than talent. The ultimate paragons of perseverance, gritty people are dogged, always eager to learn, and never complacent or easily satisfied. Crucially, they are driven by an enduring passion. They have direction and know what they want. Grit, in Duckworth's view, is therefore a combination of perseverance and passion.

Duckworth is careful to emphasize the differences between talent, grit, and achievement: "Talent," she writes, "is how quickly your skills improve when you invest effort. Achievement is what happens when you take your acquired skills and use them."[36] Grit drives all long-term achievements and is separate from talent: "Our potential is one thing. What we do with it is quite another."[37] While aptitude, skills, and a basic degree of talent do matter as determiners of success,

then, they are not as important as hard work and trying again and
again to improve what we do.

Duckworth has conducted numerous studies which clearly
show that people with grit are much more likely to succeed than individuals who lack it. Her book is peppered with anecdotes in
which the perseverant triumphs over those who are merely talented, just as in Aesop's fable of the tortoise and the hare. Truly
gritty people are passionate about their skills, which they consistently work to improve. They tend to live coherently, because all of
their mid- and low-level goals serve their one high-level passion.
Purpose, understood as "the intention to contribute to the well-being of others," is another important feature of grit.[38] We need to
believe in the importance of what we do, and to trust that it is a
valuable contribution to the larger collective. Finally, gritty people
tend to be optimistic about the power of learning as a transformative force. More generally, they believe that "our own efforts can
improve our future."[39]

The relation between grit and resilience, a form of inner
strength, is also important. Resilience is our ability to recover
quickly from difficulties, to "bounce back better" after having encountered adversity. It is our ability to pick ourselves up again after
we have fallen or been pushed. If we are resilient, we can return to
a former resourceful state without drowning in self-pity or hurting
ourselves with destructively self-critical thoughts. The Japanese
saying "Fall seven, rise eight" neatly encapsulates the role of resilience in grit.

By raising awareness about the importance of perseverance as a
key driver of success, then, Duckworth has redressed an imbalance
in our self-help landscape. Her work is an important reminder that
all good things take time and are the fruit of persistent effort. Grit
also requires the ability to learn from our failures. Gritty people
simply deal differently with failure. Rather than being embar-
rassed, shamed, or discouraged by it, they see it as a learning opportunity. Like everybody else, they will, of course, be disappointed
by setbacks. But they will always try to figure out what went wrong
and how to do better in the future. They tend to have, to cite psychologist Carol S. Dweck again, a "growth mindset" rather than a
"fixed mindset," a "passion for stretching yourself and sticking to it,

even (or especially) when it's not going well."[40] People with a growth mindset believe in the possibility of learning and of developing their abilities. People with a fixed mindset, by contrast, believe in a given set of abilities and are much less optimistic about the effects of effort on their performance.

Moreover, people with a fixed mindset tend to value success and validation and to ignore errors, while people with a growth mindset pay very close attention to their failures and associated feedback. They are genuinely interested in trying to understand where they went wrong. The journalist Matthew Syed, in *Black Box Thinking: Marginal Gains and the Secrets of High Performance* (2015), presents a compelling plea to change our attitude toward failure. When we fail, most of us feel shame, blame others, or simply try to hide our failures. But we should learn to see failure as providing helpful information. All success, after all, is based on learning from failure. Without failure, there would be no progress, no science, no growth. Syed, with his so-called "black box thinking," proposes a dramatic mindset change that completely destigmatizes failure and instead seeks to harness its benefits. We read above about Toyota's practice of *kaizen*, a classic example of black box thinking. A similarly growth-oriented attitude toward failure exists in the aviation industry. After any plane crash, considerable effort is invested in the retrieval and painstaking analysis of the information contained in the black boxes to extract lessons and feed them back into production. In that way, the frequency of accidents is systematically diminished.

Syed argues that the opposite mindset prevails in the healthcare sector, where no productive procedures are in place to learn from error. This is astounding, for the number of deaths from preventable human errors is staggeringly high—in the United States, potentially up to 100,000 each year, or the equivalent of two jumbo jets falling out of the sky every twenty-four hours.[41] Lagging behind only heart disease and cancer, preventable medical error is the third biggest killer in the United States. In the United Kingdom, a study estimates that one in every ten patients "is killed or injured as a consequence of medical or institutional shortcomings."[42] In France, the number is even higher, an estimated 14 percent.

The core difference between healthcare and aviation, Syed argues, is the attitude toward failure. Where failures are analyzed openly and analytically, and failure feedback is acted upon, growth and improvement follow naturally. In institutional cultures where cover-ups and nontransparency are standard, by contrast, blame and shame prevail. Another example in which closed-loop thinking tends to have catastrophic consequences is the justice system, which still has much to learn about how to deal even with obvious miscarriages of justice. The computer animation studio Pixar, on the other hand, is a famous case of a company that has developed a production process that harnesses learning from failure. Collecting and genuinely listening to audience feedback from the very start, Pixar patiently reworks and enhances its plotlines until they turn into films that manage to capture the hearts of a maximum number of viewers.

But our reluctance to learn from failure is not due only to institutional attitudes. Psychological reasons, too, play their part. Chief among them is our inclination to avoid, if necessary at a high cost, what the social psychologist Leon Festinger has called "cognitive dissonance."[43] Festinger argues that we have a very strong drive to establish harmony between our values, beliefs, behaviors, and external information. If we perceive an inconsistency among these, we seek immediately to eliminate this dissonance. Because it is the path of least resistance, we tend not to change our deeply held beliefs, but rather to ignore or reframe evidence that does not fit into our picture of the world. Because dissonance threatens our inner balance and self-esteem, we often filter, twist, and bend what disturbs us. This may, of course, include our own shortcomings. We invest considerable mental energy in blocking mistakes we have made from entering our conscious thought, spinning self-justifications and alternative narratives, and often blaming others. This, then, is a negative form of perseverance—a dogged attachment to our beliefs in spite of strong evidence inviting us to question them.

"If we wish to fulfil our potential as individuals and organisations," Syed concludes, "we must redefine failure." For failure is among the most important, if not the most important, "means of learning, progressing and becoming more creative."[44] His conclusion leads him to call self-esteem—perhaps the most cherished concept in the Anglo-American post-sixties personal development

landscape—"a vastly overvalued psychological trait." A too close attachment to protecting our self-esteem can easily lead us to reject
learning, because we might fear that engaging with our failures
openly makes us look weak. What we need much more than self-
esteem, Syed argues, is resilience, which he defines as "the capacity
to face up to failure, and to learn from it."[45] The royal road to self-
improvement is, then, a form of perseverance that, far from being
put off by failure, accepts it as essential.

Discussions of perseverance and related categories inevitably touch
on deeper philosophical questions. Do we all have the same capacity for sticking with our pursuits? In what ways do our genes, personality traits, upbringing, socioeconomic background, and
experiences shape this capacity? Are laziness, lack of discipline, or
character weakness to blame if we fail to succeed in life? These
questions revolve around notions of agency and responsibility.
What is in our control and what is not? And following on from
that, for what can we be held personally responsible? Just what we
can voluntarily resolve to achieve and then actually achieve, and
when, and how, continues to be the subject of much debate.
    These are all crucial questions that relate to the tension be-
tween determinism and free will. They are so important because
they directly translate into political beliefs and government policies
that affect all of us. If we think that everyone possesses the same capacity to work hard and to succeed, we will be much less inclined to
look kindly on those who do not manage to do so, and also much
less likely to offer them support. If we think that our ability to persevere is impacted by various external factors for which we cannot
be held responsible, we will be more likely to favor solid social security provisions for those in need. The ongoing shrinking of the
welfare state in the United Kingdom and the United States, major
cuts in corporate taxes, and the resulting decline in state funding
for education, health, and public transport are all justified by the
former view, based on the idea that we are ultimately responsible
for our own fate. All of us, it is assumed, have the power to pull
ourselves up by our own bootstraps—regardless of the material
conditions in which we may find ourselves. In that particular context, the idea of "self-help" can take on a sinister meaning as large

numbers of struggling people are, more or less guilt-free, left to their own devices, their predicament seen as owing to a moral failing on their part.

There are, however, statistics that trouble such assumptions. The chances of gaining a good education and a well-paying job, and of living a healthy, safe, and long life, are considerably lower for those of us who were born poor, who belong to disenfranchised minorities, or who have been the victim of physical or mental abuse.[46] Numerous studies and surveys make it clear that it is simply much harder and much less likely for those from lower socioeconomic backgrounds to take good care of their physical and mental well-being and to succeed in life. It is churlish to assert that this is entirely their own fault. The theoretical possibilities of social mobility and limitless psychological self-enhancement do not translate into statistically measurable social change. This tension between theory and social reality should trouble us, and remind us that we need to nuance our arguments on what is and what is not possible.

Of course, we should also beware of simply abandoning our belief in our own agency and efforts in favor of deterministic worldviews. This defeatist mindset, too, can lead to serious problems, as Carol Dweck and Martin Seligman have pointed out.[47] We need, then, to find a middle ground between determinism and the notion that we all have limitless powers of free will at our disposal. The good news is that, as both Duckworth and Dweck argue, we can hone our ability to persevere, irrespective of our starting point. The most reasonable conclusion is arguably that we should take a measured and humble *kaizen* approach to our own improvement, valuing gradual and incremental change for the better, however small that change may be.

CHAPTER NINE

Mentalize

WE CAN SEEK TO IMPROVE ourselves in three main domains. We may choose to work on our inner life, by trying to control our thoughts and emotional reactions or by cultivating specific qualities and virtues. We may focus on enhancing our physical bodies—for example, by improving our appearance, diet, exercise regime, or general health. Or we may wish to improve our social relations by working on the way we interact with others. All are of course interrelated. But while in the self-improvement literature of the past the focus was principally on our inner life, the social dimension of self-improvement has become much more important in the twentieth and twenty-first centuries, as has the preoccupation with improving our physical being.

There are a variety of reasons for our growing need for guidance on relating to others. Our age is marked by the possibility of social mobility—a relatively recent phenomenon—which means that we can, at least in theory, transcend our class origins and improve our economic circumstances. Our social hierarchies and etiquettes are less rigid and regulated than those of our ancestors. In the West, we also tend increasingly to understand ourselves as atomized rather than relational, which has resulted in a decline of the importance of traditional social institutions such as the family, the community, the church, and the state, and a resulting exaltation of the self as our primary site of meaning. With this elevation of the individual self come new freedoms but also numerous new psychological pressures. In the Western world, we are, for example, witnessing unprecedented levels of depression, narcissism, and loneliness.[1] Many of us find it increasingly difficult to establish meaningful and lasting relationships with others.

It was not always thus. In ancient times, the self was understood as fundamentally relational, firmly embedded within wider social and cultural contexts. Interacting correctly with others in a formally regulated way and respecting social hierarchies, traditions, and fixed codes of conduct were much more important than today. Confucian social rituals, as well as European courtly customs in the early modern period, are at the most rigid end of the spectrum. Only in the later nineteenth and twentieth centuries did social hierarchies grow more porous. But as we have seen, this loosening initially amplified the preoccupation with correct protocol. As a consequence of increased possibilities for social mobility in the Victorian era, many lower- and middle-class people who had risen above their parents' station became ever more anxious about the subtle markers of class. They feared that their manners might expose their origins. More seasoned members of the middle class, in turn, sought to distinguish themselves clearly from social climbers. As a result, both groups placed a stronger emphasis on traditional codes of conduct.

While class markers—both of the subtle and not so subtle kind—continue to matter, correctly following strictly defined codes of etiquette has ceased to be of great importance in our less overtly hierarchical times. Social status tends to be evident in other details. What continues to cause us much anxiety, however, is both the quantity and the quality of our social relations, and in this social media have shifted the balance. The introduction of the now ubiquitous "like" button, in particular, has done much damage to our mental health, not only exploiting our need for love and approval, but making a demeaning public spectacle of it. While seeking to be respected by others is a perennial human concern, likability has become one of the core themes in the self-help literature of the twentieth and twenty-first centuries. We appear to worry about being liked much more than did our more formally role-defined and community-embedded ancestors.

And yet the concern with what others may think of us is not a new one. Those who wish primarily to be respected or even feared need look no further than *The Prince* (1532), by the infamous Italian political philosopher Niccolò Machiavelli (1469–1527). And Machiavelli's lessons are still highly instructive in that domain. The evidence suggests, however, that most of us prefer being liked to being feared. Likability was already a dominant concern of the early modern courtier, for example, for their livelihoods quite literally depended on being held in high esteem by those whom they served. Given how much ink has been expended on the topic since that time, it is surprising that what remains one of the best texts on how to get others to like us was written during the Great Depression. Dale Carnegie's classic *How to Win Friends and Influence People* (1937) is still in print for a reason. Although originally aimed at salespeople and businessmen, this perennial bestseller is full of sensible, practical, and directly applicable tips for making the best of human relations. Key to Carnegie's method is the art of mentalizing—that is, stepping into the other person's shoes, trying to see the world from their point of view, and mobilizing empathy.

The skill of mentalizing is also at the heart of neuro-linguistic programming (NLP). Devised in the 1970s, NLP is now mainly used to help us better to read and influence others. NLP practitioners invest vast amounts of energy in creating rapport, by systematically emphasizing similarities. Carefully studying clues to other people's "mental maps," they use key words, body language, and themes that most closely harmonize with their conversation partners' preferences.

Meaningful relationships with others rank highly on our list of basic human needs. The advice on how we can best improve our relationships with others ranges from strategies for controlling and manipulating to approaches that advocate authenticity, compassion, and more heartfelt ways of forging bonds with people. In one way or another, however, all of them center on the concept of mentalizing—that is, our ability to understand our own emotional state of mind and that of others. Only if we grasp our own emotions can we imagine and react appropriately to the needs, feelings, beliefs, and motivations of others. Mentalizing enables us to project ourselves into somebody else's mind, and to envisage the world as they might experience it. It is related to empathizing, or becoming cognitively aware of others' feelings and even experiencing those feelings ourselves. If we do not understand our own and other people's feelings, we are very likely to find it hard, if not impossible, to form meaningful relationships. Instead we may well misread others' feelings and make false assumptions about their intentions, causing us to respond inappropriately.

Mentalizing is difficult, however, and very few of us master the art. It requires not just self-knowledge but also a genuine interest in the other, the ability to imagine what may lie beyond the boundaries of our own cognitive maps, and a willingness seriously to engage with modes of perception, beliefs, and interests that might be very different from our own. It is a form of grappling with otherness that requires both imagination and openness.

Yet if practiced to excess, mentalizing can also lead to empathy stress, paralysis, and neurosis. If we project ourselves too much into the minds of others, constantly speculating what others may feel or think, we can become cripplingly hypersensitive to other people's presumed emotions, at the cost of losing touch with our own. Furthermore, the ability to mentalize can be put to good or bad use: it can form the basis for forging deep and meaningful bonds, or be weaponized for manipulating and exploiting others. It can generate a compassionate response to other people's concerns and sufferings, or be used in populist power grabs—for populists often have an exquisite intuitive understanding of what voters want to hear.

First, let us look at the dark side of mentalizing, and the nefarious art of manipulation. The Florence-born Renaissance political thinker Niccolò Machiavelli was particularly talented at understanding what people want, and also at translating this knowledge into power. He shared his insights in a work entitled *The Prince*, which he wrote in 1513. Published posthumously in 1532, it revolutionized the mirrors of princes (*specula principium*) genre—that is, self-improvement literature for kings. Mirrors of princes texts outline the basic principles of the art of governing, and include moral reflections on the virtues a great ruler should possess in order to reign justly and peacefully over his subjects. Most traditional mirrors of princes texts emphasize the idea that moral goodness is the most essential quality in a leader and that the good ruler has to lead by moral example. It was therefore truly shocking when Machiavelli challenged this notion. For Machiavelli, the good ruler was above all an effective ruler—regardless of personal morality.

Our own leadership and business management literature, too, tends to privilege effectiveness over goodness. However, in an intriguing twist, goodness has recently been rediscovered as a tool for bringing about effectiveness and enhancing employee engagement.[2] Leadership development research suggests that being a good leader (in the ethical sense of being compassionate, empathetic, humble, and consistently virtue-driven) may also bring out the best in employees and boost financial profit.

Machiavelli witnessed many of the upheavals that defined Italian Renaissance politics, such as Cesare Borgia's (1475–1507) brutal campaign to conquer large parts of central Italy. In 1494, the Florentine people expelled the Medici family, which had ruled the city-state for sixty years. Machiavelli held various government offices in the newly restored republic. But when the Medicis managed to reconquer the city in 1512, his fortunes changed for the worse. He was summarily dismissed from his offices and imprisoned for plotting against the new rulers. Though released a few weeks later, he subsequently remained an observer of the political scene, dedicating himself to the study of history, which, he believed, held the key to effective political leadership.[3] By carefully studying the patterns of the past, Machiavelli sought to extract vital lessons for the present. Just as modern self-help tends to be structured around inspiring tales about earlier exemplary human efforts, *The Prince*, too, includes numerous case studies of political leaders from bygone eras.

Given the instability of political structures that he witnessed firsthand, it is unsurprising that Machiavelli was more interested in strategies for maintaining power than he was in ways of attaining it. In rulers of the past, he appreciated above all speedy decision-making and the capacity for unwavering action. Advocating a politics of results, much of Machiavelli's advice revolves around the question of how best to respond to aggression. Machiavelli believes that the state cannot be defended effectively without recourse to what is commonly classified as vice. If a ruler were to remain virtuous at all times, it is precisely his virtues that would eventually lead to his downfall.[4] Machiavelli therefore advocates a course of action that forgiving critics have described as realpolitik, and less sympathetic ones as amoral scheming.

According to Machiavelli, it is generally safer to be feared than loved. This is because human beings are "ungrateful, fickle, false, cowardly, covetous, and as long as you succeed, they are yours entirely; they will offer you their blood, property, life, and children." But when one's fortunes change, they will turn against you without hesitation. People have far fewer scruples about betraying someone who is loved than someone who is feared, because fear preserves us "by a dread of punishment which never fails."[5] Machiavelli's preference for being feared is, then, quite simply a question of control. While we cannot force others to love us, we can always make them fear us by threatening retribution should they let us down.

What renders Machiavelli's philosophy most modern, however, is that he cares deeply about image, openly privileging appearance over essence. We must at all times know what other people want to see and hear, he holds, and appear to fulfill their desire. It is therefore necessary for a prince "to be a great pretender and dissembler," for "men are so simple, and so subject to present necessities, that he who seeks to deceive will always find someone who will allow himself to be deceived."[6] Here and elsewhere, it is clear that Machiavelli's opinion of the people is extremely low. Focused on their short-term needs, they are more than willing to be misled, and ultimately care about the ends and not the means. While it is not necessary, and is even undesirable, for a prince to possess all the virtuous qualities, "it is very necessary to appear to have them." What matters is not to be "merciful, faithful, humane, religious, upright," but to seem to be so.[7] A prince, in other words, needs to know what people want to hear and publicly talk the right talk, but keep their ethics flexible behind the scenes. Effective rhetoric is thus one of the most essential tools for successful leadership—as, of course, many politicians today know all too well.

It is not difficult, then, to see how Machiavelli's advice for princes can be translated into more general rules for manipulating others. A recent example is *Machiavelli Mindset* (2016) by R. Shaw, who believes that "life is a ruthless war in which you'll either be a winner or a loser," and provides his readers with Machiavelli-inspired tips for "getting over the guilt."[8]

As shameless everyday Machiavellians, for example, we might do the following: Above all, we would strive to appear to be kind and always pay lip service to the virtues of the day, even when, out of the public eye, we would be prepared ruthlessly to defend our position of power. Although extremely image-conscious and concerned with what people think of us, we would not aspire to goodness as a value in itself. Instead, we would live by the idea that effectiveness is the best measure of success, and that success trumps goodness every time. We would study others carefully, because knowing their fears and desires is the prerequisite for our ability effectively to manipulate them. We would say what people want to hear, but at the same time make sure that we are respected rather than loved, so that they would avoid crossing us for fear of retaliation.

Those of us in leadership positions would ensure that our colleagues are sufficiently loyal and happy that they do not rebel against us; we would reward achievement and try to keep people on our side. At the same time, we would make it known that disloyalty will be punished. We would surround ourselves with good people, but not with people who are more accomplished than we are and who could become rivals. We would make decisions swiftly and confidently, not hesitating to throw former friends under the bus, and always keep an eye on which side our bread is buttered. We would never apologize, fiercely attack anyone who dares to criticize us, and seek to destroy their reputation rather than engage with the content of their criticism. The Machiavellian model, in short, might be effective if our sole aim is power, but is not to be emulated if we wish to sleep soundly at night.

Another self-improvement genre that enjoyed a surge in popularity in the early modern period is courtesy literature. Courtesy literature teaches courtiers good manners and morals, with a new focus not only on social etiquette but also on the more superficial aspects of human interactions such as witty chat and sharp dressing. The most famous examples of the genre include Baldassare Castiglione's

The Book of the Courtier (1528) and Giovanni della Casa's *Galateo: The Rules of Polite Behavior* (1558).

A member of an aristocratic Italian family, the poet, diplomat, scholar, and, of course, courtier Baldassare Castiglione was born in 1478. Having received an extensive humanistic education, he entered the service of Guidobaldo of Montefeltro, duke of Urbino, in 1504. He soon became the duke's most trusted courtier and an important contributor to the court's literary and artistic life. It was his happy years as a courtier in the service of Guidobaldo that inspired *The Book of the Courtier.* During his lifetime, Castiglione was known above all as a paragon of refinement and courtesy. Hugely popular in the Elizabethan era, his book inspired many imitations, and profoundly influenced European sensibilities.[9]

The Book of the Courtier is written in the style of a fictional conversation. A group of aristocrats and cultivated men and women, as well as some less refined characters, debate the ideal qualities of the perfect courtier. They agree that chief among these is nonchalance: the courtier should always give the impression of calm and casual insouciance, and carefully avoid looking as though he is making an effort. This apparent unconcern was deliberately practiced and cautiously calculated, of course, in a manner that is not unlike our present-day cultivation of cool. In addition, the courtier must at all costs "avoid ostentation or the kind of outrageous self-glorification by which a man always arouses loathing and disgust among those who have to listen to him."[10] Pompousness and narcissism were as unpopular then as they are now. And being popular and well liked at court, it is important to remember, was quite literally of existential significance to the courtier. If they bored or offended those they served, they could easily be deprived of their livelihoods, or even their lives. It is of little wonder, then, that courtiers took the art of people-pleasing so seriously. They, too, constantly had to mentalize in order to anticipate what their patrons desired and needed most.

While the courtier should be discreetly learned and cultivated, and well versed in the literary arts, he must at all times carry this learning lightly and avoid the appearance of pretentiousness and artificiality. For nobody likes to be lectured in a patronizing tone or to be made to think that they are ignorant. In his conversations, the courtier should sound like a naturally talented amateur rather than a tedious scholar. And neither should he neglect the martial arts. The ideal courtier should be both a scholar and a warrior, a thinker and a man of action. All of his accomplishments should naturally be placed at the service of a prince, for the key function of the courtier is of course to guide the prince he serves along the path of virtue. The courtier, then, is to be both entertainer and spiritual guide, a fun-loving friend as well as a mentor—albeit one who counsels only on the sly.

Castiglione places a special emphasis on the importance of entertaining and elegant speech. Eloquence requires knowledge, wit, a smooth flow of information, as well as current and nonpretentious diction. Witty and stylish speech should be peppered with "well-turned metaphors" and accompanied by "certain movements of the entire body, not affected or violent but tempered by an agreeable expression of the face and movement of the eyes giving grace and emphasis to what is said."[11]

Appearance matters, too, "since external appearances often bear witness to what is within."[12] The courtier's dress should be "sober and restrained rather than foppish," the most agreeable color for everyday attire being black and other dark shades.[13] The courtier should dress according to what sort of man he wishes to be, so that his clothes signal his aspirations. In addition, Castiglione advises us to select our friends judiciously, for like attracts like, and "a man who associates with the ignorant or wicked is taken to be ignorant or wicked."[14] Just like our outfits, then, our acquaintances are an external reflection of our character.

The Book of the Courtier also contains advice specifically for women. This is a first in the older literature of self-improvement: up until the sixteenth century, women were completely disregarded as subjects deemed worthy of improvement. Not so in Castiglione's handbook. The ideal woman, it is agreed, must have virtues of the mind in common with the courtier, but combine these intellectual and moral attributes with the "womanly" qualities of caring for family and property. In addition, ladies at court should have a quick and vivacious spirit, knowledge of many subjects, a "certain pleasing affability," and know exactly how to entertain graciously "every kind of man with charming and honest conversation, suited to the time and the place and the rank of the person with whom she is talking."[15] They should, then, be paragons of virtue as well as highly accomplished small talkers in possession of refined communication skills and astute social instincts. One of the unexpected merits of Castiglione's work is not just that he adjudges women to be subjects worthy of self-improvement, but that he takes issue with traditional misogynist views. Throughout *The Book of the Courtier*, characters holding women in low esteem are made to look crude and stupid, and a few witty women contribute intelligent rebuttals of such chauvinistic positions.

Given how economically and socially dependent they were on the prince whom they served, and on their own social capital, courtiers had no greater concern than to be perceived as agreeable and entertaining, to be known to give good advice, and to delight their prince and those around him at all times. While traditional virtues have a place in the discussion of the ideal courtier, there is a new and noticeable emphasis in Castiglione's work on appearance, rhetoric, and the outward forms of polite behavior. Yet artificiality and insincerity are repeatedly mentioned as vices to be avoided at all costs—perhaps precisely because there is a danger that all the artful mannerisms and studied people-pleasing behaviors advocated in the book might be perceived as disingenuous and manipulative.

The skill of pleasing people also became ever more essential in the context of the transformation of agricultural into industrial societies. It played a particularly important role in the early decades of the twentieth century, in a capitalist economy where the profession of the salesman rose to importance. In the late 1930s, the Minnesota-born farm boy Dale Carnegie wrote *How to Win Friends and Influence People* (1937), an overnight sensation that was to feature on bestseller lists for decades to come. Like Napoleon Hill's bestselling *Think and Grow Rich!* (1937), it clearly resonated in the era of the Great Depression.

It was also a milestone in what the cultural historian Warren Susman has called the shift from a "culture of character" to a "culture of personality."[16] Nineteenth-century self-improvement guides, Susman argues, were still broadly advocating values such as duty, citizenship, work, honor, morals, manners, reputation, and integrity. But as a direct result of rapid industrialization, urbanization, and the rise of big business, the focus in the early decades of the twentieth century shifted from inner virtue to outer charm. Personality became the new cornerstone for self-improvement.[17] Personal charisma and the powers of persuasion became increasingly essential skills that people needed to possess in order to thrive in the new economic order. Another consequence of this shift was a growing cult of extroversion, in the wake of which traits associated with introversion became ever more strongly sidelined, and even pathologized.

Although marked by quaint phrases such as "Yes, sir!" and personal anecdotes opening with "Shortly after the close of World War I ... ," the core message of Carnegie's book remains relevant today—as evidenced by the fact that it is still on sale in most bookshops.[18] And yet Carnegie's key idea is neither cheesy nor cringeworthy. *How to Win Friends and Influence People* was originally aimed at salespeople. It combines insights from applied psychology with practical advice on successful sales techniques, conquering the fear of public speaking, and the general art of engineering rewarding human relationships. That said, most of his recommendations also apply to human interactions that are not motivated by monetary transactions.

Like Machiavelli, Carnegie has an astonishingly low opinion of his fellow human beings, whom he considers to be self-obsessed and needy, defined above all by their unquenchable thirst for attention and love. People are not driven by reason, he writes, for they are "creatures of emotion, creatures bristling with prejudices and motivated by pride and vanity."[19] In addition, he believes that we are quite set in our ways. We do not like to change our worldview and generally do not appreciate it when someone challenges our deeply held beliefs: "most citizens," he writes, "don't want to change their minds about their religion or their haircut or communism or their favourite movie star."[20] It is true that our minds work hard to avoid cognitive dissonance at all times. Yet Carnegie is also a sincere advocate of forgiving others their shortcomings, and of treating them kindly and with respect. Sympathize, don't blame, but do manipulate a bit, is his motto.

Most of Carnegie's advice revolves around making others feel appreciated, thereby rendering them more compliant with our own agendas. What people want above all, Carnegie states, is to feel important and to be praised. He admonishes his readers to remember that "a person's name is to that person the sweetest and most important sound in any language."[21] He estimates that we spend 95 percent of our time thinking about ourselves. "Remember that the people you are talking to are a hundred times more interested in themselves and their wants and problems than they are in you and your problems. A person's toothache means more to that person than a famine in China which kills a million people."[22] The vast majority of the people we meet, Carnegie believes, are hungry for sympathy. If we can figure out a way to give it to them, they will love us. Carnegie thus instrumentalizes the insight that we all tend to be most interested in ourselves. However, a shrewd mentalizing maneuver is necessary not just to figure that out, but also to put that knowledge to work.

There are a number of key ways to make people like us. We need to be genuinely interested in the other person, smile, remember their first name and use it often, be a good listener, and encourage them to talk about themselves. We should also focus on the other person's interests and, in a sincere manner, make them feel important. It also helps to remember small details about people's lives and preferences, and to mention these to show that we care about them. It is helpful to compliment them on something they are wearing or saying, and to touch them lightly on the shoulder at appropriate moments.

If we wish to win people over to our way of thinking, we must begin in a friendly way and show respect for the other person's opinion (rather than telling them they are wrong). We must try to see the matter from their point of view, always allow them to save face, and find some common ground on which everyone can agree. Ideally, we will let them do most of the talking, and make them feel that the idea to which we want them to come round is really theirs. Carnegie also advises us to praise rather than criticize if we wish to change other people's behavior—a basic concept taken from the work of the behaviorist B. F. Skinner. Praise, he believes, will reinforce the good things people do, while their less appealing actions will disappear if we do not grace them with attention.[23] Another important component of the art of persuasion is to secure attention and vividly to dramatize our ideas: "You have to use showmanship," Carnegie urges. "The movies do it. Television does it. And you will have to do it if you want attention."[24] This advice is endorsed still today, for example by the journalist and communication expert Carmine Gallo, author of *Talk Like TED: The 9 Public Speaking Secrets of the World's Top Minds* (2014).

Although Carnegie shows us how to instrumentalize our fellow human beings' psychological neediness, this is not as objectionable as it may sound. After all, we all share a need for appreciation, and showing appreciation is hardly immoral. Carnegie's is a win-win world—we get what we want, and the other person feels good about themselves, too, for they get what they want most in their interactions with us. Essentially, Carnegie encourages us always to imagine what the world looks like from the other's point of view—in other words, to mentalize and practice empathy.

Understanding and giving others what they want is also central in neuro-linguistic programming. We have already encountered NLP in the chapter on the imagination, and seen how practitioners use very specific forms of visualization to reprogram our unconscious and to set us on a pathway to success. The other dominant strand of NLP techniques is designed to enhance our ability not just to communicate more effectively with others, but also to influence them. One of NLP's central concerns is the art of rapport-building. It is for that reason that NLP-based methods not only have infiltrated many a self-help book, but are also very popular in the coaching sector, a highly lucrative business. Many motivational speakers and self-help gurus who advocate NLP have a cultlike following and are multimillionaires, examples being Richard Bandler, Paul McKenna, and Anthony Robbins. Indeed, Robbins is thought to be worth between $500 and $600 million, amassed through his various self-help franchises, including mass-participation seminars with titles such as "Date with Destiny."[25]

As previously mentioned, NLP is based on the assumption that each of us has a unique way of "mapping" the world, that is, a preferred "representation system" for collecting and processing information. If we want to communicate effectively with someone, we first of all have to understand the other person's system. The language that people use can give us a powerful indication of their subjective representations of the world. Seen in this way, it is our language rather than our eyes that are the windows to our souls. If we pay careful attention to linguistic habits and frequently used metaphors, we can gain valuable information about others.

In *Instant Influence and Charisma* (2015), the British hypnotist Paul McKenna outlines various concrete strategies for boosting our charisma and our power to influence others. Charisma, he argues, is a "code" that can be learned, above all by modeling others who have it in abundance. He, too, believes that a key strategy for becoming more charismatic is building rapport with those we wish to influence. If we want others to like and trust us, we need above all to reduce our difference by amplifying what we have in common.[26] This includes aligning our physiology with that person— echoing posture, gestures, speed of movement, even the pace, tone, and volume of our conversation partner's speech. Blatant copying, however, is to be avoided in favor of subtler forms of mirroring. McKenna, too, advises us to pay close attention to other people's metaphors and styles of expression. We should also seek to ask questions aimed at finding out what their core values and beliefs are, and then respect these.

In *Neuro-linguistic Programming for Dummies* (2015), the seasoned NLP-coaches Romilla Ready and Kate Burton share more detailed techniques for building rapport and influencing others. Master communicators, they argue, have three qualities: they know what they want; they are very good at noticing the responses they get; and they have the flexibility to modify their behavior.[27] We should start all our conversations with our desired end result in mind, constantly aware of what it is we want to achieve in our interactions. The ability to adapt our communicative style is key in this process. If what we are doing is not working, we have to do something different. People with the most flexibility within a system are usually best at influencing the system.[28]

Ready and Burton also argue that rapport is about establishing trust and emphasizing our similarities with others rather than our differences. In addition to matching and mirroring, active listening, and ramping up our alikeness, they recommend that we take a genuine interest in getting to know what is important to other people.

They also advise us to pay attention to whether others are interested in detail or just the big picture. People who are sticklers for detail may be put off by blue-sky visionary thinkers who do not ground their assumptions in concrete facts, whereas free-floating big ideas people may find the detail-obsessed tedious and limited. We should also take into account our conversation partners' dominant temporal frame of mind: are they stuck in the past, alive in the present, or always talking about the future? Last but not least, we should seek to respect our conversation partners' time, energy, friends, favorite associates, and money.[29]

All of these are external, outside-in techniques, some of which may indeed work well for establishing contact with strangers. But because they are so deliberately engineered, they are not likely to result in deeper connections. In order to be truly charismatic and influential, McKenna argues, another ingredient is required: we need to appear authentic, which he understands as living in harmony with our own values. Our state of mind must be balanced when we encounter others, so that our nonverbal communications and overall energy harmonize with what we say. If we are constantly battling with self-sabotaging inner voices, doubts, fears, or other unproductive states of mind, we cannot bundle our energy and fully project it outward, toward the other person.

Truly charismatic people tend to be genuinely curious about others. At peace with who they are, they can dedicate their full attention to the external world and invest it in the quality of their interactions. It is certainly true that the more we are preoccupied with our own insecurities, the less we have to give to the outside world. For our energies are finite, and the lion's share of our attention will be directed inward. As Freud points out, the key problem for melancholics is that the majority of their psychological energy is consumed in internal psychological battles. If we fall into that category, we are likely to find it very hard to make others feel appreciated and important. Which, after all—and here McKenna fully agrees with Carnegie—is what they desire most.

NLP offers some valuable insights into how we can enhance our interactions with others. It asks us to take our conversation partners seriously by paying a deeper kind of attention and genuinely listening not just to what they have to say but also to how they say it. It is likely that being at the receiving end of this kind of concentrated active listening will make most of us feel good about ourselves. However, whether these techniques allow us to establish deeper kinds of relationship is less certain. They come with a distinctive whiff of engineering, occasionally bordering on manipulation. NLP techniques will not appeal to those of us who value more natural modes of social interaction, or who prefer to talk to others without a specific goal in mind, for the sheer pleasure of it or because it makes us feel less alone in the world. NLP is based on a distinctly transaction-based conception of human interactions. Some may find this a realistic model: many people, after all, do approach others with a "What's in it for me?" mindset, even if all they want is simply to be liked. Others, however, may find it a reductive, indeed dangerous, model of human contact.

It is perhaps no coincidence that NLP-based self-help tends to appeal particularly to those working in sales, as well as to aspiring pick-up artists.[30] Carnegie's model, too, it is worth remembering, was originally aimed at salespeople. *How to Win Friends and Influence People* ushered in a raft of self-help literature that has focused on making communication more effective—rather than, say, more pleasant, illuminating, or deep. As in Carnegie's case, NLP-based self-help often has a very explicit emphasis on sales strategies and techniques, a distinctive salesman-mindset that tends to be applied to all models of human interaction. As McKenna puts it, "One way or another, everybody is selling all day long."[31]

At the heart of Machiavelli's, Castiglione's, Carnegie's, and McKenna's advice, however, resides a very simple lesson: if we want anything at all from others—be that simply to be liked, or to achieve other, more specific outcomes such as being feared, securing favors, exerting influence, or selling something—we need to take the people with whom we interact seriously. We must grace them with genuine attention. We must listen to what they say and to how they say it, understand what they want and fear most, and communicate in a language that is similar to theirs. We must, in other words, mentalize.

Why is it that so many of us find mentalizing so hard these days? Is it because, in what has been described as the age of narcissism, we are more caught up than ever in our own psychodramas, so that we simply have less to give to others? Has our fixation on self-worth and self-esteem led us systematically to undervalue the importance of other people? Or are social media to blame? Numerous studies have shown that excessive social media use has led to an erosion of our ability to empathize, and that we are much crueler online than when we meet people face to face. Moreover, the hours we now spend socializing virtually have hampered our ability adequately to read the facial expressions and emotions of those we meet in person.[32]

Another reason for our struggles with mentalizing might be related to what sociologists call the "economization" of the social sphere, the idea that we increasingly tend to see everything through the prism of the economic, including our private selves and our interactions with others. It means, in other words, that the neoliberal dictate of efficiency enhancement is shaping all areas of our lived experience. We tend to see even our relationships with others in terms of transactions that are more or less profitable. We even speak of "social capital" and, in management contexts, refer to concepts such as empathy and emotional intelligence as "soft skills" that we may wish to hone to increase our interactional effectiveness.

It is likely that all of these factors have impacted on our ability to relate well to others, and that they have contributed to our increased need for guidance on this basic human task. But there is also a less pessimistic reading of the upsurge in self-help literature on this topic in the twentieth and twenty-first centuries. It is equally plausible that human beings have in fact always struggled with the task of mentalizing, but that our ability to do so has simply become much more pressing in our age. There is no doubt that mentalizing is a key soft skill, the possession of which leads to distinctive advantages in our service economies. It is also true that because many of our old communal structures and ways of socializing have broken down, we now need to forge our alliances more proactively. In our age of atomization and anomie, we have to seek and build our own communities.

Mentalizing also involves a paradox. In our own psychological universe, we are the subject, but in everybody else's, we are a mere object. This truth is hard to fathom, and truly accepting its implications

can be threatening to our sense of self. Genuinely acknowledging that
there are other ways of seeing the world out there, moreover, requires
not just imagination but also courage. For this admission entails the
concession that our own beliefs, values, and interpretations are not
absolute truths, but simply subjective preferences.

It is, finally, also simply very hard truly to know others. While
Carnegie's belief that appreciation is what all of us want most is
certainly true to an extent, it does not capture the complexities and
nuances of our many other needs. It is hard—very hard—to imagine what others really want, not least because they often don't
know themselves. Many great writers, including Marcel Proust in
his multivolume masterpiece *In Search of Lost Time* (1913–27),
grapple with the fundamental unknowability of others. Proust was
also of the view, however, that art and literature could help us to
improve our powers of mentalizing. As he put it, "Through art
alone are we able to emerge from ourselves, to know what another
person sees of a universe which is not the same as our own and of
which, without art, the landscapes would remain as unknown to us
as those that may exist on the moon."[33]

Novels in particular demand of us a sustained emotional and
imaginative involvement, by inviting us to project ourselves into and
to identify with the lives of the characters about whom we are reading. They have the power to enable us fully to share the perspectives
of their characters and to see the world from their point of view.
The fictional worlds conjured up by great writers are thus magnificent training grounds for honing our ability to mentalize, and to engage with ways of seeing the world that may be profoundly different
from our own.

CHAPTER TEN

Be Present

O NE OF THE MOST ubiquitous recent self-help trends is
mindfulness. Its merchandise is everywhere. But this is
also its problem: all the coloring books have harmed
its appeal, and its methods have become a cliché. Mindfulness has now peaked, and the self-help market has moved on.
Our apparent thirst for constant novelty dictates that all self-help
trends rise and fall, with variable life spans. And in so doing, they
reveal society's prevailing values and preoccupations. At the height
of its popularity, mindfulness clearly addressed an urgent collective
need.

In essence, mindfulness is about relearning how to live in the
here and now. It encourages us to direct our attention fully and
nonjudgmentally to whatever task we are currently performing. It
asks us to cultivate our ability to focus on the present by training
our minds not to flit feverishly from our past to our futures, chasing after every thought, however trivial. Rather than getting lost in
the content of our thoughts, it asks us to become aware of their
movement. At its apex, mindfulness resonated with so many of
us because we clearly felt we had lost the ability to live fully in the
present moment.

Fueled by Jon Kabat-Zinn's influential bestsellers *Full Catastrophe Living* (1990) and *Wherever You Go, There You Are* (1994), the

mindfulness vogue began in the 1990s. Significantly, it coincided with the advent of the Internet. Mindfulness's popularity then grew rapidly and in conjunction with the ever more pervasive digitization of our lives. There is no doubt that social media, our nonstop connectivity, our 24/7 shopping culture, and the effects of our radically changed communication habits are decisive causes for its widespread appeal.

The more we feel our presence bleeding away, the stronger our desire becomes to shore up our defenses against this constant leakage. Many of us are rarely alone with our own thoughts and feelings, as we are constantly exposed to what others think and feel, like and dislike. Whether we are at work or at play, in the office, relaxing at home, caring for others, or on holiday, we are chronically being distracted by the many electronic notifications, messages, and ads that vie for our attention. Few and far between are those who don't have a smart phone to hand. It is a profoundly worrying fact that our attention spans are now at an all-time low. It is unsurprising, then, that we have been so receptive to advice on how to enhance our threatened capacity to experience the present and to engage fully in what we happen to be doing.

In the marketing of mindfulness, moreover, depending on the target audience, its Buddhist origins tend to be either emphasized or played down.[1] Mindfulness is often presented as part of a package that includes loving-kindness and compassion, which appeals to those of us who are tired of Western-style individualism and its neoliberal "greed is good" values. This version of mindfulness also satisfies a desire for more altruism and connectedness in our lives. In addition, it addresses an appetite for exotic practices from cultures very different from our own that, we hope, might be able to fill our spiritual vacuum.[2]

But mindfulness can also be presented very differently, stamped with the approval of Western science. Neuroscientists and psychologists, too, have played a significant role in helping mindfulness rise to prominence.[3] By conducting clinical studies on the efficacy of ancient meditation practices, they have furnished mindfulness with solid credentials. Mindfulness is often sold simply as a highly effective stress-reduction and productivity-enhancing technique, with an emphasis on its proven benefits for our emotional and physical well-being. It thus also appeals to those who might be put off by ancient wisdom and anything that smacks of spirituality.

There are many reasons, then, why mindfulness appealed so strongly in our age of fast-paced change, nonstop communication, and competitive individualism. And yet we are far from alone in having worried about our ability to dwell in the present. While the many distractions of techno-capitalism have rendered our interest in honing our present-moment attention more pressing, the art of being present is an ancient human preoccupation with a long and rich history. Asian philosophies and religions have traditionally placed considerable emphasis on living fully in the present moment. Together with compassionate living, meditation is the primary pathway to enlightenment in Buddhist thought. Tai-chi and yoga, too, are time-honored techniques for connecting our minds more firmly to our bodies, designed to anchor our thoughts by coordinating our breath and physical movements.[4] Mentioned in ancient sacred texts such as the Vedas, the Upanishads, and the Bhagavad Gita, the word "yoga" can be translated as "to yoke." Its aim is quite literally to yoke the human spirit to the divine, and the body to the mind. But the meaning of the word has also been traced to the Sanskrit for "to concentrate."[5] Concentration, or *samādhi*, is the central category in the *Yoga Sūtras of Patañjali* (second century CE). Instead of explaining how to hone our headstand pose, the sage Patañjali provides complex holistic advice on how to improve our present-moment awareness. This crucial spiritual and cognitive dimension of yoga tends to be neglected in Western-style yoga practices, which place more emphasis on the body than on the mind.

The interest in being present is not unique to Asian cultures. In his *Meditations*, the Roman emperor Marcus Aurelius, for example, also recommends that we strengthen our attachment to the present moment. "Every hour of the day," he writes, "give vigorous attention . . . to the performance of the task in hand with precise analysis, with unaffected dignity, with human sympathy, with dispassionate justice—and to vacating your mind from all its other thoughts." We will best achieve this objective, Aurelius promises, if we perform each action as if it were the last of our life—"freed, that is, from all lack of aim, from all passion-led deviation from the ordinance of reason, from pretence, from love of self, from dissatisfaction with what fate has dealt you."[6]

Aurelius advocates the restorative powers of emptying our
minds and withdrawing into the self. We must seek refuge from
the world of appearances in our "inner citadel," he urges, and
meditate. It is not necessary to withdraw to the country, the sea, or
the hills when we can retreat into our own selves at any time.
"No retreat offers someone more quiet and relaxation than that
into his own mind," Aurelius observes, "especially if he can dip into
thoughts there which put him at immediate and complete ease." It
is for this reason that we should seek to achieve such a withdrawal
into the mind, this retreat enabling us to "renew" ourselves.[7]

The French philosopher Jean-Jacques Rousseau also cherished
the power of the now. For him, being present is a means by
which to free ourselves from toxic cultural norms, reconnecting
with our authentic self, and reaching a state of heightened sensibility. In such a state, Rousseau writes, "My soul can find a position
solid enough to allow it to remain there entirely and gather together its whole being, without needing to recall the past or encroach upon the future, where time is nothing to it, where the
present lasts for ever, albeit imperceptibly and giving no sign of
its passing, with no other feeling of deprivation or enjoyment,
pleasure or pain, desire or fear than simply that of our existence, a
feeling that completely fills our soul."[8] Where we are on our inner
temporal time line, then, is of the essence, according to both Aurelius and Rousseau. In order to be truly present, we must block our
restless minds from time-traveling, rather anchoring them firmly
in the here and now. In addition, we must deactivate our fear of
missing out and our self-pity, and temporarily halt all our wanting
and striving.

Ralph Waldo Emerson, too, was deeply concerned about our
problematic attitude toward time. Instead of privileging the past or
worrying about the future, he advises, we must relearn to honor
the present. "But man postpones or remembers," Emerson complains, "he does not live in the present, but with reverted eye laments the past, or, heedless of the riches that surround him, stands
on tiptoe to foresee the future. He cannot be happy and strong
until he too lives with nature in the present, above time."[9]

Where exactly are we when we are not present? If we aren't paying attention to the complexities and wonders of the current moment, we tend to dwell either in our pasts or our futures. These experiences can be pleasant or unpleasant. We might be reminiscing, regretting, or obsessively ruminating about bygone events; or we might be imaging a future that is possible or completely fantastical. Depending on whether our outlooks are optimistic or pessimistic, we might imagine a future filled with exciting opportunities, or else worry about all the bad things that may befall us or our loved ones.

Yet we need to expand even further the options for where our minds might wander when going absent without leave. Nowadays, technology enables us to direct our attention to people, information, or images that are physically far away from us. Our smart phones build the bridges. We can communicate very easily with people who are not in the room with us, and who may even be in another country, and we can monitor their publicly expressed thoughts. We can lose ourselves in the lives of others, following them on Instagram and Facebook or keeping an eye on their every tweet. We can, as a result, neglect to grace the people who are actually there with us, in our physical presence, with our full attention. We have all experienced the social gathering or the family meal where those who are ostensibly "present" are in fact elsewhere, caught in the realm of social media.

The command to "be present" does not sound like a particularly dramatic strategy for self-improvement. And yet, considering how hard we find it to do so, how many of our thoughts tend to revolve around either our past, our future, or faraway people and events, and how willingly we allow ourselves to be distracted, learning to be present is one of the most difficult and radical techniques for self-transformation imaginable. Once again, the ancients knew this well. Unlike us, they did not underestimate the challenging nature of the task. And neither did they downplay the ongoing commitment, practice, and effort that being present requires.

They knew another crucial secret as well. Being present is not just a question of directing our attention to the present moment. More radical shifts in our perception and consciousness are required. These relate to what psychologists now describe as "defusing," or "self as context" perception.¹⁰ These notions suggest that we are not simply the sum of our experiences, thoughts, or emotions, but that there is a self outside our current experience. Cognitive defusing challenges the credibility of our thoughts and feelings, simply by highlighting that they are just that: thoughts and feelings. It involves stepping back from our experiences and observing them in a more disinterested way. Others talk about our "observing mind"—a detached form of consciousness that is simply watching our thoughts at work. Buddhists take this line of thought furthest in their theory of the "no-self," the idea that there is in fact no permanent and separate entity called the self. All of these models are based on the idea that we should learn to pay less attention to the content of our thoughts, and focus more on their form and movements.

Buddhists believe that it is above all our ignorance about ourselves and the true nature of phenomena that is responsible for our suffering.¹¹ Buddhist scriptures teem with metaphors of sleeping, dreaming, and waking, illustrating the idea that most of us are trapped in harmful illusions. Buddhism places an extremely high value on insight—for it is insight alone that can release us from suffering. But the kind of insight that has this transformative power is not sterile and intellectual, nor purely metaphysical or abstract. Truly transformative insight can only be the fruit of persistent meditation and a lifelong dedication to being attentive to things as they really are in the here and now. Buddhist insight, then, is the reward of a radically present-oriented way of life.

The Buddha emphasizes the vital importance of controlling our mind via meditation, for "our life is the creation of our mind."¹² But Buddhist mind control is very different from the Stoic version, for it does not attempt to force our thoughts into more logical pathways. Instead, it encourages our minds to stay anchored in the present moment and simply to watch our thoughts pass by, like clouds in the sky, without becoming attached to their content. The Buddha declares: "The mind is wavering and restless, difficult to guard and restrain: let the man straighten his mind as a maker of arrows makes his arrows straight. . . . The mind is fickle and flighty, it flies after fancies wherever it likes: it is difficult indeed to restrain. But it is a great good to control the mind. . . . An enemy can hurt an enemy, and a man who hates can harm another man; but a man's own mind, if wrongly directed, can do him a far greater harm."[13]

The primary Buddhist way to hone present awareness and true insight is to practice meditation. We can meditate by observing and stilling our thoughts and by focusing on our breath, on our sensual perceptions, on mantras, on visual imagery, or, in the Zen tradition, on paradoxical statements. Designed to tame our "monkey" minds, constantly jumping from one thought, feeling, or perception to another, meditation is a technique for cultivating our ability to experience inner peace and to concentrate. The most common mental obstacles preventing us from staying present include sensual desires, hostility, dullness and lethargy, agitation and worry, and doubt. If we can overcome them, we can gradually learn to let go of our egocentric conception of the world and hence of our ignorance.

There are very good reasons for considering Buddhism a self-improvement doctrine. By advocating the powers of meditation, insight, and compassionate living, it provides a comprehensive ethical and spiritual framework for overcoming our suffering. And yet there is the knotty matter of the doctrine of the "no-self" to consider. Buddhists believe that ignorance about our true nature is the primary cause of all suffering. More specifically, they locate this ignorance in the conceit that our selves are discrete and permanent entities. The primary aim of Buddhism is to let go of this idea of the self as a separate and fixed entity, and to recognize that the self is, like everything else, impermanent and insubstantial.[14]

Anattā, the doctrine of "no-self," states that there is no permanent substance that can be called the soul. Neither is there another permanent essence of self in living beings. According to this doctrine, there are no fixed entities called "selves" at all that can own specific and lasting qualities. There are only a number of psycho-physical elements, which participate in a succession of transient events and states, rather like H_2O molecules in a river. Even our cells are subject to change. There are, then, only fleeting experiences, passing emotions, and changing beliefs.[15] This doctrine bears a striking similarity to the pre-Socratic Greek philosopher Heraclitus's belief that "everything flows."

Buddhists believe that we base our conception of the self as a fixed entity on a bundle of five aggregates, or *skandha*s: our physical form, our sensations, our cognitions, our desires, and our consciousness. All of these elements, however, are impermanent. Moreover, the aggregates of the self can group together in different formations, like a swarm of bees or a shoal of fish—a notion that is as intriguing as it is difficult to accept on a rational level. The philosopher Mitchell S. Green pragmatically objects that there is some kind of continuity to our bodily and mental existence while we are alive. Through our life spans, we tend, after all, to have *"the same overall shape and function"* and are *"being made of largely the same material as it was moments earlier."*[16] Unless we suffer from amnesia or dementia, we are also memory-linked to our earlier person-stages. He has a point. But perhaps we should take the "bundle-idea" of the self less literally.

Buddhism considers the Western conception of the self as a discrete feeling, perceiving, and thinking entity to be a cognitive distortion. The ultimate purpose of Buddhist meditation is the dissolution of this illusion. "Pluck out your self-love as you would pull off a faded lotus in autumn," the Buddha advises.[17] For if we truly let go of our common notion of selfhood, we would become more humble. Our desires, fears, and undertakings would appear to us much less pressing, even insignificant. It is of course paradoxical that many of us now use traditional Buddhist mindfulness techniques to strengthen our egos and to make them more resilient, when in fact Buddhism views this very attachment to ego as the main cause of our suffering. The irony of the scenario is not lost on critics of the current mindfulness vogue.[18]

By practicing Buddhist mindfulness and meditation, then, we can cultivate a metacognitive form of present-moment awareness. Its purpose is to help us realize that we are not our incessantly chattering thoughts, and that we can still them. As a second step, this insight will allow us to overcome our egocentricity, and to accept that our very conception of the self as a separate and autonomous unit with a fixed essence is an illusion. What we think of as our selves are porous and fleeting bundles of components that are themselves in flux. Only when we grasp this can we appreciate the interconnectedness and relationality of all beings, and understand that we are part of a universe that stretches far beyond the limited boundaries of the self.

Western interest in Buddhist thought is not a new phenomenon. Periodically waxing and waning, its fortunes in the West have been fueled by trade, colonialism, immigration, and globalization. There is no doubt, however, that this interest has grown significantly more pronounced in recent decades. In the second half of the twentieth century, mounting disenchantment with capitalist materialism and traditional Christianity resulted in an appetite for alternative modes of spirituality. A "Zen Boom" captured the countercultural imagination of hippies and other spiritual seekers in the late 1960s. Philip Kapleau's *The Three Pillars of Zen* (1965) and the Japanese teacher Shunryu Suzuki's *Zen Mind, Beginner's Mind* (1970) became instant classics. After the Chinese invasion of Tibet in 1950, exiled Tibetan lamas fled to the West, prompting an interest in Tibetan Buddhism and culture. In turn, Western students began to join Buddhist monasteries in Asia, later returning to teach others what they had learned. Tenzin Gyatso, the current Dalai Lama, is not just the most illustrious but also the most influential Buddhist thinker, many of his Buddhist self-help books having become bestsellers in the West. Multitudes of lay teachers, finally, have helped spread Buddhist meditation practice, offering retreats, workshops, and classes across Europe and the United States.[19]

Our cultural fascination with mindfulness, then, did not come out of nowhere. It builds on a long-standing interest in Buddhist practices in the West—one that has been kindled further by Hollywood films such as *Kundun* and *Seven Years in Tibet*, both released in 1997. Although there is now a vast body of mindfulness-based self-help literature available, the most influential texts of that genre are without doubt the American Jon Kabat-Zinn's *Full Catastrophe Living* (1991) and the shorter and more readable *Wherever You Go, There You Are* (1994). Kabat-Zinn (b. 1944), now an emeritus professor of medicine, studied with Zen teachers such as Philip Kapleau and Thich Nhat Hanh. In 1979 he founded the Mindfulness-Based Stress Reduction (MBSR) program of the Stress Reduction Clinic at the University of Massachusetts Medical Center. MBSR-inspired programs are now offered by numerous other organizations and clinics across the world.

Kabat-Zinn understands mindfulness as a skill that can be trained. While acknowledging the Buddhist origins of the practice, he considers mindfulness a technique the essence of which is universal.[20] He thus seeks to detach mindfulness from its Buddhist context, transplanting it into a universal scientific framework. Above all, he considers it a highly efficient tool for stress reduction, but one that also comes with positive ethical side-effects. In *Full Catastrophe Living*, he defines mindfulness as "the awareness that arises by paying attention on purpose, in the present moment, and non-judgementally."[21] Awareness is a form of attention, a way of exercising discernment. Proper mindfulness is about non-doing and non-striving. It is a way of being that involves observing our thoughts and then letting them go, not getting attached to their content.

Seven mental attitudes are additional core pillars of mindfulness practice. They are non-judging, patience, a beginner's mind, trust, non-striving, acceptance, and letting go.[22] Of those, non-judging is the most important. We can practice it by trying not to get caught up in our opinions, our likes and dislikes, and by refraining from evaluating people and experiences as either good or bad. Instead, we should accept them just as they are in this moment. Patience is a related form of wisdom "which demonstrates that we understand and accept the fact that sometimes things must unfold in their own time."[23]

Generally, Kabat-Zinn believes, there is far too much doing in our lives, and not enough being. Our hectic lifestyles mean that we can quite literally no longer catch our breath. In recent decades, our stress levels have increased dramatically. Practicing mindfulness, he argues, has a range of significant health benefits. It not only helps us to regulate our stress, but also strengthens our immune systems, reduces inflammation, and counteracts mind-wandering and rumination. It helps with perspective-taking, concentration, learning, memory, the regulation of our emotions, and threat appraisal. And it can nurture self-acceptance, kindness, and self-compassion.

Perhaps most importantly, mindfulness can assist us in not getting too caught up in the drama of our selves, in paying more attention to the form of our thoughts and becoming less attached to their content. "It is remarkable how liberating it feels to be able to see that your thoughts are just thoughts and that they are not 'you' or 'reality,' " Kabat-Zinn writes.[24] This deliberate devaluation of the content of our thoughts is also a core tenet of acceptance and commitment therapy (ACT), and features centrally in Eckhart Tolle's philosophy of the power of now. Kabat-Zinn also points out important links to the Buddhist notion of no-self, noting that there is no continuous discrete self but instead only a process of continual self-construction, which he calls "selfing."[25] Selfing is a mental activity, a process of grasping and holding together. If we manage to watch ourselves disinterestedly in the act of selfing, we succeed in defusing our selves from the content of our thoughts.

Aptly, the first chapter of *Full Catastrophe Living* is entitled "You Have Only Moments to Live." The present moment, Kabat-Zinn argues, is all we have, for the present "is the only time that we have to know anything. It is the only time we have to perceive, to learn, to act, to change, to heal, to love."[26] In its most basic sense, meditating simply means "being in the present on purpose."[27] And yet Kabat-Zinn knows all too well how difficult this task is. Indeed, it takes a lifetime of continuous practice. For our minds are constantly battling with the "incredible pull of the Scylla and Charybdis of past and future, and the dreamworld they offer us in place of our lives."[28] Mindful living à la Kabat-Zinn, then, is the art of conscious, intention-driven, and present-focused living. It is a way of being that continuously fights the twin threats of unawareness and automaticity.

The idea that we are not our thoughts, that we need to distance ourselves from the content of those thoughts, and that our true self is located somewhere beyond them is also a central tenet in Eckhart Tolle's cult-book *The Power of Now: A Guide to Spiritual Enlightenment* (1998). Tolle, who was born in Germany in 1948 and now lives in Canada, has been described in the *New York Times* as "the most popular spiritual author in the nation."[29] He counts Oprah Winfrey as one of his many fans.

Tolle had suffered from anxiety and depression for most of his early life. After experiencing an inner transformation, he dropped out of his PhD studies at the University of Cambridge and became a spiritual teacher instead. Before his epiphany, which he recounts in *The Power of Now*, he often thought, "I cannot live with myself any longer." This debilitating thought, however, also became the engine for his transformation: "Am I one or two?" he wondered. "If I cannot live with myself, there must be two of me: the 'I' and the 'self' that 'I' cannot live with."[30] He wondered whether they could both be real at the same time. After this strange realization he was drawn first into a vortex of energy and then into a void, from which he emerged much later in a state of bliss. He understood that his suffering must have forced his consciousness "to withdraw from its identification with the unhappy and deeply fearful self, which is ultimately a fiction of the mind." His false, suffering self fell away, revealing his true nature in the form of pure consciousness.[31]

The key to living in the present, Tolle writes, is to stop identifying with our minds, with the stream of involuntary and incessant thinking we tend to equate with our personal essence. Our true selves are located beyond our shifting emotions and compulsive thinking. Like the Buddhists and Kabat-Zinn, Tolle believes that our very notion of self is a fiction of the mind. We need to learn to witness our thought patterns rather than identify with them. He, too, argues that we must let go of our attachment to our egos.

Most of our thoughts and emotions revolve around the past or future as we compulsively vacillate between memory and anticipation. Our past furnishes us with an identity, and narratives of cause and effect, while "the future holds the promise of salvation, of fulfilment in whatever form."[32] But both are illusions. We should instead learn to be present as "watchers" of our minds. Watching is all we need to do, and it includes refraining from analyzing and judging.

Much like Kabat-Zinn, Tolle asserts that the present moment is all we ever really possess. Not only is now the most precious thing there is, it is the only thing there is. "Give attention to the present," he urges, "give attention to your behaviour, to your reactions, moods, thoughts, emotions, fears, and desires as they occur in the present."[33] Tolle sees being present as the royal road to salvation: "True salvation," he writes, "is a state of freedom—from fear, from suffering, from a perceived state of lack and insufficiency and therefore from all wanting, needing, grasping, and clinging. It is freedom from compulsive thinking, from negativity, and above all from past and future as a psychological need."[34] There is nothing we can ever do or attain that will get us closer to salvation than this moment. By freeing ourselves from our enslavement to our minds, he writes, we can radically transform our consciousness. And this radical transformation of consciousness is precisely what is needed to save not only ourselves, but also humanity at large and our planet—the latter idea being the focus of Tolle's second book, *A New Earth: Create A Better Life* (2005).

The basic problem of humanity, then, is rooted in the mind, or rather in "our misidentification with mind."[35] Thinking has become our core disease, Tolle believes. Our identification with our mind, which causes our thoughts to become compulsive, is the root cause of all our suffering. We have become slaves to our minds, and we need to move beyond them again, not allowing what is merely a formidable instrument to become our tormentor. Our deeper self, our conscious presence, can only be located behind thought. With a nod to Buddhism, he calls this the realm of "no-mind." Tolle does not identify this detachment from our thoughts as mindfulness, however. Instead he describes it as consciousness without thought, or concept-less consciousness. The principle of nonjudgmentally observing our thoughts while remaining purposefully anchored in the present, though, remains the same.

The idea that we need to distinguish between the form and the content of our thoughts has also been explored by psychiatrists and psychologists. In *The Brain That Changes Itself* (2007), Norman Doidge reports on the pioneering research into obsessive-compulsive disorder (OCD) of Jeffrey M. Schwartz. Schwartz has developed a treatment that helps those suffering from OCD, but his findings are relevant for all of us. His treatment involves a simple act of relabeling. Rather than thinking we are being attacked by germs or that our house is on fire because we have forgotten to turn off the stove, we should remind ourselves that the problem is not germs, but an attack of OCD. As Doidge observes, "Schwartz is teaching patients to distinguish between the universal *form* of OCD (worrisome thoughts and urges that intrude into consciousness) and the *content* of an obsession (i.e., the dangerous germs). The more patients focus on content, the worse their condition becomes." This simple act of relabeling produces distance from the content of the obsession and allows sufferers to view it in a way that is similar to how Buddhists perceive suffering in meditation: "they observe its effects on them and so slightly separate themselves from it."[36] Schwartz's OCD sufferers, then, are trained to stay in the present, consciously reminding themselves of what is happening right now. They are invited to observe their minds OCD-ing, rather than engaging seriously with the content of their thoughts.

The same differentiation between form and content is also at the heart of acceptance and commitment therapy. In *The Happiness Trap* (2007), Russ Harris explains that unlike cognitive behavioral therapy, ACT does not encourage us to challenge our negative thoughts and feelings. It asks us simply to notice and accept them, and then let them go. The commitment to nonjudgmental observation, to acceptance, to watching our thoughts come and go without becoming attached to their content, and of course, to staying in the here and now clearly aligns ACT with ancient Buddhist principles. The same is true of ACT's emphasis on the distinction between our observing and our thinking selves.

Harris also encourages us to defuse our thoughts from our identity and consciousness. He invites us to practice thinking something like "Thank you, mind" whenever it bombards us with unproductive thoughts or bullies us with counterproductive beliefs, and not to take the contents of what it produces too seriously. When we experience troubling thoughts, he suggests that we remind ourselves that we are not our thoughts and that our thoughts are not the reality; rather, they are just words, opinions, beliefs, stories, and assumptions—essentially mental noise. We can create distance from unhelpful thoughts simply by adding a tag line: "I am having the thought that . . ." For example, instead of thinking "I am unlovable" and simply accepting it to be the case, if we reframe as "I am having the thought that I am unlovable," we already disempower the thought. This strategy of stepping back and observing our minds at work in the present moment is what unites Buddhist thought, mindfulness-based self-help, Tolle's philosophy, and ACT interventions.

Mindfulness and other present-moment-oriented self-help practices, however, are not without their critics. The American academic Ronald E. Purser has produced some of the most stinging attacks on what he calls the "McMindfulness" industry. It is true that mindfulness has been highly commercialized (though so have many other self-help trends). The mindfulness industry is estimated to be worth $4 billion annually, and there are more than 100,000 books for sale on Amazon that feature some form of "mindfulness" in the title.[37] Andy Puddicombe's Headspace app alone has been valued at $250 million, and its annual revenues are estimated to be over $50 million.[38] Mindfulness-based programs are now offered in schools, on Wall Street, in Silicon Valley, and in government agencies in the United Kingdom and the United States. For many years, Google employed an in-house mindfulness guru, Chade-Meng Tan, whose official job title was "Jolly Good Fellow." Mindfulness talks have been popular in recent years at the World Economic Forum in Davos, where the world's most influential business leaders and politicians congregate. Perhaps most controversially, the US military has adapted an MBSR-inspired program to improve combatants' "operational effectiveness."[39]

And yet it seems wrong to blame mindfulness itself for the ways in which it has been instrumentalized and commercialized. First and foremost, it is a technique, and one that, just like any technology, can be put to good or less good use. Raging, as Purser does, against lunchtime mindfulness classes as one of the insidious ways in which an exploited workforce can be pacified misses the point. Seeking to enhance the resilience and well-being of employees is not a crime, and its alternative—letting people burn out and then firing them—is surely the less preferable option. Moreover, mindfulness is a private practice, one that cannot simply, let alone involuntarily, be imposed from the outside. The worst-case scenario is that corporate mindfulness workshops are ineffective. The best-case scenario is that they help people better to manage their stress. It is highly unlikely that mindfulness, in whatever form, has the power to turn us into "better-adjusted cogs in the capitalist machinery," as Purser alleges.[40]

Other critics, too, argue that mindfulness (and indeed self-help more generally) individualizes and medicalizes stress, rather than addressing its social causes. By privatizing our suffering, they say, Kabat-Zinn and others offer a depoliticized diagnosis that is victim-blaming.[41] Mindfulness, so the argument goes, is complicit in upholding the exploitative neoliberal status quo because it does not promote political change. But this is a puzzling charge. It is a bit like reproaching a cushion for being an unsuitable tool for killing birds. While political change can be a laudable aim, it is traditionally the task of social and political activists, as well as unions, politicians, and legislators. We cannot reasonably expect the teachers and practitioners of mindfulness to take on that task. Mindfulness of the kind promoted by Kabat-Zinn is above all a self-help tool, designed to reduce stress and enhance focus and happiness levels, as well as our resilience, health, and general well-being. There is nothing wrong with these aims.

It is true, though, that we should be wary of those who present Western-style mindfulness as an intrinsically revolutionary and socially transformative movement with the potential to change the world. To claim as much is indeed a case of overselling and dubious branding. Secular mindfulness is a self-help tool, nothing more and nothing less. It is misguided to assume that the ever more widespread practice of mindfulness will automatically translate into higher levels of social compassion. And neither should we assume that mindfulness can solve systemic political, social, and environmental problems. It clearly hasn't done so, not even at its peak. At the same time, we should also be careful not simply to dismiss out of hand all the acts of micro- and macro-kindnesses that may result from it.

The dynamic between personal development and political engagement is more complex than many make it sound. Each time we board a plane, after all, we are advised in the case of a loss of cabin pressure to put our own oxygen masks on first so that we can then help others more effectively. Similarly, the French-born Buddhist monk Matthieu Ricard argues that we have to transform ourselves before we will be able to transform the world. "To want to rush headlong into working for the good of others, without getting prepared first," he writes, "is like wanting to carry out a medical operation immediately in the street, without taking the required time to learn medicine and build hospitals." We all have to begin with putting our own house in order. "The first thing to do if you want to help others," writes Ricard, "is to develop your own compassion, altruistic love, and courage enough to be able to serve these others without betraying your original intention. Remedying our own egocentrism is a powerful way of serving those around us. We must therefore not underestimate the importance of personal transformation."[42] Improving ourselves and wishing to improve society are, then, not mutually exclusive aims. They can go hand in hand, as Ricard and Thich Nhat Hanh, among others, have demonstrated. In fact, in a growing number of activist circles, too, the boundaries between inner and outer transformation are being redrawn, with many younger activists practicing mindfulness or pursuing psychological or spiritual development in other ways.[43]

Moreover, mindfulness is decidedly not a new opiate for the masses. It is far too simplistic to believe that enhancing our resilience necessarily results in our becoming submissive servants in an exploitative neoliberal system. For the outcomes of mindfulness meditation are unpredictable. We may well become less stressed and more focused, but what we do with our enhanced energy is by no means predetermined. We may become more productive and add more value to the companies for which we work, or we may gain the courage to quit our jobs, or finally to confront difficult bosses and demand changes in our organization. We may drop out or else decide to take on a leadership role, to shape things in accordance with our own, perhaps more compassionate, vision. We may find it in ourselves to campaign for political reform, join a volunteer corps abroad, eat less red meat, or offer to buy food for our elderly neighbors during a lockdown.

And neither should we dismiss Western-style mindfulness as an act of cultural appropriation. Again, a more nuanced perspective is called for. Mindfulness is often taught by Asians who have come to the West to spread the message. Rather than insisting that it is a form of cultural appropriation, we should see the popularity of mindfulness in the Western world as signifying an openness to, and a willingness to learn from, other cultures. There is nothing wrong in acknowledging that other cultures might simply be much better than we are when it comes to living in the present moment. After all, they have valued and honed this skill for millennia. We, by contrast, are only just beginning to catch up. And this, surely, has to be a good thing.

Conclusion

WHAT WOULD HISTORIANS OF the future make of our current self-help landscape? No doubt they would remark on the sheer diversity of the books that populate the bestseller lists. Our self-help literature ranges from the rigorously evidence-based to the wildly esoteric, from performance enhancement–driven approaches to manuals telling us simply to do as we please. It includes authenticity-based advice alongside recipes for how to manipulate others effectively. There are works that seek to turn us into more ruthless competitors and others that show us how we can become more compassionate and altruistic. Some writers argue that we should be more like machines, while others seek to persuade us that we need to learn from nature. There are books that suggest techniques for controlling our minds, and others that advocate abandoning control and letting ourselves go. It is quite possible that those historians of the future will be confused or frustrated by such diversity. However that may be, this eclecticism is a telling feature in its own right.

It indicates that our problems are multifaceted, and that there are many different ways of framing and addressing them. As in the political realm, where populism is experiencing an upsurge precisely because it offers simple answers to ever more complex and urgent problems, some self-help also has a tendency to simplify. But we are complex beings, and so are our challenges. Simplistic solutions tend not to work for the multilayered nature of our sorrows. We must accept this complexity, and the fact that untangling our inner knots will take time and effort.

At the same time, beneath the apparent variety of our self-help approaches and models, there are some shared fundamental aims. While the means may differ, the aspirations are often very similar. There is, for instance, a widely shared desire for connectedness and meaning. There is a need for control (of our cognitions and emotions, but also of other people). There is an increasingly pronounced tendency to advocate more sustainable as well as more minimalist ways of living, and a call for us to reconnect with nature. A significant number of self-help books today address anxieties related to the rapidly growing digitization of our daily lives, suggesting ways in which we can relearn to focus our attention on the present moment and shore up our defenses against distraction. Much of the current self-literature seeks to make us more resilient and better able to deal with fast-paced external changes and economic uncertainty.

Our self-help culture differs from that of the ancients in a number of ways. Nowadays, we tend to believe that we should be happy most of the time. Many of us expect a life that is largely free of calamities. An increasing number of us feel entitled to celebrity and wealth. Most of us hope for lives that are better than those of our parents. Yet in the past, it was more commonly (and realistically) assumed that life is primarily suffering and that bad things are bound to happen. The Buddhists and the Stoics subscribed to a much less cheerful conception of human existence than we in the West do today. The early Christians believed that humanity was not just profoundly flawed but doomed, and that we require salvation.

We differ from our self-improving ancestors in many other ways as well. In the self-improvement literature of the past, the emphasis was placed squarely on the virtues. Yet reflections on goodness have all but disappeared from modern self-help. Our focus tends to be on personality rather than character, and on our effectiveness in achieving successful careers. We also want instant results, without having to invest too much effort. Accordingly, many of our self-help writers promise dramatic and immediate transformations. The ancients, by contrast, knew that self-improvement is a lifelong project, one that is never completed and that requires hard work. They cherished a slow and incremental approach to the improvement of the self. Our ancestors' emphasis was on gentle and gradual reform, while we tend to expect instant transformation.

No less importantly, most of our self-help literature today tends to rest on the assumption that we are competitive by nature. We are often portrayed as autonomous agents in a hostile environment. This is in striking contrast to earlier conceptions of human beings as relational, interdependent, and social, the individual being part of a wider community, to which we were bound for better or worse. In Confucian China, self-improvement was considered an essential aspect of improving society more generally. The self-improving individual was thought to have a ripple effect, leading by example and inspiring others to follow suit.

The eighteenth-century German philosopher Immanuel Kant, too, believed that we have a social duty to improve ourselves. Kant is most famous for his categorical imperative, which states that we should only ever do what we would be happy for all others to do, too. If we would not wish others to behave as we do, if we would not wish to see our actions universalized, we should refrain from them. We might, for example, think that there is no harm at all in our disregarding a sign telling us not to walk on a lawn or not to feed the ducks. But, applying Kant's categorical imperative, we would need to ask ourselves whether we would be happy for everyone to do the same, with the inevitable result being the destruction of the lawn and some very unhealthy ducks.

Kant was also strongly of the view that the duty of care we show for others must extend to ourselves. In the *Groundwork of the Metaphysics of Morals* (1785), he argues that we have a responsibility to improve ourselves to the greatest extent possible. He asks us to consider the example of someone who "finds in himself a talent which could, by means of some cultivation, make him in many respects a useful man." If that person decides not to develop that talent, those natural capacities, Kant argues, he is neglecting a fundamental duty.[1] It follows that we have a duty to self-improve. For were we *not* to develop our natural talents, our personal choice could not become universal law. We could not thrive as a human being.[2] Confucius, by contrast, considers self-improvement essential for the development of society at large. He thinks of self-improvement as a fundamentally pro-social act.

The Victorian Samuel Smiles, who founded modern self-help, also maintains that there is a crucial link between individual and national improvement, although his argument is based on a conception of "energetic individualism" rather than a relational view of the self.[3] This difference is crucial. National progress, Smiles writes, "is the sum of individual industry, energy, and uprightness, as national decay is of individual idleness, selfishness, and vice. . . . It follows that the highest patriotism and philanthropy consist, not so much in altering laws and modifying institutions, as in helping and stimulating men to elevate and improve themselves by their own free and independent individual action."[4] Smiles emphasizes the wider social importance of self-improvement, and calls for the government to support us in this quest. However, his statement also foreshadows the British prime minister Margaret Thatcher's famous claim that there is no such thing as society. We alone are responsible for our fate (economic and otherwise), Smiles argues, and it is in our power to influence it. There is no acknowledgment of any social or psychological obstacles to our efforts.

Here and elsewhere, the potential political implications of self-help theories become evident. There are self-help books that carry their politics on their sleeves, like Smiles's. Jordan B. Peterson's *12 Rules for Life: An Antidote to Chaos* (2018) falls into the same category. An unabashed contribution to the culture wars, Peterson's guide aims to make young white men who have a problem with equality legislation feel better about themselves. Yet the politics of the majority of self-help texts are not so plainly stated.

Good self-help has to navigate two persistent dangers: our tendency either to overestimate or to underestimate our capacity to self-improve. The former can lead to a constantly belabored and self-blaming self, with unrealistic expectations that are detached from our psychological and socioeconomic realities.[5] Self-help guides that crudely overvalue our willpower, agency, and capacity for change can thus turn into toxic fairy tales that warp our sense of the possible.

At a wider social level, overestimating our capacity to change can translate into callous politics. If we believe that we all have the same high potential to self-improve, we are likely to condemn those who do not manage to turn their lives around. We might, for instance, blame the obese for failing to eat more healthily, blame those in abusive relationships for not leaving them, blame the physically and mentally ill for their conditions, and the poor for not making the requisite effort to become wealthy. If we believe our own actions are all that matter in our forward progress, we might dismiss out of hand such factors as genetic predisposition, social milieu, and trauma that render the task so much harder for some of us.

Yet underestimating our potential to improve ourselves can have equally damaging consequences. We might privilege natural ability and talent over potential. When only what is already fully developed matters, we tend to hide our failings, exaggerate our achievements, and deny gaps in our knowledge. We will dramatically underestimate the importance of learning and perseverance, of slow and incremental improvement. We might feel helpless and depressed because we believe that our abilities are fixed and that our efforts can make no difference.[6]

Beyond the individual, if we do not believe in our essential improvability as a society, we are likely to stop investing in *Bildung* and the development of talent. We will underestimate the importance of education, and we may not give support where it could have a decisive impact. We might refuse to invest in prison reform and rehabilitation programs; those struggling with addictions will be left to suffer without intervention. We might conclude that there is no point in wasting limited healthcare budgets on the obese. A society that underestimates our fundamental capacity to improve would be a profoundly dystopian one.

It is not always the case that a particular culture will either over- or underestimate our capacity to self-improve. The United States is a striking case in point. It is undoubtedly the country in which the idea of self-improvement is most fully embedded within its national culture. The belief in a fundamental entitlement to happiness, in the possibility of dramatic self-reinvention, and the myth of the self-made millionaire remain powerful salvation-promising stories. At the same time, however, the United States is one of the few Western nations that still has the death penalty. And capital punishment is of course grounded in the idea that the nature of an individual can be completely determined by a particular act, and that no genuine self-improvement is possible.

If there is a lesson in all this, it is that self-improvement matters enormously, not just at the level of the individual life but at that of society as a whole. Inner and outer transformation go hand in hand, and we will not be able to tackle our most urgent crises—climate change, social inequality, psychological alienation, and the erosion of our democracies chief among them—if we do not also change the very ways we think about ourselves and others. As the long history of self-improvement demonstrates, changing ourselves can take many forms, some more suited to achieving a fair and just society than others. Today's self-help industry is one of those forms. But it, too, is multifarious. Knowingly or unknowingly, it draws on a long and vibrant tradition, and articulates in new ways the ten abiding themes of the ancient art of self-improvement.

Notes

Preface

1. Jonathan Rowson, *The Moves That Matter: A Chess Grandmaster on the Game of Life* (London: Bloomsbury, 2019), 37.

Introduction

1. Grand View Research, "Personal Development Market Size, Share and Trends Analysis Report by Instrument (Books, e-Platforms, Personal Coaching/Training, Workshops), by Focus Area, by Region, and Segment Forecasts, 2020–2027," July 2020, www.grandviewresearch.com/industry-analysis/personal-development-market. See also Steve Salerno, *SHAM: How the Self-Help Movement Made America Helpless* (New York: Three Rivers Press, 2005), 8.
2. Seneca, *Letters from a Stoic: Epistulae Morales ad Lucilium*, trans. Robin Campbell (London: Penguin, 2004), 64.
3. See Adam Alter, *Irresistible: The Rise of Addictive Technology and the Business of Keeping Us Hooked* (New York: Penguin, 2017); and Cal Newport, *Digital Minimalism: On Living Better with Less Technology* (London: Penguin Business, 2019).
4. See, e.g., Stephen R. Covey, *The 7 Habits of Highly Effective People: Powerful Lessons in Personal Change* (New York: Free Press, 2004), 288.
5. Micki McGee, *Self-Help, Inc.: Makeover Culture in American Life* (New York: Oxford University Press, 2005), 51.
6. See George Lakoff and Mark Johnson, *Metaphors We Live By* (Chicago: University of Chicago Press, 2003).
7. Quoted in Massimo Pigliucci, *How to Be a Stoic: Ancient Wisdom for Modern Living* (London: Rider, 2017), 153.

8. Jordan B. Peterson, *12 Rules for Life: An Antidote to Chaos*, foreword by Norman Doidge (London: Allen Lane, 2018), 8.

9. Abraham Maslow, "A Theory of Human Motivation," *Psychological Review* 50 (1943): 370–96.

10. Carl Rogers writes about our "actualizing tendency," which he understands as "the inherent tendency of the organism to develop all its capacities in ways which serve to maintain or enhance the organism." See Carl Rogers, "A Theory of Therapy, Personality, and Interpersonal Relationships as Developed in the Client Centered Framework," in *Psychology: A Study of a Science*, vol. 3: *Formulations of the Person and the Social Context*, ed. S. Koch (New York: McGraw-Hill, 1959), 196.

11. For a comparative analysis of these and other basic human needs theories, see Thane S. Pittman and Kate R. Zeigler, "Basic Human Needs," in *Social Psychology: Handbook of Basic Principles*, ed. A. W. Kruglanski and E. T. Higgins (New York: Guilford Press, 2007), 473–89.

12. Robert Kegan, *The Evolving Self: Problem and Process in Human Development* (Cambridge, MA: Harvard University Press, 1982), 107.

13. Thanks to Jens Klusemann for discussing these needs with me.

14. For a more detailed exploration of the term *Bildung* and its relationship to self-improvement, see Anja Röcke, *Soziologie der Selbstoptimierung* (Berlin: Suhrkamp, 2021), 85–91.

15. Carol S. Dweck, *Mindset: Changing the Way You Think to Fulfil Your Potential* (London: Robinson, 2017).

Chapter One. Know Thyself

1. Plato, "Apology," in *Complete Works*, trans. G. M. A. Grube et al. (Indianapolis: Hackett, 1997), 21.

2. Galen, *On Temperaments. On Non-Uniform Distemperment. The Soul's Traits Depend on Bodily Temperament*, ed. and trans. Ian Johnston (Cambridge, MA: Harvard University Press, 2020); and Merve Emre, *The Personality Brokers: The Strange History of Myers-Briggs and the Birth of Personality Testing* (London: Penguin, 2018).

3. C. G. Jung, *Psychological Types*, trans. R. F. C. Hull and H. G. Baynes (London: Routledge, 2017).

4. See Richard E. Nisbett, *The Geography of Thought: How Asians and Westerners Think Differently—and Why* (Boston: Nicholas Brealey, 2003).

5. See Julian Baggini, *How the World Thinks: A Global History of Philosophy* (London: Granta, 2018).

6. Ibid., 187.

7. See R. J. Hankinson, *The Cambridge Companion to Galen* (Cambridge: Cambridge University Press, 2008).

8. For more on melancholia, see, e.g., Jennifer Radden, ed., *The Nature of Melancholy: From Aristotle to Kristeva* (Oxford: Oxford University Press,

2000); and Matthew Bell, *Melancholia: The Western Malady* (Cambridge: Cambridge University Press, 2014).

9. Marsilio Ficino, *Three Books on Life: A Critical Edition and Translation with Introduction and Notes*, ed. Carol V. Kaske and John R. Clark (Tempe, AZ: Medieval & Renaissance Texts & Studies, 1989), 371.

10. This book has been updated, sometimes significantly, annually since 1975. For the most recent edition, see Richard N. Bolles and Katherine Brooks, *What Color Is Your Parachute 2021: A Practical Manual for Job-Hunters and Career-Changers* (Berkeley, CA: Ten Speed Press, 2020).

11. Norman Doidge, *The Brain That Changes Itself: Stories of Personal Triumph from the Frontiers of Brain Science* (London: Penguin, 2008), 243.

12. Sigmund Freud, "Mourning and Melancholia," in *The Standard Edition of the Complete Psychological Works of Sigmund Freud*, ed. and trans. James Strachey (London: Vintage, 2001), 14:244.

13. Ibid., 246.

14. Louise L. Hay, *You Can Heal Your Life* (London: Hay House, 2006), 3.

15. Steve Peters, *The Chimp Paradox: The Mind Management Programme for Confidence, Success and Happiness* (London: Vermilion, 2012).

16. Daniel Goleman, *Emotional Intelligence: Why It Can Matter More Than IQ* (London: Bloomsbury, 1996), 36.

17. Ibid., xii.

18. Ibid., 43.

19. C. G. Jung, *Psychological Types*, trans. R. F. C. Hull and H. G. Baynes (London: Routledge, 2017), 407.

20. Joseph Campbell, with Bill Moyers, *The Power of Myth*, ed. Sue Flowers (New York: Broadway Books, 2001), 124.

21. Ibid., 148.

22. Ibid., xv.

23. Ibid., 123.

24. Jung, *Psychological Types*, 349.

25. Ibid., 309.

26. Ibid., 337.

27. Ibid., 356.

28. Ibid., 310.

29. Insights Discoveries website, www.insights.com (accessed 13 February 2020).

30. Richard Wiseman, *59 Seconds: Think a Little, Change a Lot* (London: Pan Books, 2015), 303–4.

31. Ibid., 302.

32. Ibid., 305.

33. See, e.g., Gregory J. Boyle, "Critique of Five-Factor Model (FFM)," in *The Sage Handbook of Personality Theory and Assessment*, vol. 1, ed. Gregory J. Boyle, Gerald Matthews, and Donald H. Saklofske (Los Angeles: Sage, 2008), 295–312.

34. See Dan P. McAdams, "What Do We Know When We Know a Person?" *Journal of Personality* 63, no. 3 (1995): 365–96.
35. It is also worth mentioning that personality testing has become a $2 billion industry. See Emre, *The Personality Brokers*.
36. Jens Klusemann's test is a welcome exception in this regard. See Jens Klusemann and Christopher Niepel, "Entwicklung und erste Überprüfung des dialog Persönlichkeitsinventars (dpi) für den Einsatz im Coaching," *Zeitschrift für Arbeits- und Organisationspsychologie* 61, no. 1 (2017): 31–44.
37. See Mitchell S. Green, *Know Thyself: The Value and Limits of Self-Knowledge* (New York: Routledge, 2018), 135.

Chapter Two. Control Your Mind

1. For general information on Stoicism, see, e.g., John Sellars, *Stoicism* (London: Routledge, 2006); Suzanne Bobzien, *Determinism and Freedom in Stoic Philosophy* (Oxford: Oxford University Press, 2002); and Alegra Keimpe et al., eds., *Cambridge History of Hellenistic Philosophy* (Cambridge: Cambridge University Press, 1999).
2. Seneca, *Letters from a Stoic: Epistulae Morales ad Lucilium*, trans. Robin Campbell (London: Penguin, 2004), 15.
3. Ibid., 230.
4. Epictetus, *Of Human Freedom*, trans. Robert Dobbin (London: Penguin, 2010), 11.
5. Ibid., 81.
6. Seneca, *Letters*, 69.
7. Epictetus, *Of Human Freedom*, 14.
8. Ibid., 52.
9. Ibid., 13.
10. Ibid.
11. Marcus Aurelius, *Meditations*, trans. Martin Hammond (London: Penguin, 2006), 48.
12. Diskin Clay, "Introduction" to Marcus Aurelius, *Meditations*, trans. Martin Hammond (London: Penguin, 2006), xxxiii.
13. Marcus Aurelius, *Meditations*, 47–48.
14. Ibid., 17, 32.
15. Ibid., 113.
16. Ibid., 31.
17. Ibid., 57.
18. Ibid., 10.
19. Quoted in Massimo Pigliucci, *How to Be a Stoic: Ancient Wisdom for Modern Living* (London: Rider, 2017), 153.

20. Phineas Parkhurst Quimby, *The Quimby Manuscripts: Containing Messages of New Thought, Mesmerism, and Spiritual Healing from the Author*, ed. Horatio W. Dresser (n.p.: Pantianos Classics, 1921), 73.

21. Mary Baker Eddy, *Science and Health with Key to the Scriptures* (Boston: Writings of Mary Baker Eddy, 2000), viii.

22. Ibid., 109.

23. Ibid., 40.

24. See, e.g., Emma Kate Sutton, "Interpreting 'Mind-Cure': William James and the 'Chief Task . . . of the Science of Human Nature,' " *Journal of the History of Behavioural Sciences* 48, no. 2 (Spring 2012): 115–33.

25. William James, *The Varieties of Religious Experience* (Cambridge, MA: Harvard University Press, 1985), 92–93.

26. William Walker Atkinson made similar claims in *Thought Vibration or the Law of Attraction in the Thought World* (Chicago: The Library Shelf, 1906).

27. Napoleon Hill, *Think and Grow Rich! The Original Version, Restored and Revised* (Anderson, SC: Mindpower Press, 2007), 9.

28. Ibid., 21.

29. Rhonda Byrne, *The Secret,* 10th anniv. ed. (New York: Simon & Schuster, 2016), xv, 7, 9.

30. Ibid., 11.

31. Ibid., 15.

32. Ibid., 28.

33. Ibid., 43.

34. Ibid., 41.

35. See David D. Burns, *Feeling Good: The New Mood Therapy* (New York: Harper, 1999), xxiii–xxix.

36. Albert Ellis, *Reason and Emotion in Psychotherapy* (New York: Citadel Press, 1962); and Aaron T. Beck, *Cognitive Therapy and the Emotional Disorders* (New York: Meridian, 1979).

37. Burns, *Feeling* Good, xxx.

38. Ibid., 61.

39. Ibid., 57.

40. Martin Seligman and Mihaly Csikszentmihalyi, "Positive Psychology: An Introduction," *American Psychologist* 55, no. 1 (2000): 5–14. See also Mihaly Csikszentmihalyi, *Flow: The Classic Work on How to Achieve Happiness,* rev. and updated ed. (London: Ryder, 2002).

41. Martin Seligman, *Learned Optimism: How to Change Your Mind and Your Life* (London: Nicholas Brealey Publishing, 2006), 14, 167–84.

42. For the latter assumption, see, e.g., Lewina O. Lee et al., "Optimism Is Associated with Exceptional Longevity in 2 Epidemiologic Cohorts of Men and Women," *PNAS* 116, no. 37 (2019): 18357–62.

43. See, e.g., Russ Harris, *The Happiness Trap. Based on ACT: A Revolutionary Mindfulness-Based Programme for Overcoming Stress, Anxiety, and Depression* (London: Robinson, 2008), 28.

44. Jonathan Rowson, *The Moves That Matter: A Chess Grandmaster on the Game of Life* (London: Bloomsbury, 2019), 36.

Chapter Three. Let It Go

1. Numerous versions of this popular self-help parable are in circulation on the web. Everyone tells it slightly differently. This version, which I slightly modified, can be found online at www.thechurning.net/there-are-no-opportunities-or-threats-the-parable-of-the-taoist-farmer, 1 September 2020.

2. For a discussion of the philosophical, cosmological, spiritual, and mystic dimensions of the *Tao te ching*, see Chad Hansen, "Daoism," *Stanford Encyclopedia of Philosophy*, https://plato.stanford.edu/entries/daoism, 28 June 2007.

3. See Irene Bloom, "Metaphysics and Government in the Laozi," in *Sources of Chinese Tradition*, vol. 1: *From Earliest Times to 1600*, ed. Wm. Theodore de Bary and Irene Bloom, 2nd ed. (New York: Columbia University Press, 1999), 78.

4. See, e.g., D. C. Lau, "The Problem of Authorship," in Lao-tzu, *Tao te ching*, trans. D. C. Lau (New York: Alfred A. Knopf, 2017), 89–103 [all subsequent references are to this edition]; and Alan Chan, "Laozi," *Stanford Encyclopedia of Philosophy*, https://plato.stanford.edu/entries/laozi, 21 September 2018.

5. See Hansen, "Daoism."

6. For an excellent summary and analysis of Lao-tzu scholarship, see Chan, "Laozi." Chan also provides a good overview of questions of provenance, textual variants, and different traditions of commentaries.

7. See Chan, "Laozi."

8. See Sarah Allan, "Introduction" to Lao-tzu, *Tao te ching*, xiii.

9. See Chan, "Laozi."

10. Lao-tzu, *Tao te ching*, 27. Further references in the text to this work cite the appropriate chapter number.

11. See Chan, "Laozi."

12. See Hansen, "Daoism."

13. The traditional dates of the Buddha's life are given as approximately 560–480 BCE, but many scholars now assume that he must have been born later and died around 405 BCE. See Mark Siderits, "The Buddha," *Stanford Encyclopedia of Philosophy*, https://plato.stanford.edu/entries/buddha, 14 February 2019.

14. Damien Keown, *Buddhism: A Very Short Introduction* (Oxford: Oxford University Press, 2013), 53.

15. *The Dhammapada*, trans. Juan Mascaró (London: Penguin Classics, 2015), 42.

16. Ibid.

17. Saint Augustine, *Confessions*, trans. Henry Chadwick (Oxford: Oxford University Press, 2008), 146.

18. Ibid., 147.

19. Ibid., 146.

20. Ibid., 141.

21. Ibid., 151.

22. Deepak Chopra, *The Seven Spiritual Laws of Success: A Practical Guide to the Fulfillment of Your Dreams* (New Delhi: Excel Books, 2000), 81.

23. See, e.g., Russ Harris, *The Happiness Trap* (London: Robinson, 2008).

24. Viktor E. Frankl, *Man's Search for Meaning: The Classic Tribute to Hope from the Holocaust* (London: Rider, 2004), 115.

25. Harris, *The Happiness Trap*, 5.

26. See also Steven C. Hayes, *A Liberated Mind: The Essential Guide to ACT* (London: Vermilion, 2019).

27. Robert Kegan, *The Evolving Self: Problem and Process in Human Development* (Cambridge, MA: Harvard University Press, 1982), 31, 50.

28. Jean-Jacques Rousseau, *Of the Social Contract*, in *Of the Social Contract and Other Political Writings*, trans. Quintin Hoare (London: Penguin, 2012), 10.

29. See Christopher Bertram, "Jean-Jacques Rousseau," *Stanford Encyclopedia of Philosophy*, https://plato.stanford.edu/entries/rousseau, 26 May 2017.

30. Abraham Maslow, "A Theory of Human Motivation," *Psychological Review* 50 (1943): 370–96.

31. Wilhelm Reich, *The Mass Psychology of Fascism*, trans. Vincent R. Carfango (London: Souvenir Press, 1972).

32. Sigmund Freud, "'Civilized' Sexual Morality and Modern Nervous Illness" (1908), in *The Standard Edition of the Complete Psychological Works of Sigmund Freud*, ed. and trans. James Strachey (London: Vintage, 2001), 9:187.

33. Sigmund Freud, "Civilization and Its Discontent" (1930), in *The Standard Edition of the Complete Psychological Works of Sigmund Freud* 21:115.

34. John C. Parkin, *F**k It: The Ultimate Spiritual Way* (Carlsbad, CA: Hay House, 2014), 1.

35. Ibid., 9.

36. Ibid., 18–19.

37. Quoted from Spencer Johnson, *Who Moved My Cheese? An Amazing Way to Deal with Change in Your Work and in Your Life* (London: Vermilion, 1998), frontmatter review comment.

38. Ibid., 60.

39. Ibid., 46.

Chapter Four. Be Good

1. For a detailed philosophical, psychological, and biological discussion of theories of altruism, see Matthieu Ricard, *Altruism: The Science and Psychology of Kindness* (London: Atlantic, 2015).

2. See, e.g., ibid.; E. W. Dunn, L. Aknin, and M. I. Norton, "Spending Money on Others Promotes Happiness," *Science* 319 (2008): 1687–88; and Paul Dolan, *Happy Ever After: Escaping the Myth of the Perfect Life* (London: Allen Lane, 2019).

3. See Daniel K. Gardner, *Confucianism: A Very Short Introduction* (Oxford: Oxford University Press, 2014), 1. General information about Confucius, his times, and his philosophy in this chapter is based on Gardner's lucid study, as well as on Wm. Theodore de Bary and Irene Bloom, eds., *Sources of Chinese Tradition*, vol. 1: *From Earliest Times to 1600*, 2nd ed. (New York: Columbia University Press, 1999). See also Benjamin I. Schwartz, *The World of Thought in Ancient China* (Cambridge, MA: Harvard University Press, 1985); Bryan W. Van Norden, ed., *Confucius and the Analects: New Essays* (Oxford: Oxford University Press, 2002); and Bryan W. Van Norden, *Introduction to Classical Chinese Philosophy* (Indianapolis: Hackett, 2011).

4. Confucius, *The Analects*, trans. Annping Chin (London: Penguin, 2014), 109.

5. See Philip J. Ivanhoe, *Confucian Moral Self-Cultivation* (Indianapolis: Hackett, 2000).

6. See Gardner, *Confucianism*, 22–24.

7. Confucius, *The Analects*, 113.

8. See Gardner, *Confucianism*, 28.

9. See Richard Wiseman, *59 Seconds: Think a Little, Change a Lot* (London: Pan Books, 2015), 32.

10. Mencius, "Selections from the *Mencius*," in de Bary and Bloom (eds.), *Sources of Chinese Tradition* 1:130.

11. Ibid., 129.

12. Ibid., 147.

13. Xunzi, "Selections from the Xunzi," in de Bary and Bloom (eds.), *Sources of Chinese Tradition* 1:180.

14. Ibid., 166.

15. See Gardner, *Confucianism*, 72.

16. For more on Buddhist ethics, see, e.g., Peter Harvey, *An Introduction to Buddhist Ethics: Foundations, Values, and Issues* (Cambridge: Cambridge University Press, 2000).

17. Damien Keown, *Buddhism: A Very Short Introduction* (Oxford: Oxford University Press, 2013), 8.

18. His Holiness the Dalai Lama and Howard C. Cutler, *The Art of Happiness: A Handbook for Living* (London: Hodder & Stoughton, 2009).

19. The label Buddhism does of course encompass a wide variety of traditions and beliefs, with Theravada ("doctrine of the elders") and Mahayana (the "Great Vehicle") constituting the two main schools. The compassion of the bodhisattva, who even after his enlightenment devoted himself to serving others, features more centrally in the Mahayana tradition that dominates Central and East Asian Buddhism.

20. Quoted in Ricard, *Altruism*, 6.

21. Ibid., 691.

22. Quoted in ibid., 6.

23. Damien Keown, *Buddhist Ethics: A Very Short Introduction* (Oxford: Oxford University Press, 2005), 7.

24. See ibid., 23.

25. Aristotle, *The Nicomachean Ethics*, trans. David Ross (Oxford: Oxford World Classics, 2009).

26. See Christopher Shields, "Aristotle," *Stanford Encyclopedia of Philosophy*, https://plato.stanford.edu/entries/aristotle, 25 September 2008, substantively revised 25 August 2020.

27. See Edith Hall, *Aristotle's Way: How Ancient Wisdom Can Change Your Life* (London: Bodley Head, 2018), 7.

28. See ibid.

29. Aristotle, *The Nicomachean Ethics*, 12.

30. Quoted in Hall, *Aristotle's Way*, 7.

31. See Lesley Brown, "Introduction" to Aristotle, *The Nicomachean Ethics*, xiii.

32. Richard Kraut, "Aristotle's Ethics," *Stanford Encyclopedia of Philosophy*, https://plato.stanford.edu/entries/aristotle-ethics, 1 May 2001, substantively revised 15 June 2018.

33. See ibid.

34. See Hall, *Aristotle's Way*, 116.

35. Quoted from Daniel Goleman, *Emotional Intelligence: Why It Can Matter More Than IQ* (London: Bloomsbury, 1996), ix.

36. See John Lydon, *Anger Is an Energy: My Life Uncensored* (London: Simon & Schuster, 2014).

37. See Kraut, "Aristotle's Ethics."

38. See Brown, "Introduction," xv.

39. Hall, *Aristotle's Way*, 26.

40. Ibid., 41.

41. *The New Testament: The Authorized or King James Version* (New York: Everyman's Library, 1998), 115.

42. Ibid., 39.

43. Ibid., 7–8.

44. Stephen R. Covey, *The 7 Habits of Highly Effective People: Powerful Lessons in Personal Change* (New York: Free Press, 2004).

45. Quoted in Ichiro Kishimi and Fumitake Koga, *The Courage to Be Disliked: How to Free Yourself, Change Your Life, and Achieve Real Happiness* (London: Allen & Unwin, 2017), 21.

46. See ibid., 163.

47. Ibid., 165, 169.

48. Viktor E. Frankl, *Man's Search for Meaning: The Classic Tribute to Hope from the Holocaust* (London: Rider, 2004), 85.

49. Ibid., 104.

50. Ibid., 115.

51. Martin Seligman, *Learned Optimism: How to Change Your Mind and Your Life* (Boston: Nicholas Brealey, 2006), 282.

52. Ibid., 286.

53. Ibid., 288.

54. Ibid., 287.

55. See, e.g., Jeremy Carrette and Richard King, *Selling Spirituality: The Silent Takeover of Religion* (London: Routledge, 2005); Byung-Chul Han, *Psycho-Politics: Neoliberalism and New Technologies of Power* (London: Verso, 2017); and Ronald E. Purser, *McMindfulness: How Mindfulness Became the New Capitalist Spirituality* (London: Repeater, 2019).

56. See, e.g., Lene Rachel Andersen and Tomas Björkman, *The Nordic Secret: A European Story of Beauty and Freedom* (Stockholm: Fri tanke, 2017); Tomas Björkman, *The World We Create: From God to Market* (London: Perspectiva Press, 2019); Jonathan Rowson, *The Moves that Matter: A Chess Grandmaster on the Game of Life* (London: Bloomsbury, 2019); and Zachary Stein, *Education in A Time Between Worlds: Essays on the Future of Schools, Society, and Technology* (San Francisco: Bright Alliance, 2019).

57. See, e.g., the research collective Perspectiva, https://systems-souls-society. com; the media platform Rebel Wisdom, https://rebelwisdom.co.uk; and the Emerge project, www.whatisemerging.com (all accessed 18 December 2020).

58. Deepak Chopra, *The Seven Spiritual Laws of Success: A Practical Guide to the Fulfillment of Your Dreams* (New Delhi: Excel Books, 2000), 30–31.

59. See, e.g., Greta Thunberg, *No One Is Too Small to Make a Difference* (London: Penguin, 2019); and Anonymous, *This Is Not A Drill: An Extinction Rebellion Handbook* (London: Penguin, 2019).

60. Marian Wright Edelman, *Lanterns: A Memoir of Mentors* (Boston: Beacon Press, 1999), 7.

Chapter Five. Be Humble

1. See David Robson, "Is This the Secret of Smart Leadership?" BBC, www.bbc.com/worklife/article/20200528-is-this-the-secret-of-smart-leadership, 31 May 2020.

2. See Bradley P. Owens et al., "Expressed Humility in Organizations: Implications for Performance, Teams, and Leadership," *Organization Science*

24, no. 5 (2013): 1517–38; and Elizabeth J. Krumrei-Mancuso et al., "Links between Intellectual Humility and Acquiring Knowledge," *Journal of Positive Psychology* 15, no. 2 (2019): 155–70.

3. Arménio Rego et al., "How Leader Humility Helps Teams to Be Humbler, Psychologically Stronger, and More Effective: A Moderated Mediation Model," *Leadership Quarterly* 28, no. 5 (2017): 639–58; Amy Y. Ou et al., "Do Humble CEOs Matter? An Examination of CEO Humility and Firm Outcomes," *Journal of Management* 20, no. 10 (2020): 1–27; and Irina Cojuharenco and Natalia Karelaia, "When Leaders Ask Questions: Can Humility Premiums Buffer the Effects of Competence Penalties?" *Organizational Behavior and Human Decision Processes* 156 (2020): 113–34.

4. See Jean M. Twenge and W. Keith Campbell, *The Narcissism Epidemic: Living in the Age of Entitlement* (New York: Atria, 2013).

5. Quoted in Matthieu Ricard, *Altruism: The Science and Psychology of Kindness* (London: Atlantic, 2015), 290.

6. Morris Rosenberg, *Society and the Adolescent Self-Image* (Princeton, NJ: Princeton University Press, 1965).

7. On the self-esteem movement and its wider impact, see Will Storr, *Selfie: How We Became So Self-Obsessed and What It Is Doing to Us* (London: Picador, 2017).

8. Quoted in Ricard, *Altruism*, 293–94.

9. See Linda Woodhead, *Christianity: A Very Short Introduction*, 2nd ed. (Oxford: Oxford University Press, 2014).

10. See Henry Chadwick, "Introduction" to Saint Augustine, *Confessions*, trans. Henry Chadwick (Oxford: Oxford University Press, 2008), xxiv.

11. See Max von Habsburg, "Introduction" to Thomas à Kempis, *The Imitation of Christ*, trans. Robert Jefery (London: Penguin, 2013), xvii–xviii.

12. Kempis, *The Imitation of Christ*, 172.

13. Ibid., 22.

14. Ibid., 136–37.

15. Ibid., 136.

16. Ibid., 33.

17. Ibid., 43.

18. Ibid., 7.

19. Ibid., 16.

20. Ibid., 25.

21. Eckhart Tolle, *The Power of Now: A Guide to Spiritual Enlightenment* (London: Hodder & Stoughton, 1999).

22. Gloria Steinem, *Revolution from Within: A Book of Self-Esteem* (London: Corgi, 1993), 356.

23. Clarissa Pinkola Estés, *Women Who Run with the Wolves: Contacting the Power of the Wild Woman* (London: Rider, 2008), 4.

24. Elli H. Radinger, *The Wisdom of Wolves: How Wolves Can Teach Us to Be More Human*, trans. Shaun Whiteside (London: Michael Joseph, 2019), 18.

25. Ibid., 68.
26. Ibid., 120.
27. Ibid., 220.
28. Stéphane Garnier, *How to Live Like Your Cat* (London: Fourth Estate, 2017), 29.
29. See Jennifer McCartney, *The Little Book of Sloth Philosophy: How to Live Your Best Sloth Life* (London: HarperCollins, 2018), 95.
30. They include Rob Dircks, *Unleash the Sloth! 75 Ways to Reach Your Maximum Potential by Doing Less* (2012); McCartney, *The Little Book of Sloth Philosophy*; and Sarah Jackson, *A Sloth's Guide to Taking It Easy: Be More Sloth with These Fail-Safe Tips for Serious Chilling* (2018). Other examples are Talia Levy and Jax Berman's *Sloth Wisdom* (2015) and Ton Mak's *A Sloth's Guide to Mindfulness* (2018). Although about the trait, not the animal, Wendy Wasserstein's self-help parody *Sloth: The Seven Deadly Sins* (2007) is also of interest in this context.
31. See McCartney, *Little Book of Sloth Philosophy*.
32. Ibid., 2.
33. Charles Foster, *Being a Beast: An Intimate and Radical Look at Nature* (London: Profile, 2016), 1.
34. Annie Davidson, *How to Be More Tree: Essential Life Lessons for Perennial Happiness* (London: Lom Art, 2019), 5.
35. Michael Marder, *Plant-Thinking: A Philosophy of Vegetal Life* (New York: Columbia University Press, 2013), 90.
36. Mark O'Connell, *To Be a Machine: Adventures among Cyborgs, Utopians, Hackers, and the Futurists Solving the Modest Problem of Death* (London: Granta, 2017), 134.
37. Ibid., 6.
38. Ibid., 11.
39. Ibid., 73.
40. Ibid.
41. Ibid., 139, 141, 150.
42. Ibid., 33.
43. See John G. Daugman, "Brain Metaphor and Brain Theory," in W. Bechtel et al., *Philosophy and the Neurosciences* (Oxford: Blackwell, 2001), 23–36.
44. O'Connell, *To Be a Machine*, 64.
45. Ibid., 142.
46. Ibid., 135.
47. Stefanie Marsh and Serge Faguet, "I, Robot: The Silicon Valley CEO Who Thinks Biohacking and Robotics Will Let Him Live Forever," *Guardian Weekend*, 22 September 2018, 17.
48. Ibid., 18.
49. See Greta Wagner, *Selbstoptimierung: Praxis und Kritik von Neuroenhancement* (Frankfurt am Main: Campus, 2017).

50. This parable circulates in different versions on the Internet (it is also sometimes called "The Mexican Fisherman and the Harvard MBA"). It often features in investment banking and entrepreneurial self-help manuals, with a slightly different ending. I have retold it here in my own words.

Chapter Six. Simplify

1. See, e.g., podcasts with Jordan Hall, Daniel Schmachtenberger, John Vervaeke, and Jamie Wheal at https://rebelwisdom.co.uk (accessed 21 December 2020).

2. See, e.g., Shunmyō Masuno, *Zen: The Art of Simple Living* (New York: Michael Joseph, 2019).

3. Marsilio Ficino, *Three Books on Life. A Critical Edition and Translation with Introduction and Notes*, ed. Carol V. Kaske and John R. Clark (Tempe, AZ: Medieval & Renaissance Texts & Studies, 1989), 135.

4. Jean-Jacques Rousseau, *Reveries of the Solitary Walker*, trans. Russell Goulbourne (Oxford: Oxford University Press, 2011), 11.

5. Ibid., 103.

6. For two excellent recent studies on solitude and loneliness, see David Vincent, *A History of Solitude* (London: Polity, 2020); and Fay Bound Alberti, *A Biography of Loneliness: The History of an Emotion* (Oxford: Oxford University Press, 2020).

7. See Patrick Barkham's insightful article "Can Nature Really Heal Us?" *Guardian*, www.theguardian.com/books/2020/mar/14/wild-ideas-how-nature-cures-are-shaping-our-literary-landscape, 14 March 2020.

8. See, e.g., Richard Mabey, *Nature Cure* (London: Chatto & Windus, 2005); Isabel Hardman, *The Natural Health Service: What the Great Outdoors Can Do for Your Mind* (London: Atlantic Books, 2020); Quing Li, *Shinrin-yoku: The Art and Science of Forest Bathing* (London: Penguin Life, 2018); Yoshifumi Miyazaki, *Shinrin-yoku: The Japanese Way of Forest Bathing for Health and Relaxation* (London: Aster, 2018); Nick Barker, *ReWild: The Art of Returning to Nature* (London: Aurum Press, 2017); and Simon Barnes, *Rewild Yourself: 23 Spellbinding Ways to Make Nature More Visible* (London: Simon & Schuster, 2018).

9. See Jonathan Hoban, *Walk with Your Wolf: Unlock Your Intuition, Confidence, and Power* (London: Yellow Kite, 2019). Other examples include Shane O'Mara's *In Praise of Walking: The New Science of How We Walk and Why It's Good for Us* (London: Bodley Head, 2019); and Erling Kagge's *Walking: One Step at a Time* (London: Viking, 2019).

10. Examples include Anthony Storr, *Solitude* (London: HarperCollins, 1997); Anneli Rufus, *Party of One: The Loners' Manifesto* (New York: Marlowe & Co., 2003); Sara Maitland, *How to Be Alone* (London: Macmillan, 2014); Michael Harris, *Solitude: In Pursuit of a Singular Life in a Crowded*

World (New York: Random House, 2018); and Erling Kagge, *Silence: In the Age of Noise* (London: Penguin, 2018).

11. Quoted in Barkham, "Can Nature Really Heal Us?"

12. See, e.g., Alan Levinovitz, *Natural: The Seductive Myth of Nature's Goodness* (London: Profile, 2020).

13. See Barkham, "Can Nature Really Heal Us?"

14. Henri David Thoreau, *Walden* (London: Penguin, 2016), 11.

15. Ibid., 13.

16. Ibid., 7.

17. Ibid., 86.

18. Ibid., 85.

19. For more details on the movement, see, e.g., Cecile Andrews and Wanda Urbanska, eds., *Less Is More: Embracing Simplicity for a Healthy Planet, a Caring Economy, and Lasting Happiness* (Gabriola Island, BC: New Society, 2009); Jerome M. Segal, *Graceful Simplicity: Toward a Philosophy and Politics of the Alternative American Dream* (Berkeley: University of California Press, 2003); and David Shi, *The Simple Life: Plain Living and High Thinking in American Culture*, new ed. (Athens: University of Georgia Press, 2007).

20. See "What Is Voluntary Simplicity?" by the The Simplicity Collective, http://simplicitycollective.com/start-here/what-is-voluntary-simplicity-2 (accessed 31 March 2020).

21. Ibid.

22. Duane Elgin, *Voluntary Simplicity: Toward a Way of Life That Is Outwardly Simple, Inwardly Rich* (New York: William Morrow, 1983), 33–34.

23. Quoted in "What Is Voluntary Simplicity?".

24. See ibid.

25. Online at www.mrmoneymustache.com (accessed 30 December 2020).

26. Other examples include Mrs. Hinch, *Hinch Yourself Happy: All the Best Cleaning Tips to Shine Your Sink and Soothe Your Soul* (London: Michael Joseph, 2019); and Fumio Sasaki, *Goodbye, Things: On Minimalist Living* (New York: W. W. Norton, 2017).

27. James Wallman, *Stuffocation: Living More with Less* (London: Penguin, 2015).

28. Marie Kondo, *The Life-Changing Magic of Tidying* (London: Vermilion, 2014), 213.

29. Dominique Loreau, *L'art de la simplicité: How to Live More with Less*, trans. Louise Rogers Lalaurie (London: Trapeze, 2016), 31.

30. For more on Japan and how its history has shaped its current culture, see Scott Haas, *Why Be Happy?: The Japanese Way of Acceptance* (New York: Hachette, 2020).

31. Loreau, *L'art de la simplicité*.

32. Ibid., 127.

33. Ibid., 89.

34. See Michael Pollen, *In Defense of Food: An Eater's Manifesto* (London: Penguin, 2008).

35. Adam Alter, *Irresistible: The Rise of Addictive Technology and the Business of Keeping Us Hooked* (New York: Penguin, 2017), 28.
36. See ibid., 40.
37. Ibid., 110.
38. See ibid., 14.
39. Cal Newport, *Digital Minimalism: On Living Better with Less Technology* (London: Penguin Business, 2019), 104.
40. Ibid., 106–7.
41. Jean M. Twenge, "Have Smartphones Destroyed a Generation?" September 1997, www.theatlantic.com/magazine/archive/2017/09/has-the-smartphone-destroyed-a-generation/534198/.
42. Newport, *Digital Minimalism*, 136.
43. See Alter, *Irresistible*, 1.
44. Quoted in Newport, *Digital Minimalism*, 9, 11.
45. Alter, *Irresistible*, 9.
46. Ibid.
47. Newport, *Digital Minimalism*, 24.
48. Ibid., 39.
49. Ibid., xvii.

Chapter Seven. Use Your Imagination

1. See, e.g., Rob Hopkins, *From What Is to What If: Unleashing the Power of Imagination to Create the Future We Want* (Hartford, VT: Chelsea Green, 2019).
2. Various psychologists, including Martin Seligman and Carol Dweck, have shown this to be the case.
3. See Massimo Pigliucci, *How to Be a Stoic: Ancient Wisdom for Modern Living* (London: Rider, 2017), 151.
4. Saint Augustine, *Confessions*, trans. Henry Chadwick (Oxford: Oxford University Press, 2008), 147.
5. Quoted in Matthieu Ricard, *Altruism: The Science and Psychology of Kindness* (London: Atlantic, 2015), 147–48.
6. Thank you, Nick Phillis, for sharing this.
7. Samuel Smiles, *Self-Help: With Illustrations of Character, Conduct, and Perseverance*, ed. Peter W. Sinnema (Oxford: Oxford University Press, 2002), 7.
8. Back cover text of Jack Canfield, Mark Victor Hansen and Amy Newmark, *The Original Chicken Soup for the Soul*, 20th anniv. ed. (n.p.: Chicken Soup for the Soul, 2013).
9. Smiles, *Self-Help*, 21.
10. Martha C. Nussbaum, *Cultivating Humanity: A Classical Defense of Reform in Liberal Education* (Cambridge, MA: Harvard University Press, 1997).
11. Quoted in Carmine Gallo, *Talk Like TED: The 9 Public Speaking Secrets of the World's Top Minds* (London: Pan Books, 2017), 41.
12. See ibid., 51.

13. Immanuel Kant, *An Answer to the Question: "What Is Enlightenment?,"* trans. H. B. Nisbet (London: Penguin, 2009), 1.

14. William Wordsworth, "Preface to *Lyrical Ballads, with Pastoral and Other Poems*" (1802), in William Wordsworth and Samuel Taylor Coleridge, *Lyrical Ballads 1798 and 1802* (Oxford: Oxford University Press, 2013), 104.

15. Percy Bysshe Shelley, "A Defence of Poetry," in *The Major Works* (Oxford: Oxford University Press, 2009), 682.

16. Jean-Jacques Rousseau, *Reveries of the Solitary Walker,* trans. Russell Goulbourne (Oxford: Oxford University Press, 2011), 70.

17. Ralph Waldo Emerson, "Self-Reliance," in *Nature and Selected Essays,* ed. Larzer Ziff (London: Penguin, 2003), 175–203.

18. Ibid., 185.

19. Ibid., 193.

20. Ibid., 203.

21. See Julian Baggini, *How the World Thinks: A Global History of Philosophy* (London: Granta, 2018).

22. Quoted in ibid., 46.

23. See Shane Weller, *Modernism and Nihilism* (Basingstoke, UK: Palgrave Macmillan, 2011).

24. Friedrich Wilhelm Nietzsche, *Thus Spoke Zarathustra,* trans. R. J. Hollingdale (London: Penguin, 2003), 41–43.

25. Quoted in R. J. Hollingdale, "Introduction" to ibid., 16.

26. Nietzsche, *Thus Spoke Zarathustra,* 51.

27. Anthony Robbins, *Awaken the Giant Within: How to Take Control of Your Mental, Emotional, Physical, and Financial Destiny* (London: Simon & Schuster, 1992), 345.

28. See Alfred Yankauer, "The Therapeutic Mantra of Emile Coué," *Perspectives in Biology and Medicine* 42, no. 4 (1999): 490.

29. For a full history of Couéism, its influences, and its legacy, see Hervé Guillemain, *La méthode Coué: Histoire d'une pratique de guérison au XXe siècle* (Paris: Seuil, 2010).

30. Emile Coué, *Self Mastery through Conscious Autosuggestion: A Classic Self Help Book* (London: New Creative, 2011), 11.

31. Ibid., 13.

32. Ibid., 15.

33. Ibid., 14.

34. Ibid., 23.

35. Ibid., 22.

36. Ibid., 57.

37. See Martin Seligman, *Learned Optimism: How to Change Your Mind and Your Life* (Boston: Nicholas Brealey, 2006).

38. Richard Bandler and John Grinder, *Frogs into Princes: Neuro-linguistic Programming* (Lafayette, CA: Real People Press, 1979).

39. For critical evaluations of NLP's scientific claims, see, e.g., Michael Heap, "The Validity of Some Early Claims of Neuro-linguistic Programming," *Skeptical Intelligencer* 11 (2008): 1–9; Tomasz Witkowski, "Thirty-Five Years of Research on Neuro-linguistic Programming—NLP Research Data Base: State of the Art or Pseudoscientific Decoration?" *Polish Psychological Bulletin* 41, no. 2 (2010): 55–66; and Christopher F. Sharpley, "Research Findings on Neurolinguistic Programming: Nonsupportive Data or an Untestable Theory?" *Journal of Counseling Psychology* 34, no. 1 (1987): 103–7.

40. Romilla Ready and Kate Burton, *Neuro-linguistic Programming for Dummies*, 3rd ed. (Chichester, UK: Wiley, 2015), 318.

41. Ibid., 83.

42. See Paul McKenna, *Instant Influence and Charisma* (London: Bantam, 2015).

43. Alain de Botton, "Introduction" to *The School of Life: An Emotional Education* (London: Hamish Hamilton, 2019), 2.

Chapter Eight. Persevere

1. See Angela Duckworth, *Grit: Why Passion and Resilience Are the Secrets to Success* (London: Vermilion, 2017); and Carol S. Dweck, *Mindset: Changing the Way You Think to Fulfil Your Potential* (London: Robinson, 2017).

2. For more information on the test, see VIA Institute on Character, https://viacharacter.org/about (accessed 23 June 2020).

3. Quoted in Duckworth, *Grit*, 48.

4. See, e.g., Matthew Syed, *Black Box Thinking: Marginal Gains and the Secrets of High Performance* (London: John Murray, 2016).

5. Sarah Harvey, *Kaizen: The Japanese Method for Transforming Habits One Small Step at a Time* (London: Bluebird, 2019).

6. See Peter W. Sinnema, "Introduction" to Samuel Smiles, *Self-Help: With Illustrations of Character, Conduct, and Perseverance*, ed. Peter W. Sinnema (Oxford: Oxford University Press, 2002), vii–xxviii.

7. See Nicola Humble, "Introduction" to *Mrs. Beeton's Book of Household Management* (Oxford: Oxford University Press, 2008), xxi.

8. See Kenneth O. Morgan, ed., *The Oxford Popular History of Britain* (Oxford: Oxford University Press, 1993); and Peter Mathias, *The First Industrial Nation: The Economic History of Britain 1700–1914* (New York: Routledge, 2001).

9. See Kathryn Hayes, "The Middle Classes: Etiquette and Upward Mobility," *British Library*, www.bl.uk/romantics-and-victorians/articles/the-middle-classes-etiquette-and-upward-mobility, 15 May 2014.

10. See ibid.

11. See Humble, "Introduction," vii–xxx.

12. Smiles, *Self-Help*, 3.

13. Ibid., 4.
14. Ibid., 39.
15. Ibid., 3.
16. Ibid., 18.
17. Ibid., 191.
18. Ibid., 192.
19. M. Scott Peck, *The Road Less Traveled: A New Psychology of Love, Traditional Values, and Spiritual Growth* (New York: Touchstone, 1985), 15.
20. Ibid., 16–17.
21. Ibid., 19.
22. Ibid., 35.
23. Ibid., 81.
24. Ibid., 271.
25. Ibid., 277.
26. See "The Video Which Made Jordan Peterson Famous," https://www.youtube.com/watch?v=O-nvNAcvUPE&t=158s 12 October 2016.
27. Jordan B. Peterson, *12 Rules for Life: An Antidote to Chaos*, foreword by Norman Doidge (London: Allen Lane, 2018), 79.
28. Ibid., 80.
29. Stephen R. Covey, *The 7 Habits of Highly Effective People: Powerful Lessons in Personal Change* (New York: Free Press, 2004), 43.
30. Ibid., 46–47.
31. Ibid., 71.
32. Ibid., 148.
33. Ibid., 288–89.
34. Charles Duhigg, *The Power of Habit: Why We Do What We Do and How to Change* (London: Random House, 2013), 19.
35. Ibid., 92.
36. Duckworth, *Grit*, 51.
37. Ibid., 17.
38. Ibid., 173.
39. Ibid., 203.
40. Dweck, *Mindset*, 7.
41. See Syed, *Black Box Thinking*, 52–53.
42. Ibid., 10.
43. See Leon Festinger, *When Prophecy Fails* (Minneapolis: University of Minnesota Press, 1956).
44. Syed, *Black Box Thinking*, 283.
45. Ibid., 292.
46. See *State of the Nation Report on Social Mobility in Great Britain*, summarized at www.gov.uk/government/news/state-of-the-nation-report-on-social-mobility-in-great-britain, 16 November 2016. See also Jo Marchant, *Cure: A Journey into the Science of Mind over Body* (New York: Crown, 2016), 151–52.

47. See Martin Seligman, *Learned Optimism: How to Change Your Mind and Your Life* (Boston: Nicholas Brealey, 2006).

Chapter Nine. Mentalize

1. See Martin Seligman, *Learned Optimism: How to Change Your Mind and Your Life* (Boston: Nicholas Brealey, 2006); and Jean M. Twenge and W. Keith Campbell, *The Narcissism Epidemic: Living in the Age of Entitlement* (New York: Atria, 2013).

2. See, e.g., Grant Soosalu and Martin Oka, "Neuroscience and the Three Brains of Leadership," October 2014, available at www.mbraining.com /mbit-and-leadership.

3. Niccolò Machiavelli, *The Prince*, trans. W. K. Marriott (New York: Everyman's Library, 1992), 68.

4. Ibid., 71.

5. Ibid., 76.

6. Ibid., 80.

7. Ibid., 80–81.

8. R. Shaw, *Machiavelli Mindset: How to Conquer Your Enemies, Achieve Audacious Goals, and Live without Limits from "The Prince"* [*sic*] (London: CreateSpace Independent Publishing Platform, 2016), 1.

9. See George Bull, "Introduction" to Baldesar Castiglione, *The Book of the Courtier*, trans. George Bull (London: Penguin, 2003), 12, 14.

10. Castiglione, *Book of the Courtier*, 59.

11. Ibid., 172.

12. Ibid.

13. Ibid., 135.

14. Ibid., 137.

15. Ibid., 212.

16. Warren Susman, *Culture as History: The Transformation of American Society in the Twentieth Century* (Washington, DC: Smithsonian Institution Press, 2003), 271–85.

17. See Susan Cain, *Quiet: The Power of Introverts in a World That Can't Stop Talking* (London: Penguin, 2012).

18. Dale Carnegie, *How to Win Friends and Influence People* (London: Vermilion, 2006), 119.

19. Ibid., 13.

20. Ibid., 130.

21. Ibid., 87.

22. Ibid., 97.

23. Ibid., 234ff.

24. Ibid., 196–97.

25. Steve Salerno, *SHAM: How the Self-Help Movement Made America Helpless* (New York: Three Rivers Press, 2005), 75–87.

26. Paul McKenna, *Instant Influence & Charisma* (London: Bantam Press, 2015), 72.
27. Romilla Ready and Kate Burton, *Neuro-linguistic Programming for Dummies*, 3rd ed. (Chichester, UK: Wiley, 2015), 145.
28. Ibid., 141.
29. Ibid., 102–3.
30. See, e.g., Neil Strauss, *The Game: Undercover in the Secret Society of Pickup Artists* (Edinburgh: Cannongate, 2005).
31. Paul McKenna, *Instant Influence and Charisma* (London: Bantam, 2015), 180.
32. See Cal Newport, *Digital Minimalism: On Living Better with Less Technology* (London: Penguin Business, 2019), 99–109.
33. Marcel Proust, *Time Regained and A Guide to Proust, In Search of Lost Time*, vol. 4 (London: Vintage, 2000), 254.

Chapter Ten. Be Present

1. See Ronald Purser, *McMindfulness: How Mindfulness Became the New Capitalist Spirituality* (London: Repeater Books, 2019); and David Forbes, *Mindfulness and Its Discontents* (London: Fernwood, 2019).
2. See Jeremy Carrette and Richard King, *Selling Spirituality: The Silent Takeover of Religion* (London: Routledge, 2005).
3. For a discussion of some of the clinical trials that have established the efficacy of mindfulness meditation, see, e.g., Jon Kabat-Zinn, *Full Catastrophe Living: How to Cope with Stress, Pain, and Illness Using Mindfulness Meditation*, rev. and updated ed. (London: Piatkus, 2013), xli–xlv; and Jo Marchant, *Cure: A Journey into the Science of Mind over Body* (New York: Crown, 2016), 153–73. See also the selected publications on the Oxford Mindfulness Centre research website, www.psych.ox.ac.uk/research/mindfulness (accessed 7 January 2020).
4. See B. K. S. Iyengar, *Light on the Yoga Sūtras of Patañjali* (London: Thorsons, 2002).
5. Georg Feuerstein, *The Yoga Tradition: Its History, Literature, Philosophy, and Practice*, 3rd ed. (Prescott, AZ: Hohm Press, 2008).
6. Marcus Aurelius, *Meditations*, trans. Martin Hammond (London: Penguin, 2006), 11.
7. Ibid., 23.
8. Jean-Jacques Rousseau, *Reveries of the Solitary Walker*, trans. Russell Goulbourne (Oxford: Oxford University Press, 2011), 55.
9. Ralph Waldo Emerson, "Self-Reliance," in *Nature and Selected Essays* (London: Penguin, 2003), 189.
10. See Russ Harris, *The Happiness Trap. Based on ACT: A Revolutionary Mindfulness-Based Programme for Overcoming Stress, Anxiety, and Depression* (London: Robinson, 2008); Steven C. Hayes and Spencer Smith, *Get out*

of Your Mind and into Your Life: The New Acceptance and Commitment Therapy (Oakland, CA: New Harbinger, 2005); and Steven C. Hayes, K. D. Strosahl, and K. G. Wilson, *Acceptance and Commitment Therapy* (New York: Guilford Press, 2012).

11. See Mark Siderits, "The Buddha," *Stanford Encyclopedia of Philosophy*, https://plato.stanford.edu/entries/buddha, 17 February 2011, substantively revised 14 February 2019.

12. *The Dhammapada*, trans. Juan Mascaró (London: Penguin Classics, 2015), 1.

13. Ibid., 5–6.

14. Damien Keown, *Buddhism: A Very Short Introduction* (Oxford: Oxford University Press, 2013), 39.

15. See Mitchell S. Green, *Know Thyself: The Value and Limits of Self-Knowledge* (New York: Routledge, 2018), 128.

16. Ibid., 130.

17. *The Dhammapada*, 35.

18. See, e.g., Carrette and King, *Selling Spirituality*, 101; and Purser, *McMindfulness*.

19. On the transmission of Buddhism in the West, see, e.g., Richard Hughes Seager, *Buddhism in America* (New York: Columbia University Press, 2012); and James William Coleman, *The New Buddhism: The Western Transformation of an Ancient Tradition* (Oxford: Oxford University Press, 2001).

20. Kabat-Zinn, *Full Catastrophe Living*, ixii.

21. Ibid., xxxv.

22. Ibid., 21.

23. Ibid., 23.

24. Ibid., 66.

25. Jon Kabat-Zinn, *Wherever You Go, There You Are: Mindfulness Meditation for Everyday Life* (London: Piatkus, 1994), 238.

26. Ibid., 16.

27. Ibid., 17.

28. Ibid., xiii.

29. Jesse McKinley, "The Wisdom of the Ages, for Now Anyway," *New York Times*, 23 March 2008, www.nytimes.com/2008/03/23/fashion/23tolle.html.

30. Eckhart Tolle, *The Power of Now: A Guide to Spiritual Enlightenment* (London: Hodder & Stoughton, 1999), 1.

31. Ibid., 3.

32. Ibid., 40.

33. Ibid., 75.

34. Ibid., 122.

35. Ibid., xviii.

36. Norman Doidge, *The Brain That Changes Itself: Stories of Personal Triumph from the Frontiers of Brain Science* (London: Penguin, 2008), 171.

37. See Purser, *McMindfulness*, 151.
38. Ibid., 163.
39. For a critique of mindfulness programs used by the military, see Christopher Titmuss's blog "Are Buddhist Mindfulness Practices Used to Support International War Crimes?" www.christophertitmussblog.org/are-buddhist-mindfulness-practices-used-to-support-international-war-crimes, 19 May 2014.
40. Purser, *McMindfulness*, 108.
41. E.g., Byung-Chul Han, *Psycho-Politics: Neoliberalism and New Technologies of Power*, trans. Erik Butler (London: Verso, 2017); and Carrette and King, *Selling Spirituality*.
42. Matthieu Ricard, *Altruism: The Science and Psychology of Kindness* (London: Atlantic, 2015), 678–79.
43. See, e.g., the portraits of activists, socially conscious entrepreneurs, and other change-makers on the Emerge project website, www.whatisemerging.com/profiles (accessed 23 December 2020).

Conclusion

1. Immanuel Kant, "Morality and Rationality," in *Ethics: Essential Readings in Moral Theory*, ed. George Sher (New York: Routledge, 2012), 336.
2. For a more nuanced and thorough discussion of Kantian self-improvement, see, e.g., Robert N. Johnson, *Self-Improvement: An Essay in Kantian Ethics* (Oxford: Oxford University Press, 2011).
3. Samuel Smiles, *Self-Help: With Illustrations of Character, Conduct, and Perseverance*, ed. Peter Sinnema (Oxford: Oxford University Press, 2002), 20.
4. Ibid., 18.
5. See Byung-Chul Han, *Psycho-Politics: Neoliberalism and New Technologies of Power*, trans. Erik Butler (London: Verso, 2017); Alain Ehrenberg, *The Weariness of the Self: Diagnosing the History of Depression in the Contemporary Age*, trans. David Homel et al. (Montreal: McGill-Queen's University Press, 2010); and Micki McGee, *Self-Help, Inc.: Makeover Culture in American Life* (New York: Oxford University Press, 2005).
6. See Angela Duckworth, *Grit: Why Passion and Resilience Are the Secrets to Success* (London: Vermilion, 2017); Carol S. Dweck, *Mindset: Changing the Way You Think to Fulfil Your Potential* (London: Robinson, 2017); and Martin Seligman, *Learned Optimism: How to Change Your Mind and Your Life* (Boston: Nicholas Brealey, 2006).

Acknowledgments

FOR SUPPORT, FRIENDSHIP, PRECIOUS insights, and stimulating discussions, I wish to thank Enid Allison, Kate Alshaker, Clemence Ardin, Peter Atkins, Judith Bovensiepen, Peter Buse, Agnès Cardinal, Jeremy Carrette, Cecile Cheval, Sarah Colvin, Mary Cosgrove, Andreas Essl, Gavin Eustace, Marie Eustace, Angelos Evangelou, Chloe Galien, Andreas Gehrlich, Scott Haas, Elizabeth Hartley, Katja Haustein-Corcoran, Ben Hutchinson, Marie Hutchinson, Lindi Jefferson, Will Jefferson, Marie Jettot, Stephàne Jettot, Tim Julier, Annette Kern-Stähler, Jana Klusemann, Jens Klusemann, Marie Kolkenbrock, Rachel Lehmann, Gordon Lynch, Micki McGee, Laura Mooney, Stephen Morris, Sighard Neckel, Patricia Novillo-Corvalàn, Katharina Paschkowsky, Joanne Pettitt, Nick Phillis, Anna Pollard, Ana de Quimpo, Peter Read, Katrin Ridder, Anja Röcke, Amelia Saberwal, Duna Sabri, Ernst Schaffner, Eva Schaffner, Tanya Mozias Slavin, Axel Stähler, Ali Stewart, Nùria Triana Toribio, Katherine Voice, Greta Wagner, Liz Weller and Saranne Weller.

I also wish to thank my wonderful agent, Jennifer Bernstein, and my extremely perceptive editor, Jennifer Banks, two brilliant women whose feedback has been invaluable. Thanks are also due to Anne Canright for her smart copyediting, which has significantly improved this text, and to Joyce Ippolito and Abigail Storch from Yale University Press for all their fantastic work.

I would like to express my thanks to the Wellcome Trust for funding a project on human energy which somehow morphed into this book. I am deeply grateful for a Leverhulme Research

Fellowship (2019–20), which enabled me to complete a large part of my research. A Hamburg Institute for Advanced Studies (HIAS) fellowship (2020–21) allowed me to finish the writing of my book—thanks are due to everyone at the HIAS, especially Astrid Bothmann-Lucko, Frank Fehrenbach, Sonja Gräber-Magocsi, Tanja Kruse Brandao, and Anna Neubauer, and to my co-fellows Katrin Hammerschmidt, Dietmar von der Pfordten, Sonja Prinz, and Chenxi Tang. I am also very grateful to the ZEIT-Stiftung Ebelin und Gerd Bucerius for funding the HIAS fellowship.

I would like to thank my daughter, Helena, who is my opposite in so many ways and therefore my perfect teacher. Last but not least, I wish to thank my partner, Shane Weller, who is a pessimist and a nihilist by creed. He does not believe in our ability to improve ourselves; like Beckett, he holds that we go on because we must go on, worstward ho. But he does believe in improving texts, and his feedback on my writing has been invaluable. My arguments (with almost all of which he fundamentally disagrees) have become sharper and more focused, and my early drafts have benefited enormously from his incisive thoughts.

With love and sadness this book is dedicated to my friend Verena Trusch (1978–2016)—the most magnificent, persistent, and inspiring self-improver I have ever known.

Index